Materials In Today's World

Second Edition

*Crystals of ultrapure chromium produced by chemical vapor deposition
Magnification ×10 — see text on page 79.*

Materials In Today's World

Second Edition

Peter A. Thrower
The Pennsylvania State University

McGraw-Hill, Inc.
College Custom Series

*New York St. Louis San Francisco Auckland Bogotá
Caracas Lisbon London Madrid Mexico Milan Montreal
New Delhi Paris San Juan Singapore Sydney Tokyo Toronto*

McGraw-Hill's College Custom Series consists of products that are produced from camera-ready copy. Peer review, class testing, and accuracy are primarily the responsibility of the author(s).

Materials In Today's World

2 3 4 5 6 7 8 9 0 PCP PCP 9 0 9 8 7 6

ISBN 0-07-050711-2

Editor: M.A. Hollander
Cover Illustration: Detail from the author's photograph of chromium produced by chemical vapor deposition.
Cover Designer: Jeffrey Boyd
Printer/Binder: Port City Press

ABOUT THE AUTHOR

Peter A. Thrower is professor of materials science in the Materials Science and Engineering Department of the Pennsylvania State University in State College, Pennsylvania. He received a B.A. degree in physics from Cambridge University and was later awarded a Ph.D. degree by the same university. Dr. Thrower teaches graduate and undergraduate courses in materials science and has particular interests in making the subject interesting to students entering the major, and to those who have no leaning towards things scientific whatsoever. His own research interests are concerned with carbon materials, and he has been Editor-in-Chief of the international scientific journal *Carbon* since 1983.

COVER PHOTO: Crystals of ultrapure chromium produced by chemical vapor deposition - see text on page 79.

This book is dedicated to my parents, who understand by faith (Hebrews 11 v.3).

CONTENTS

Preface to the second edition

This book was originally based on, and especially written for, a General Education course taught at The Pennsylvania State University. It was not written for science majors and specialists, but rather for the student with a basic high school science background who wishes to understand and know something about the exciting materials developments which are affecting us all in today's world. It is now five years since this book was first written, and seven years since this course was first formulated. During this time enrollment has grown from around sixty to almost a thousand each semester. What could be more relevant in bringing science to the non-major than those materials which we depend on for many of our everyday activities? The course is popular because the material is interesting.

I never cease to wonder at the materials developments of the last few decades which have had such an amazing influence on so much of what we do. As a skier I am aware of the tremendous differences in equipment which have occurred in the last thirty years. Composites and polymers have created boots and skis which were but a dream when I made my first 'run'. The same can probably be said of all other sporting activities. When I was a student we did not have portable cassette players and pocket calculators; they are the result of quite recent materials' developments. Advances in semiconductors, electronics and computers are still continuing at a tremendous pace, and the revolution promised by optical fiber communication is perhaps the one development we can realistically anticipate in the lifetimes of today's students.

There has been nothing more rewarding in my 26 years at Penn State than having students who 'hate' science get excited about learning the reason why Corning Ware® can go from freezer to burner without breaking, why body panels on today's cars can be much thinner than they were twenty five years ago, or understanding the difference between high and low density polyethylenes and some of the problems of polymer recycling.

It has been interesting to learn of the different uses to which this book has been put, not the least of which has been as an introduction to materials for freshmen students who plan to major in the subject, but who do not yet have the background in physics, chemistry and mathematics to embark on courses in their proposed major. Indeed many of our students complain about the lack of materials courses in their first two years of study. Perhaps this expanded and revised edition will find more use in this area.

This new edition tries to answer some of the requests and suggestions received from many people by introducing some new topics, providing examples of the problems given to my students, and reorganizing previous material to give what is perhaps a more logical sequence. I will admit to having had an aversion to multiple choice exams, but large enrollments have forced me to use them. Grade correlations between these and written exams have been remarkably good.

As stated in the first edition, "some of the explanations and discussion used are simplistic, sometimes to the point of being slightly inaccurate; analogies are often imperfect, units are not handled rigorously, etc. To those who would object to this I would simply say that while the view is probably best from the top of the mountain, it is better to climb partway up and see something, rather than stay in the valley (of ignorance). There are those who only have the time or the ability to climb so far. It is for them that this volume is written. I hope that it will better prepare today's students for the exciting materials developments which await them in future years, and provide some understanding of the new materials which are already affecting our daily lives."

I am again grateful to many present and former colleagues for their numerous suggestions. Especially noteworthy are my former department head, Dr. Michael Coleman, who encouraged the conception of this course and has provided valuable comments on the new material on polymers, and my current department head, Dr. Richard Tressler, who continues to enthusiastically support my efforts to bring Materials Science to the masses. In preparing this new edition I am particularly grateful to Dr. Elizabeth Kupp, who gave such marvelous help as my teaching assistant during the 1994-95 academic year, and who volunteered to read this current manuscript. Without her help it would have undoubtedly have contained more errors that it now has.

Last, but by no means least, I must thank my wife Carol for her patience and encouragement during the writing of this revision. She has also read and provided valuable comments on some of the new material.

Peter A. Thrower
Department of Materials Science and Engineering
The Pennsylvania State University, PA 16802   *October 1995*

Acknowledgments:

I am grateful to Tom Ruznak for help with some of the photographs taken for this book, to Pat Winand for the photographs on page 14, and to Paul Howell for the photographs on pages 109 and 120.

1. INTRODUCTION

Materials have always played a major role in man's development. Indeed history recognizes this by the names often assigned to stages in this development. The stone, bronze and iron ages are named according to the then best available materials for implements and weapons.

During these early times man became aware of the ability to change the nature and properties of the materials available. To heat a paste of clay and water and produce a pot resembling stone must have given early man a sense of achievement and control over the matter around him which was totally new. Before 4000 B.C. came the use of metals, with naturally occurring (native) copper being shaped for both ornament and implement. At this stage it was learned that heat helped to soften the metal and hence aided the forming process. There then followed (3000 - 1000 B.C.) the importance of bronze, a metal formed by mixing molten copper and tin. This is perhaps the first man-made **alloy**, a mixture of metals.

Of course at the same time there were many elaborate techniques developed for forming gold and silver into beautiful jewelry. Many of these manufacturing methods have had to be rediscovered in recent years. It may be hard to believe that such arts could be lost, but it is a fact that many of the techniques used to make the jewelry found in the ancient tombs of the middle east had to be reinvented.

The iron age followed, but there were no facilities to melt the pure metal and it was only iron which contained large amounts of carbon which could be melted and cast into shapes, hence the term **cast iron**. The crude iron which was formed and shaped by hammering always contained large inclusions and lots of impurities which weakened the material.

Iron ore obtained from the earth, mostly in the form of iron oxides, was heated in a charcoal hearth. The carbon in the charcoal reacted with the iron oxide to produce carbon dioxide and iron, the former escaping as a gas and leaving iron behind as a spongy mass which could be formed by hammering etc., as already mentioned. Continued heating caused some of the carbon atoms to move into the iron producing what we now know as steel. Eventually the iron would take up enough carbon to form cast iron, which is quite brittle.

We should note here that there were quite drastic changes occurring in the iron during all this, but the metal workers were totally unaware of them. In fact some of their conclusions were the opposite of the truth. Fire was known to have a purifying influence. In biblical times the concept of "refined by fire" was well established. It was therefore natural to assume that the harder, stronger and more brittle material was the result of purification whereas it was the dissolving of carbon in the iron which was producing the effect. Nowadays we are well aware that impurities can have a dramatic effect on the properties of materials, sometimes bad and sometimes beneficial but the ancient blacksmiths were unaware of these facts. In fact we shall see that defects and impurities in a material are what largely dictate its properties.

Many materials which have been made in man's history were developed by empirical, or we could even say accidental, techniques. The manufacturing methods worked! The steel in some old Japanese swords is a good example of this. The reason for the remarkable properties of this material was not known until relatively recently and the manufacturing techniques had to be rediscovered.

During the following years it is obvious that a large body of knowledge was developed which was purely empirical, meaning that it was known that a certain treatment, heating, alloying, hammering, etc. produced a certain effect on the metal's properties but the reasons were either completely unknown or wrong. The sixteen century saw the publication of the first three books which catalogued this knowledge, the most famous of which is probably *De Re Metallica*, which means 'about metallic things'.

During the eighteenth and nineteenth centuries iron and steel became cheaper and their properties, mainly strength, were improved. However little was still known about their structure. In 1864 an Englishman called Henry Sorby was responsible for a major breakthrough. He developed a technique for chemically removing, or etching, the surface layer of a polished metal specimen and then examining it in a microscope by reflected light. For the first time it was possible to see that the material consisted of a number of small grains or crystals. Different grains appeared to have different brightnesses under the reflected light microscope he used. For the first time it was clear that the metallic mass was made of a large number of crystals which were oriented in different directions, well fitted together and joined along grain boundaries.

This first view of the **microstructure** of a metal was very revealing but it was not until the twentieth century that one can say that materials science really developed. The question of 'how' they behaved was replaced by the 'why' of this behavior. Modern techniques of x-ray diffraction, electron microscopy etc. have now enabled us to see into the structures of materials and hence understand why different materials behave the way they do. As a result of this understanding we have been able to suggest ways of intentionally altering and improving the properties of materials. That is really what materials science is all about.

Departments of Materials Science at universities were first formed in the 1960's. Most of them were based on existing Metallurgy Departments, because metals were then the materials about which most was known. Some universities also had Ceramic Science departments and these too were incorporated into the new departments. Today there are Departments of Materials Science in most major universities, each of them having some activity in metals, ceramics and polymers, the three major classes of materials. Polymers are the new kid on the block but their importance has escalated so much in the last twenty five years that they now touch almost all aspects of our everyday lives. There are today over 60,000 different plastics (polymers) available to us and the number consistently grows by at least 5 - 6 each week! Hardly a week goes by without our hearing something about the impact of polymers on our environment. Plastics are 'here to stay' in at least two senses of the phrase!

Most recently there has been more importance placed on electronic and photonic materials, materials which are used in information processing using either electric or light signals. The urge to be able to process more information more quickly, whether it be for high speed computing, or for transmitting hundreds of TV signals along one cable at the same time, has produced new challenges for the materials scientist. Some experts see this as a new and separate discipline within the wide realm of materials.

Much of what we are able to do today technologically is limited by the materials at our command. New materials were required to develop the space shuttle and still other materials will be needed for the development of the National Aerospace Plane (NASP) which is projected to fulfill the role of the space shuttle while taking off and landing like a regular aircraft. Light and strong metal alloys, ceramics which can be bent and will not shatter, and polymers which can withstand high temperatures are all materials for which we have a current quest. Indeed a major thrust, which is alluded to many times in this text, is the pursuit of lighter and stronger materials which can be used at higher and higher temperatures. Perhaps many of these goals will never be attained but there are also some which are becoming a reality today.

20th Century's Techno Leaps

The first airplane stayed airborne for just 12 seconds; 66 years later, there was a man on the moon. The first electronic television had a 5-inch screen; 21 years later, trans-Atlantic television shows were broadcast via satellite. Such leaps in technology characterize our world since 1900.

1900

1901-Vacuum cleaner
1903-Airplane
1905-Dial telephone
1906-Light bulb
1908-Model T Ford

1910

1910-Electric washing machine
1911-Atomic nuclear structure
1913-Electric refrigerator
1914-Wireless telephone

1920

1920-Radio broadcasts
1921-Chromosome heredity
1921-Coast-to-coast telephone service
1925-Mechanical television
1926-35mm camera
1928-Cartoons with sound

1930

1930-Human blood types
1930-Tape recorder
1932-Atom split
1936-Jet
1939- Electronic television

1940

1943-Nuclear chain reaction
1943-Electronic computer
1944-DNA
1944-Missile
1948-Transistor
1948-Microwave
1949-Polaroid Land camera

1950

1950-Credit card
1952-Atomic bomb test
1955-Optical fibers
1957-Soviet satellite
1959-Microchip

1960

1960-Communications satellite
1962-Industrial robot
1963-Nuclear reactor
1967-Heart transplant
1969-Man on moon

1970

1971-Silicon chip
1975-Personal computer
1975-Videocassette recorders
1976-Supersonic jet
1977-Neutron bomb
1978-Test tube baby

1980

1980-Stealth bomber
1980-Gene cloning
1981-Space shuttle
1982-Permanent artificial heart
1986-Soviet space station

These are some of the technologies likely to take us...

...through the 1990s

■ Computer voice recognition
■ Artificial intelligence
■ Genetic cures for disease
■ Spaced-based assembly plant

Research and Project Editor: WENDY GOVIER
Sources: Smithsonian Institute, Ribbons of Time, American Chronicle, Inventions and Discoveries, The Timetables of Science, MacMillan World History Factfinders

Knight-Ridder Tribune News/BILL BAKER and RAY PUTMON

The tabulation of '20th Century's Techno Leaps' on the opposite page includes many innovations which were the result of new materials developments. Tungsten filaments for electric light bulbs, fine particle magnets for magnetic tape used in both audio and video tape recorders, special chemicals for processing the photos from Polaroid cameras, optical fibers for telephone communications and medical instrumentation, light weight materials for space travel, pure silicon for all our modern electronic equipment, special plastics for the artificial heart, etc. All are new materials developments.

Is today the polymer age or the semiconductor age? Will tomorrow be the superconductor age? Only time will tell whether future generations will look back on today's world and refer to it in terms of the materials we use, as we do with the stone, bronze and iron ages. However we can be sure that the development of new materials will play an important and very significant role in our history.

This book is designed to give some insight into why materials behave as they do and to show how properties can be changed and improved. Some of today's newer materials are highlighted in more detail as specific examples of our recent accomplishments. Here is science as it affects our everyday lives! It is hoped that the material covered here can be understood with very little scientific and mathematics background and will, above all, be interesting and informative.

2. THE SEARCH FOR NEW MATERIALS

New materials may be roughly divided into two types: (a) those that are made by combining **elements** which have not been previously combined, and (b) those that are made by modifying existing materials.

We have just used the term "element". A chemical element is essentially a basic building block for materials. It is "a substance which cannot be resolved by chemical means into simpler substances". We are all familiar with the elements oxygen, iron, copper, carbon, aluminum, hydrogen, nitrogen . . . . We may be less familiar with germanium, nickel, boron, titanium, tungsten . . . We may have never heard of, and will probably never see a clump of gadolinium, dysprosium, holmium . . . . There are about a hundred elements which are arranged by scientists into an array known as the Periodic Table (shown below). The number given to the element denotes the number of electrons and protons it contains. Elements in the same column have somewhat similar properties. You

THE PERIODIC TABLE

(W. D. Callister, Jr., *Materials Science and Engineering*, John Wiley, New York, 1985. Fig. 2.6)

may know that silicon (Si) and germanium (Ge) are semiconductors, and that neon (Ne) and argon (Ar) are inert gases, and by the end of this book you should be aware of some other similarities such as carbon (C) and silicon (Si), and oxygen (O) and sulfur (S). Note that the great majority of elements are metals and that nearly all the non-metals are in the upper right corner of the table.

Many scientists memorize at least the first fifty of so elements in the periodic table, but there is no need for you to do so. When the author was in high school he remembers a chemistry teacher saying, "**He** **Li**kes **B**eef **B**ut **C**an **N**ot **O**btain **F**ood", and this little memory aid for the first row of the periodic table has never been forgotten. Perhaps you too will find it useful.

We mentioned earlier that there are really two types of new material. Most of these are of the second type, i.e. they are made by modifying existing materials. Sometimes this means just purifying them, the outstanding example of which is silicon. We shall have much more to say about this element later, but for the time being it is sufficient to say that the element commonly exists combined with oxygen in the form of sand (SiO_2 - known as silica). We can extract the silicon from sand but the material produced is not very useful because of impurities. We shall later see that regular window glass has a blue/green tinge (look at it through the edge) because of the iron present in the silica.

The development of silicon fit for semiconductor use required the production of a very high purity form of the element (99.9999999% pure) which then needed to have small amounts of a specific impurity element (e.g. boron, phosphorus) added. We call this intentional addition of impurity "doping" and it is a vital part of the production of silicon for the electronic components in your personal electronic equipment, transistor radios, hi-fi equipment, calculators, cars, etc. The development of silicon for transistors required a modification of the available material, involving purification and doping. At the beginning of the 1960's there was barely a mention of these so-called 'solid-state electronics' in the author's undergraduate physics curriculum. Perhaps these materials would one day prove valuable! Just look how far we have come in the last 35 years as a result of this major materials development. We shall look at two simple uses of doped silicon in our case studies.

In another of our case studies we shall discuss the new High Strength Low Alloy Steels (HSLA Steels). Steels have been made and used for well over a century, but these are steels which are modified so that they are made of very small crystals, which increases strength. This is another example of a new material made by modifying an existing one. In this case it is the change in the processing of the material that is mainly responsible for its different properties.

Corning Ware® is a material which is found in most households. It too is a relatively new material which is formed by modifying a glass. There are even some stories that it was discovered by accident, something scientists call 'serendipity' and which happens more often than we like to admit! We shall look at what it is that makes this material withstand extreme temperature variations, enabling you to take it straight from freezer to burner.

Another example of a new material which, incidentally is still the subject of considerable research, is the group of metal alloys (metal mixtures) made by combining aluminum (Al) and lithium (Li). This new group of materials is both lighter and stronger than aluminum alone, and has obvious uses in modern aircraft. A recent TV program showed design engineers debating the use of these alloys in the new Boeing 777 aircraft, even for such mundane components as the seat frames. Any weight saving is important in an aircraft wherever obtained. We shall discuss these materials later in a case study.

The most outstanding recent example of a new material made by mixing elements in a way never before attempted are the so-called high temperature superconductors. These have involved mixtures of copper (Cu), oxygen (O), lanthanum (La) and strontium (Sr) (some elements you may have never heard of) with some later additions of barium (Ba), yttrium (Y) and scandium (Sc) (which may also be new to you). Nobody would have guessed twenty years ago that this combination of elements would produce electrical conductors let alone super-conductors. Unfortunately the promise of room-temperature superconductors, which was the subject of much discussion at the time, seems as remote today as ever it was. The search for new materials continues.

3. WHAT IS MATERIALS SCIENCE?

The relatively new science of materials is usually described as the science of the relationships between the structure and the properties of materials. Both these terms, properties and structure, have many aspects and are perhaps best explained by taking some specific examples.

Properties concerns both physical and chemical properties. How does the material react to the various forces and environments to which it is exposed? Magnetic fields, heat, physical loads (weights), wear, acids etc.

Structure concerns a wide spectrum of sizes, from the structure of the individual atoms which make up the solid to the design and shape of the part being used. We shall define five different scales of structure: electron(ic), atom(ic), crystal, micro and macro, in increasing size order.

To further explain what we mean by structure we shall look at what is certainly the element demonstrating the widest range of structures known to us. That element is carbon.

CARBON

Diamond and graphite

If you look at the periodic table on page 7 you will find carbon designated by its chemical symbol C. Above the C is the number 6, while underneath is the number 12.011. The first is what we know as the **atomic number**. All atoms are made up of a nucleus of positively charged particles called protons and neutral (no charge) particles called neutrons. This nucleus is surrounded by negatively charged particles called electrons which move around the nucleus in a manner similar to the way the planets move around the sun. The atomic number simply tells us the number of electrons belonging to one atom. We shall discuss this subject in more detail in Chapter 5 when we consider chemical bonding.

The second number is the **atomic weight** or relative mass of a single atom, and is given in what are known as atomic mass units (amu). While there is perhaps no need to remember the exact figures for this study, we should note that the atomic weight tells us that 6.02×10^{23} carbon atoms weigh 12.011 grams.

These units (amu) are therefore very, very small. (In case you are unfamiliar with this notation, 6.02×10^{23} means 6.02 multiplied by ten twenty three times, i.e. 602,000,000,000,000,000,000,000.)

As mentioned above, the carbon atom has six electrons and, as we shall see in Chapter 5, four of these electrons, called the **valence** electrons, are available to form linkages or bonds to other atoms. How these electrons are used to form bonds relates to the **electron(ic) structure** of the material.

There are two common different forms of carbon with which you are probably familiar, and several other related forms. The two familiar forms are diamond and graphite; two more different materials you could hardly imagine!

Diamond is a transparent, colorless, crystalline material which is very hard (scratches glass). It is an electrical insulator but a good conductor of heat. It is also rare and very expensive. The only place we are likely to see it is in jewelry, although small and imperfect crystals are used in glass-cutters and on cutting and grinding wheels.

Graphite is an opaque, black, crystalline material which is very soft and slippery but is very strong and stiff in one plane. It also conducts heat and electricity pretty well. It is quite cheap, costing around a dollar a pound. We encounter it in the black lead pencils we still use. It also is used as a lubricant and as an electrode in the small A-, C- and D-cell batteries we use to power our portable electronics.

We should first state that both materials have the same **atomic structure**, meaning that they are both made up of the same carbon atoms. Every material, however pure, contains some impurity atoms which alter the atomic structure or make-up of the material, but we shall ignore this for now. The main difference between these two materials lies in their **electronic structures** (bonding arrangements), which in turn give rise to different **crystal structures** (arrangements of atoms in space).

In diamond each carbon atom uses all four valence electrons to form linkages, or bonds, with four surrounding carbon atoms on the corners of a tetrahedron. This produces a three-dimensional network of atoms with strong bonds going in all directions. (A tetrahedron is a four-sided pyramid each side of which is an equilateral triangle. The easiest way of drawing a tetrahedron is to place a carbon atom at the center of a cube and place other carbon atoms on alternate corners of the cube, as illustrated in the following diagram.)

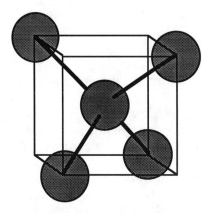

A carbon atom bonded to four others on the corners of a tetrahedron

In graphite each carbon atom uses only three electrons to form bonds with three other carbon atoms in what we call a layer plane, and the fourth electron is released by the atom and allowed to move freely between these layer planes. This produces a two-dimensional planar hexagonal arrangement of atoms with strong bonds being confined to the planes. The graphite crystal is formed by stacking these planes on top of each other in an alternating sequence, as shown in the following diagram. Because the layer planes of carbon atoms in graphite are held together very weakly they can slide over each other easily and hence give graphite its lubricating property. This property also allows a pencil to write. Indeed the word graphite comes from the Greek word for writing. We shall later see that it is the fourth "free" electron which causes graphite to conduct heat and electricity and be opaque.

Diamond   Graphite
(R. Cotterill, *The Cambridge Guide to the Material World*, Cambridge University Press, 1985, p.54)

This leaves us with microstructure and macrostructure to talk about. We mentioned **microstructure** in Chapter 1 in reference to the first microscopic observation of crystals in metals. We now know that all metallic materials consist of an assembly of crystals. Microstructure is a term used to describe the characteristics of these crystals. How big are they? What shape are they? How are they arranged? We therefore say that microstructure defines the size, shape and orientation of the crystals.

The following two photographs of polycrystalline silicon carbide were taken in an electron microscope, where we are actually looking through a very thin piece of material. Each area of approximately the same shade is a little crystal or grain (we often use the term **crystallite** in referring to such small crystals, about a micron (μm) or two in *size* (a micron is a millionth of a meter). You can also see that the crystallites are about the same size in all directions, something we call an **equiaxed** microstructure, this refers to the *shape* of the crystallites. For equiaxed, block-like crystallites there is no *orientation* to consider.

1 micron   1 micron

Two photographs of polycrystalline silicon carbide taken in an electron microscope. The grains are about one micron (μm) across. Note that many of the angles at the corners of grains are approximately 120°.

Now let's look at how this relates to graphite. Graphite crystals such as found in the electrode of a D-cell battery tend to be flake-like (lamellar or tabular), a result of the layered crystal structure. They may be a micron or so wide but are not nearly as thick. In this material therefore the crystallites tend to lie parallel to each other as will a pack of cards if thrown onto a table. All we have said here describes the microstructure, the size (~1μm), the shape (tabular), and the orientation (parallel) of the crystals. Such a microstructure is typical of all graphites, although the crystallite sizes may differ.

If you go to buy a diamond, as many of you will, you may be advised to look at the four C's - color, clarity, cut and carat. We shall later look at some of the causes of color (Chapter 23), especially as it occurs in gemstones. At this point it is sufficient to state that color is often produced by impurities. We have already mentioned (Page 8) that small amounts of iron impurity in window glass give it a blue/green tinge, and we shall later discuss the importance of impurities in optical fibers.

The lack of any free electrons in diamond (they are all used to form bonds with other carbon atoms) allows light to pass right through it, i.e. the material is transparent. The addition of a few boron atoms to diamond (changing the **atomic structure**) give it a blue tinge whereas the addition of a few nitrogen atoms turns it slightly yellow. This occurs naturally in nature and is the reason for the slight color of some diamonds. Strangely enough a slightly yellow tinge makes a diamond less valuable, whereas a blue diamond is more valuable. By the way, look at the periodic table and note that boron and nitrogen lie either side of carbon and so, respectively, have one fewer and one more electron than carbon.

Many diamonds contain flaws, which are features of the **micro-structure**. Flaws are usually in the form of small black inclusions which are not really impurities because they are microscopic regions where the carbon atoms have decided to arrange themselves in the graphite crystal structure rather than that of diamond. There may also be some planar flaws which are essentially places where two crystals join. These you certainly want to avoid. Your diamond should be a single crystal rather than polycrystalline. Polycrystalline diamonds are best crushed and used as abrasives in drill bits or cutting wheels. There is considerable research interest nowadays in the laboratory production of polycrystalline diamond films for electronics, and we shall see why there is this interest when we consider semiconductors (Chapter 24).

The value of a diamond can be greatly enhanced by expert cutting. Today's solitaire diamonds have what is known as a 'brilliant' cut in which the angles between the facets have been carefully calculated to produce the maximum fire and sparkle in the stone. Years ago diamonds were usually cut to conserve the maximum volume of the stone whereas today we sacrifice some of the stone for extra brilliance. A gem cutter will often spend weeks studying a large rough stone, usually costing millions of dollars, before making the first cut (what a responsibility!) This is because larger diamonds are proportionally more valuable than smaller ones. On the other hand cutting into smaller stones is often necessary to eliminate some major flaws. The shape (cut) and size of the diamond are descriptions of the **macrostructure**.

Other forms of carbon

In the last few years there has been considerable excitement about a new form of carbon called **fullerene**. A fullerene molecule consists of sixty carbon atoms arranged in a sphere as they would be if one were placed on each corner of the panels in a soccer ball, which has 20 hexagons (6-sided panels) and 12 pentagons (five-sided panels). The name reflects the fact that the atoms are arranged in the form of the geodesic domes created by Buckminster Fuller. In a crystal these spheres stack together in the same way that you would arrange balls for the break on a pool table. At the moment these 'buckyballs' are expensive and have no practical importance.

Soot is very impure carbon which has no crystal structure. It may contain some small regions it which there are very small graphite layers, but these layers are not arranged in any ordered manner. We therefore say that the material has short-range order, but no long-range order. Such materials are called **amorphous**, the atoms have no regular arrangement. Soot is a messy material which has more uses than we probably realize. We know it as something which periodically has to be swept from chimneys and in industrial areas it is a nuisance as it soils our clothes and laundry. However we probably do not realize that it is essentially purified soot which is used as a colorant for inks, cosmetics (mascara) and candy (liquorice) and as an important reinforcing agent in car tires, where it also serves to keep light out. The material, known as **carbon black**, is produced under very carefully controlled conditions in special furnaces, and different processing enables the production of different microstructures.

The microstructure of carbon black is usually similar to a string of malted milk balls melted together. The outer layer is somewhat crystalline (this is where there are rather imperfect graphite layer planes present) while the centers are totally amorphous, without even any short-range atomic order. Some of these materials are called "black pearls" to reflect the structure shown below. The microstructure is quite complex, and the sizes of the spheres and the lengths of the strands vary depending on the method of manufacture.

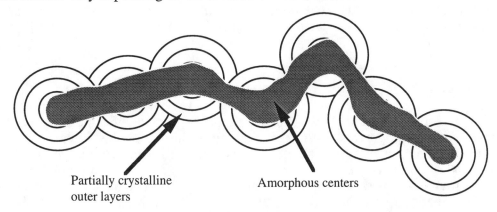

Partially crystalline
outer layers

Amorphous centers

Diagram illustrating the microstructure of a carbon black particle.

Carbon fibers are another form of carbon which you have probably encountered. They are nowadays quite common in tennis and squash rackets, skis, golf clubs and other sporting goods. If you have ever used such an article you will know that it combines light weight with a high stiffness, properties which are also desirable for aircraft frames etc. The bonds between the carbon atoms in the graphite layers are very strong which makes these planes very strong and rigid. In carbon fibers these layers are arranged to lie along the fiber length so that when you pull on the fiber you are pulling along these layers and hence pulling on the strong bonds between the atoms in the layers. This is an excellent example of how structure affects properties. We shall discuss carbon fibers and their use in composites in chapter 21.

Activated carbons are porous carbons used, for example, in filters for water purification. This carbon usually comes in the form of granules which are enclosed in a cartridge which we attach to the faucet   There are also some cigarettes which use activated carbon filters, and in industry there are numerous important applications. The structure of activated carbon is very complex. **Glassy carbon** is a hard brittle material in which graphite-like ribbons are all tangled up. It leaves no mark on paper as a result. Its only current use is as crucibles in chemical laboratories. We merely mention these two materials as further illustrations of the wide variety of carbon materials available.

All the materials mentioned so far are simply carbon and hence have the same atomic structures. Although there are certainly small amounts of impurity present, as is true of all materials, this is of no consequence here except as mentioned for diamonds. Diamond and graphite have different electron and crystal structures. All the materials mentioned can have a variety of micro- and macrostructures.

SILICON

As a further example we take a material, or element, which can be said to have exerted the greatest influence on society during the last several years. Silicon is the basis of almost all electronics, and in today's world is involved in so many of our activities, both work and leisure. It has produced revolutions in the availability of personal electronics in the form of pocketable cassette and CD players, the ignition system and instrumentation in our automobiles, household electronics such as security systems, microwaves, etc. In the areas of computers and video games the advances can still be seen on a less than annual basis.

It is perhaps difficult to believe that when Hewlett-Packard introduced their first pocket calculator some 25 years ago it cost $395 and had a waiting list of six months. In today's dollars this was over $1000. Today we can buy a much smaller unit with more capabilities for under $20! The changes brought about by the silicon 'chips' which control the plethora of electronic devices around us are truly tremendous.

Silicon comprises about 25% of the earth's surface. It commonly exists in nature in the form of sand - silicon oxide (SiO_2). We shall later (Chapter 8) discuss one of the ways super-pure silicon can be obtained for use in a wide variety of electronic components, but here we simply want to ask what it is that makes this material a semiconductor. The answer lies in the way the electrons are arranged and held in the solid, in other words the **electron structure**.

If you look once more at the periodic table you will see that silicon lies immediately under carbon, and we have already noted (Page 8) that "elements in the same column have somewhat similar properties." Like carbon, silicon has four outer or valence electrons and is also able to form bonds with four surrounding silicon atoms. In fact it does so in an identical manner such that the **crystal structure** of silicon is identical to that of diamond. Each silicon atom is again bonded to four other silicon atoms which lie at the corners of a tetrahedron. There is therefore no need to show an illustration of the crystal structure of silicon because the diagram would be identical to that given earlier for diamond (Page 13). There is no form of silicon with the crystal structure of graphite.

Although carbon (diamond) and silicon have identical crystal structures and the *atoms* have similar electronic structures, the materials are quite different. Whereas pure diamond is transparent and colorless, silicon is opaque and has a shiny metallic luster. Why? The reason lies in the fact that the bonds between atoms in silicon are not nearly as strong as those in diamond. The electrons doing the bonding are somewhat loose and some of them occasionally break free in the same way that they do in metals. In other words the electronic structures in the two *solids* are quite different. We shall explore this in more detail in chapter 24.

We saw earlier in this chapter that adding the impurity atoms boron and nitrogen to diamond changes the color. These elements are situated either side of carbon in the periodic table (Page 7). If we do the same thing with silicon, where the corresponding elements are aluminum and phosphorus, we change the electrical properties tremendously and open this material to a host of new applications. The impurities in diamond are added in nature, but in semiconductors we intentionally add the required impurities, a process called **doping**. In fact we can add different impurities to different areas of our silicon and hence produce the 'chips' which we hear so much about nowadays. In the doping process we change the atoms - the **atomic structure** of the material.

As already mentioned, there is only one possible crystal structure for silicon, and it is perhaps worth noting that crystal structure is usually the one level of structure which we have no control over. We cannot just go into a material and arrange the atoms to suit. However, we can sometimes make a material amorphous, with the atoms randomly arranged, i.e. no crystal structure. Amorphous silicon has been of interest for use in solar cells (Chapter 25).

SILICON OXIDE

There is one example in nature of a material which has a large number of crystal structures. This is silicon oxide. In this material the silicon atom again forms four bonds, but this time with oxygen atoms. These oxygen atoms are also situated on the corners of a tetrahedron. To visualize it all you have to do is look at the tetrahedron of carbon atoms shown earlier in this chapter and imagine that the central atom is silicon and the outer four are oxygens. (Notice how many similarities in structure we have encountered in looking at carbon, silicon and silicon oxide - three quite different materials).

Oxygen is an atom which has two valence electrons available to form bonds and so wants to join up with two silicon atoms. The natural result of this is that the corners of one tetrahedron are shared with others, i.e. each oxygen atom can be considered to sit on the corners of two tetrahedra at the same time. This is what happens in the crystal structure illustrated below. Thus the four oxygen atoms are each shared between two tetrahedra, and in essence only two (four halves) oxygen atoms belong to the silicon atom. This gives us the chemical formula SiO_2. Note that this structure is what would be obtained by placing an oxygen midway between the silicon atoms in the structure of silicon just examined. This material is known as cristobalite.

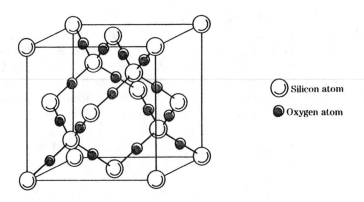

The crystal structure of cristobalite (SiO_2).
(W. F. Smith, *Principles of Materials Science and Engineering,* McGraw Hill, New York, 1986. Fig. 10.22.
Reproduced with permission of the publisher)

There are two other arrangements of these tetrahedra for which all the corners are shared. They are more complicated than in cristobalite and there is no need to go into details. These two other forms are known as tridymite and quartz. Of these three possible arrangements of the tetrahedra, quartz is probably the only one you have heard of. It is a clear, colorless crystal which is sometimes used as a (poor) fake diamond. It is also the crystal in quartz watches. If we make the crystals very small the material becomes opaque and white and is very strong We commonly encounter this material as Corning Ware®. We call this material a glass ceramic because it starts life as glass, more than 90% of which is then changed to a crystalline ceramic by 'seeding' it with very small crystals of titanium oxide, which cause SiO_2 crystals to form from the glass. It is also sometimes called **pyroceram** (because it is a ceramic which tolerates large sudden changes in temperature: pyro - heat). We shall discuss it in Chapter 19.

Glass has these tetrahedra arranged in a random manner and is considered an amorphous material. It is another example of a material in which the atoms have short-range order (tetrahedra) but have no long-range order. The following diagram of the atomic arrangement in glass portrays it as a distorted cube of cristobalite, but most glasses are far more complex because they have had other atoms added to modify the properties. Sometimes these impurities come between the tetrahedra producing weaker connections thus making a glass which softens at a lower temperature (see Chapter 7).

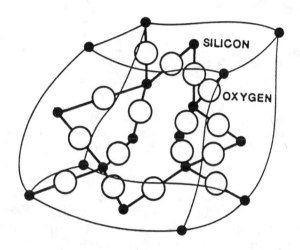

The random three-dimensional network of a silica glass (SiO_2).
(K. Easterling, *Tomorrow's Materials*, The Institute of Metals, London, U.K., 1988. Fig. 5)

In nature the tetrahedra are also arranged in a number of other ways. In one they are linked together in sheets as shown in the following diagram. (You are looking down on tetrahedra sitting on a flat sheet so that they share the three corners on the base). These sheets stack as shown in the side view with other atoms between their peaks. This material is called **talc** - the slippery mineral found in talcum powder. The other atoms hold the sheets of tetrahedra together very weakly so that they can slide over each other producing a slippery material.

The above arrangement (talc) is one example of how the tetrahedra share three corners, with other atoms between the unshared corners. There are other arrangements where either three or two corners are shared. One of the latter is the rare and valuable gemstone known as emerald. All these materials have different **crystal structures** (arrangements of the atoms) and different **atomic structures** (other atoms connected to the unshared corners of the tetrahedra.) This whole range of materials is known as the silicate minerals.

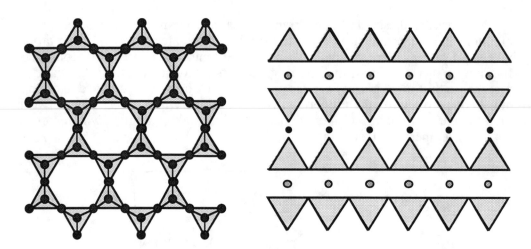

In the left hand diagram you are looking down on a sheet of silica tetrahedra.
The right hand diagram shows how these sheets stack together to form talc.
Potassium atoms ◎; Magnesium atoms ●

In the above discussion we mentioned Corning Ware® which is found in the form of cooking pans in most kitchens. These give an excellent example of the importance of the **macrostructure** of materials. You will see that the corners are rounded. Not only does this make the article easier to clean but it, more importantly, reduces the chances of breakage. Sharp corners are places where breakage is likely to occur, or to use the technical jargon, fracture can be initiated. This is somewhat like making a sharp fold in a piece of paper before tearing it so that the tear goes (maybe) where you want it to.

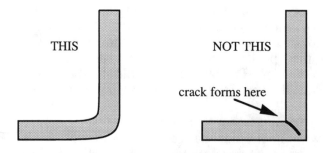

Diagram illustrating how a sharp corner acts as a place
where breakage starts, or fracture initiates.

Processing

Materials science is "the science of the relationships between the structure and the properties of materials", to quote the introduction to this chapter, but there is more to it than that. If we want to change a property by changing the structure, how do we go about it? The answer is that we have to do it by processing, i.e. the ways we treat the material during manufacture.

Here again we have a topic which has so many aspects. Perhaps an analogy will help. Most people have perhaps baked a cake or something similar. The recipe usually starts with the list of ingredients, which is important. But what follows is perhaps even more important, instructions on how to combine them and treat them. Which ingredients do you blend first? Do you first mix the flour and sugar and then add the eggs, or should the order be different? Do you just throw the eggs in the bowl straight from the shell, or do you beat them first? Do you bake in a shallow or a deep pan? Do you bake for ten minutes at 450°F or forty minutes at 350°F? All these actions are part of the processing, and variations will result in different products. There may also be some art (experience) involved. How many times has one followed another person's recipe to the letter, only to find that the product turned out to be completely different!

The processing of materials is in many ways analogous to baking a cake. The ingredients are important, but how we treat them is just as important, if not more so. Sometimes traditional procedures are more of an art than a science! Here are some general questions the materials scientist has to answer.

Metals are usually formed from a melt. How fast do we cool them? Do we stop the cooling at any point and hold the temperature there? If so, for how long? What happens if we plunge our red hot metal into ice water?

Ceramics are usually formed from powders. How fine should the powder be? What liquid should we mix it with to make a formable paste? What temperature should we fire it to in the kiln? For how long? Does it matter how we cool it?

We have already mentioned other aspects of processing for specific materials: e.g.

We insert impurity atoms into silicon, changing the atomic structure.

We add TiO_2 to glass to promote fine scale crystal formation, and thus produce a glass ceramic, changing atomic and micro structure.

We cut facets on a diamond to give brilliance, changing the macro structure.

All these are examples of **processing** to change properties.

As a result of these interrelationships we sometimes draw the following triangle describing the relationships between these three variables.

PROPERTIES

STRUCTURE   **PROCESSING**

The properties of a material depend on its structure, and the structure, and hence the properties, can be changed by different processing methods. **Materials Science** is concerned with learning about these relationships and how we can tailor properties by intentionally changing structure by the processing.

Up to ~ 30/40 yrs. ago we tended to accept the materials provided by nature (providence), or we had materials which had been developed almost accidentally with no knowledge of how their properties had been produced. Nowadays we understand why they behave the way they do and can often see how to change and improve them. This is the way many new materials are produced.

4. THE DIFFERENT CLASSES OF MATERIALS

Before we go further let's look at the three major classes of materials: metals, polymers and ceramics. Usually we classify semiconductors, glasses, and possibly carbons, as ceramics although they may not exactly fit the descriptions given below. There are exceptions to almost every rule!

Let's start with **METALS** - What do we know about them?

They are usually recognizable because they are opaque and have a shine or luster. If they are dull it is usually because the surface has been oxidized by contact and reaction with the air. If we scratch them we remove this oxide layer and reveal new shiny metal. You may want to try this with a piece of aluminum, where the surface is a thin layer of aluminum oxide.

Although some are brittle we know that many are quite ductile. We can bend a copper wire into any shape. We form body panels of cars from steels by placing them in a press with a mold of the part to be formed. We are also aware that if we keep bending a metal (e.g. a paper clip), it becomes hard and brittle so that it eventually breaks.

Steels are quite strong and are used as I (eye) beams in constructing large buildings. Here we have metals which don't bend easily and carry a lot of weight. Steel is the traditional strong metal. We can therefore immediately appreciate that there are considerable differences between the strengths and stiffnesses of metals.

There are only three common metals (iron, nickel and cobalt) which are magnetic, but there are some circumstances in which even these are not magnetic. Note that most metals, including many steels, are not magnetic.

Metals usually conduct heat and electricity well, although we know from cooking pans that copper and iron conduct heat better than stainless steel, which is usually given an aluminum or copper base to overcome this deficiency. We do not usually make seats of bare metal because they conduct the heat away from our bodies rather quickly and hence feel cold to our touch. Electrical wiring in our houses in usually copper. We never think of using stainless steel wires to conduct electricity.

Most elements are metals. There are some common traditional metals such as aluminum, copper, iron, gold, silver, etc. There are also some rather rare metals such as gadolinium, osmium, ruthenium and holmium.

Many metals we encounter in today's world are mixtures (alloys). The gold wedding band is a copper-gold alloy, and different color golds are produced by mixing different metals with the gold. Stainless steel is a mixture of iron, chromium and nickel, with a little carbon for good measure. Some magnets are mixtures of iron, aluminum, nickel and cobalt. There is no end to the number of metal alloys we can make. Not only do we have a choice of eighty metallic elements but we also have a choice of the proportions we mix them in. This truly provides an infinite number of possibilities.

Except when produced under very special circumstances, metals are crystalline. The crystallite size is controlled by changing the way the material is cooled from the melt, a process called 'heat treating.'

POLYMERS (from the Greek, poly - many; meros - part, many parts) are modern materials although many naturally occurring materials (wool, cotton, skin, rubber, etc.) are polymeric. They are usually based on a chain of carbon atoms. Different polymers have different things attached to the chain (a much simplified description as we shall later see).

Most are **plastic**, meaning that they can be easily bent into a different shape, hence the more common term - but some can be brittle. Polymers are usually considered to be either thermoplastics, meaning that they become more flexible when heated, or thermosets, meaning that heat causes them to set hard and rigid.

Polymers are usually thermal and electrical insulators. They are used for thermal insulation in houses and for insulation in electrical wiring and junction boxes etc. There are some recent developments in conductive plastics but they are beyond the scope of our discussion and are not something we are likely to encounter in our daily lives for a while.

Polymers are not magnetic.

Today we see polymers all around us - acrylic and nylon clothing, polycarbonate football helmets & protective lenses, polyurethane coverings for chairs, polystyrene food & beverage containers (styrofoam), polyethylene dishpans, polyvinyl chloride pipes, etc. Every year sees the development of hundreds of new polymers.

CERAMICS are non-metallic materials which were originally thought of only as oxides. The name comes from the Greek for "burnt earth" - because when you burn something it combines with the oxygen in the air. Modern ceramics are often produced by combining metals with boron (borides), carbon (carbides) and nitrogen (nitrides). However, you will probably not find these around the home except in small specialized applications such as coatings on drill bits. They are expensive and are mainly used in military and aerospace applications but their special properties are finding more and more applications in automobiles, for example.

Traditional ceramics are often based on clay, which is a silicate mineral (Chapter 3). We see these traditional materials in porcelain and stoneware plates, bathroom fixtures, and bricks & pipes for building materials.

Glass and cement are both ceramics, as are silica (SiO_2) and alumina (Al_2O_3) particles on sand paper, and silicon carbide (SiC) on carborundum paper.

Ceramics are usually thought of as brittle and not easily bent. Compare the dropping of a pewter and a porcelain or glass beer tankard! The metal tankard will do no more than dent while the ceramic articles will almost certainly break catastrophically (shatter).

Ceramics do not conduct heat very well and can withstand high temperatures. They are used as thermal insulators in fireplaces (firebricks) and in insulation for houses (fiberglass). Large industrial furnaces used for steel manufacture are lined with ceramic bricks because they can stand up to the high temperatures and are also insulating.

Ceramics don't conduct electricity. We see them used as electrical insulators on telegraph poles (less seen nowadays) and on high voltage electrical transmission lines. Yes, there are now ceramic superconductors but they are rather special.

Some ceramics are magnetic. Ceramics are used for the little magnets that hold notes to refrigerator doors, and the door seals consist of ceramic magnet powders mixed into a plastic. Ceramic magnets are also used extensively in TV sets and other electrical components. Their advantages over metal magnets are that they do not conduct electricity and do not rust.

Ceramics are usually crystalline, and like metals, their grain sizes can be controlled during the processing of the material, but in this case it is usually a result of the grain size of the ground powder used - finer powders give smaller grain sizes..

Glass and many other ceramics are transparent. We shall see that transparency is due to purity and that some materials are not as pure as we may think.

SEMICONDUCTORS - are a special class of materials.

Silicon and germanium are the elements which most readily come to mind. They have similar electron structures and the same crystal structures.

Gallium arsenide (GaAs) is a newer semiconductor of which you may have heard. We shall see (Page 256) that it has many of the same structural characteristics of silicon and germanium. Its importance for the future is that electrons can travel faster in it than in the conventional semiconductors. Since these electrons are what carry the information in a computer, one can see that GaAs holds a possible key to even faster computers. At least one company makes a radar detector based on GaAs with the claim that it gives you an earlier warning of the fate that may be awaiting you!

GLASSES are really a special class of ceramics. They are usually thought of as oxide based materials, but today there are important materials such as glassy carbon and glassy metals. We shall consider some of these briefly later.

Glasses are always brittle (but can be very strong) and are amorphous.

5. BONDING

The Structure of Atoms

Atoms have a nucleus composed of two types of particles, neutrons which have no electrical charge and are therefore neutral, and protons which have a positive electrical charge. This nucleus is surrounded by electrons which have a negative electrical charge. The number of surrounding electrons is equal to the number of protons in the nucleus so that the atom is electrically *neutral* because it contains equal numbers of electrons and protons.

A simple model of an atom compares it to the solar system, electrons go round the nucleus in fixed orbits, just as the planets orbit the sun. These orbits give rise to **electron shells**. The further away from the nucleus the larger the shell and the larger the number of electrons which can be accommodated in it.

The first shell can contain 2 electrons, corresponding to the two lightest elements, hydrogen and helium.

H   He

The second shell can contain 8 electrons, giving the elements lithium, beryllium, boron, carbon, nitrogen, oxygen, fluorine and neon.

Li   Be   B   C   N   O   F   Ne

The third shell can contain 18 electrons. Elements corresponding to the filling of this shell can be seen on the Periodic Table (Page 7).

The maximum number of electrons which can be accommodated in a shell is $2n^2$, where n in the number of the shell, so the fourth shell could contain a maximum of 32 electrons. However, nature keeps things simple - the first 8 electrons (e⁻'s) in the shell are what make an atom stable. Look at the periodic table and you will see that the right-hand column contains what we call the **inert gases**. These are gases which do not react with other elements to form compounds. With the exception of helium, which can only have a maximum of two electrons in its one and only shell, they all have eight electrons in their outer shell. As an example the electron structure of argon is shown.

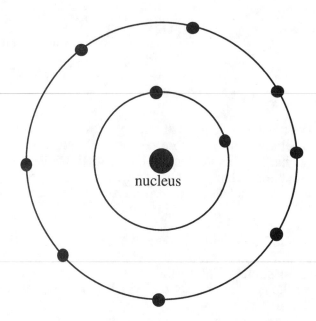

The electron structure of the inert gas argon.

Some of these inert gases may be familiar to you. Radon is something we have heard about recently in houses as a radioactive hazard. Xenon is sometimes found in photo flash tubes, and everyone has heard of neon lights.

Helium	2	e⁻'s in	1st shell
Neon	8	-----	2nd ----
Argon	8	-----	3rd ----
Krypton	8	-----	4th ----
Xenon	8	-----	5th ----
Radon	8	-----	6th ----

Atoms which have eight electrons in their outer shell are very stable and all atoms strive to achieve this state. In many respects it is the desire to have an outer shell of 8 electrons, sometimes called an "octet", which is responsible for chemical bonding. The different types of bond that exist between atoms are often due to the different ways the atoms decide to redistribute their electrons to achieve the desired eight. Just think what people could do if everybody wanted to have only eight dollars. Some would just let their excess cash go to a pool (maybe to pay off the national debt!) Others with, for example six and two, would get together and share. Yet others, for example seven and nine, could engage in a give-and-take arrangement. This example, however silly, is illustrative of the three major ways atoms use their electrons to form bonds with each other.

There are five main types of bond, and they are very instrumental in determining the properties of materials, although sometimes their role is minor. We shall therefore spend some time describing them and some of their major characteristics which affect the properties of materials.

Metallic bonds

About eighty of the hundred or so elements are metals. What makes these elements metals? It is simply the way the electrons hold the atoms together. Naturally we call the bonds that hold these atoms together **metallic bonds**.

Metals are elements which have a tendency to release their electrons. In a pure metal the electrons are therefore released from the outer electron shell, leaving a unit which has a net positive charge because there is now no longer the same number of electrons surrounding the atom as there are protons in the nucleus. We call this unit an **ion**. Because it is positively charged we call it a **cation**.

From a variety of experiments which are outside the scope of this discussion we know that, on average, each atom releases approximately one electron. A simple model of the metallic solid is therefore of a number of singly charged cations surrounded by **free electrons**. One of the fundamentals of physics with which you are probably familiar is that like charges (positive-positive & negative-negative) repel each other, whereas unlike charges (positive-negative) attract each other. Of course the cations are positively charged and the electrons are negatively charged which means that there is an attraction between them. It is this attraction which holds the atoms together. This **electrostatic attraction** between the cations and the electrons has certain characteristics which are important in determining the properties of metals.

The bond produced is quite strong. We cannot be too precise on this point because there are large variations. The bond between the atoms in mercury is quite weak, a fact that is demonstrated by the fact that mercury (Hg) is a liquid at room temperature. When materials are heated the energy goes into making the atoms vibrate, and eventually this vibration energy is enough to break the bonds and the material melts. At room temperature the bonds between the mercury atoms have been broken. On the other hand the bonds in tungsten (W) are very strong. We use tungsten filaments in light bulbs and the tungsten does not melt! In fact tungsten does not melt until its temperature reaches 3400°C (6350°F).

The electrons in a metal are instantaneously moving in all directions at the same time. It is important to realize that they are free of the atoms, or cations, even though they are what is holding the material together. We some times refer to them as a **sea of electrons** or an **electron glue**. When we put a voltage across a piece of metal we put a force on the electrons which forces them to travel preferentially in one direction. We call this an **electric current**. This is simply why metals are electrical conductors.

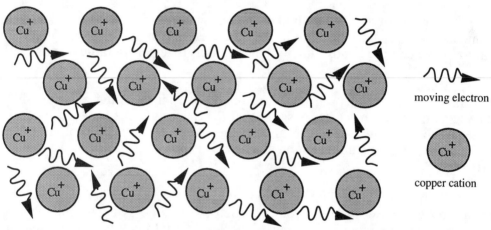

moving electron

copper cation

Illustration of how free electrons move randomly between the cations and form a metallic bond.

Metallic bonds have **no directionality**. This is a really important concept which requires amplification. Because the electrons act as a sort of glue, the metal atoms can arrange themselves in almost any way they want to. The bonds do not point in any direction. Think of the atoms being held together as if they were wooden balls held together by a glue that never really dries, rather than by nails. Nails would be directed and fix the balls in position, whereas the glue that never sets would allow the balls to be moved around. There are several consequences of this glue concept. The two most important are:

(i) The atoms can pack closely; there is nothing to stop them from getting as close as possible, which is something they want to do. As a consequence metals are quite heavy or dense.

(ii) The atoms can move over each other and change positions relatively easily. This is the basic reason why metals can be formed by pressing, hammering, etc.

We shall later see that there is much more to these two concepts, but it is true to say that they are due to the non-directionality of the metallic bonds.

Covalent bonds

While metal atoms share their electrons throughout the piece of metal, there are some materials in which atoms share electrons with specific nearby atoms in order to achieve the stable octet (8) which they wish to attain. The best way to understand this is to look at a specific example. We have spent some time talking about carbon materials (Page 11). The carbon atom is element number 6, which means it has six electrons, two in the first shell and four in the second. These four outer electrons are the **valence electrons**. In diamond a carbon atom gets its octet by sharing these four electrons with four neighboring atoms as shown in the following diagram. Each pair of shared electrons between adjacent atoms constitutes what we call a **covalent bond** (co- meaning 'together').

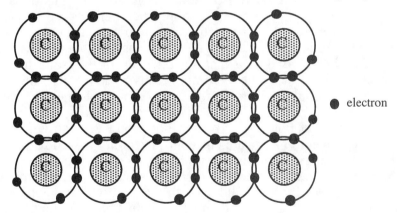

Illustration of how carbon atoms in diamond share electrons so that each has eight.

Notice each atom has four bonds each of which contains two electrons (electron pairs). Electrons are all negatively charged and therefore all four electron pairs repel each other. The bonds are pushed as far away from each other as possible, with the result that there is an angle of 109.5° between them. This is what causes the four surrounding carbon atoms to be situated on the corners of a tetrahedron with the other atom at the center. The following diagram of the diamond crystal structure specifically illustrates this point.

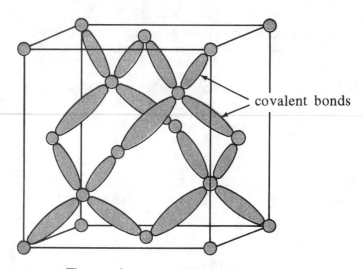

The crystal structure of diamond.
(W. F. Smith, *Principles of Materials Science and Engineering,* McGraw Hill, New York, 1986. Fig. 2.19. Reproduced with permission of the publisher)

From the above discussion you can see that covalent bonds are **directional**, i.e. they place the surrounding atoms in fixed positions, as nails would fix wooden balls in position, as mentioned earlier. As a consequence the atoms in solids which are held together by covalent bonds cannot stack as closely as they do in metals, and the resulting materials are usually not as dense. Another result of this directional bonding is that it is difficult for the atoms to move past each other, and the materials do not deform as easily as do metals. Since there are no free electrons, materials with covalent bonds do not conduct electricity.

Finally we must note that covalent bonds are very strong, in fact the strongest bonds known in nature are covalent. Diamond is well recognized as a very hard, strong material, and the strength of the covalent bond in graphite is taken advantage of in carbon/graphite fibers. Silicon and germanium also have four outer electrons, and in the solid have the same atom arrangement (crystal structure) as do the carbon atoms in diamond, but the bonds are longer and not as strong as they are in diamond.

Covalent bonds are what hold the two atoms together in a molecule of oxygen (O_2) or a molecule of nitrogen (N_2). They are also important in many ceramic materials, and are what hold the carbon atoms together in long-chain polymer molecules. This is one reason why polymers are tough materials: the chains are difficult to break because of the very strong covalent bonds between the carbon atoms forming them.

Ionic bonds

Another way of achieving an octet of electrons in the outer electron shell is for atoms to exchange electrons among themselves. The most often used, and most simple, example is that of sodium chloride or common salt (NaCl).

Sodium (element number 11) has just one outer electron, while chlorine (element number 17) has seven outer electrons. If the chlorine takes one electron from the sodium they then both have an outer shell of eight electrons.

Now the Na has lost an electron so has one more positive charge on the nucleus than the number of electrons. This atomic entity is an ion (Na$^+$) and, because it is positively charged, it is called a **cation.** The chlorine has one more electron than the number of positive charges on the nucleus which produces an **anion** (Cl$^-$) which is negatively charged. These positive and negative charges attract each other (**electrostatic attraction**) and hence produce an ionic bond.

In some respects the bond produced is similar to a metallic bond. The ions can attract each other in *any* direction. The electrons are in spherical shells around the atoms and there is therefore no preferred bonding direction. The **ions** can therefore pack as closely as possible and they do. The following diagram illustrates this situation for sodium chloride (common salt).

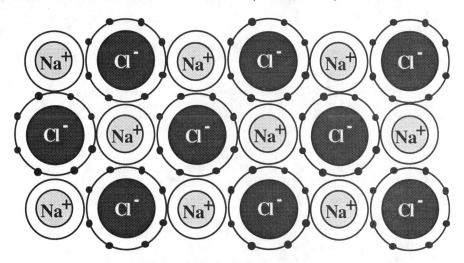

The packing of ions in sodium chloride.

Note that the cation is usually smaller than the corresponding neutral atom because the larger positive charge on the nucleus pulls the surrounding electrons in more. For similar reasons the anion is larger than the corresponding neutral atom. We therefore are now concerned with the packing of two different sizes of ions and the way the ions pack depends on their relative sizes. In general they pack as efficiently as possible as illustrated in the following diagram.

The small cation will not pack as shown on the left, but will be surrounded by three anions as shown in the center. However a larger cation (right) will be surrounded by four anions.

Ionic bonds are typically very strong and are important in many ceramics.

The three bond types considered so far - **covalent, ionic, metallic** - are known as the three **primary bonds**. They are the strongest bonds and one or more of them is involved in holding together the atoms in any useful solid material.

Before we go on let's summarize some of their important differences and characteristics.

• ionic bonds involve the transfer of electrons; covalent and metallic bonds involve the sharing of electrons.

• covalent bonds are directional; ionic and metallic bonds are non-directional.

• metallic bonds involve attraction between cations and a sea of electrons; ionic bonds involve attraction between cations and anions. Covalent bonds do not involve electrostatic attraction.

In addition to these three bonds there are some much weaker bonds between atoms and molecules and these sometimes dictate the properties of a material, especially the strength. After all, a chain is only as strong as its weakest link. These other bonds, which we call **secondary bonds**, are often the weak points in materials.

Hydrogen bonds

This secondary bond is the one with which we are probably most familiar. It is the bond which holds water molecules together in ice.

Water consists of molecules of H_2O. The molecule is angular (not straight) with the hydrogens making an angle of 105° with the oxygen atom (the three atoms form an isosceles triangle). The hydrogen atoms are *covalently* bonded to the oxygen atoms but the electrons in the bonds are shifted somewhat towards the oxygen. Or to look at it another way, they spend more time with the oxygen atom than they do with the hydrogen atoms. This makes the molecule more negative at the oxygen atom and more positive at the hydrogen atoms.

This situation produces what we call a **polar molecule**. Just as a magnet has magnetic poles, north and south, with the north having an attraction for the south, a polar molecule has electrical poles, positive and negative, with there being an attraction between unlike poles in the same way that there is an attraction between positive cations and negative anions in an ionic bond.

Diagram of a polar water molecule with covalent bonds between the atoms.

This imbalance in charges is a permanent feature of the molecule, i.e. it is like a triangle with a positive charge on two corners and a negative charge on the other. This charge is much smaller than the single electron charge such as there would be on a chlorine anion or a sodium cation because the electron is not totally displaced as is the case in an ionic bond. The small charge results from the fact that the electron favors the oxygen rather than the hydrogen.

When two molecules of water come together at a low enough temperature the positively charged ends of the molecule are attracted by the negative end of an adjacent molecule with the formation of a bond between them. Just like the ionic bond, this **hydrogen bond** is the result of electrostatic attraction. However, it is much weaker because the charges involved are much smaller. This is why solid ice melts at quite a low temperature. The bonds between the molecules are quite weak.

We should also note another difference between ionic and hydrogen bonds. Ionic bonds hold ions together: hydrogen bonds hold molecules together.

We already mentioned that the water molecule contains an angle of 105°. This is not much different from the angle between the corners of a hexagon (120°). It is therefore perhaps not surprising that when these water molecules are joined together by hydrogen bonds to form ice these angles are slightly stretched to 120° so that the molecules arrange themselves into hexagons as shown below.

This arrangement gives the ice crystals a **hexagonal symmetry** and accounts for the shape of snowflakes. You are probably aware that each snowflake is unique and has the form of a complex six-pointed star.

The arrangement of water molecules in ice crystals.

Another interesting fact about ice, which we can explain from what we know about the bonding between water molecules, is that it is lighter than water. Think about it! Nearly all liquids become denser when they freeze and the solid sinks to the bottom. This is not the case with water, which is why ice forms on the top of a pond rather than sinks to the bottom, or ice floats in your soda.

The hydrogen bonds are **directional** bonds in the sense that they point in the direction of the hydrogen atoms in the molecule. This forces the adjacent molecules into the arrangement shown above, a hexagon with a large space in the middle. This is what accounts for the lower density of ice. In the liquid the molecules can pack more closely than the bonding allows them to in the solid.

Hydrogen bonds are common between molecules which contain hydrogen. They are often important bonds between long chain polymer molecules. While they are not as strong as the primary bonds, they are somewhat stronger than the bonds (van der Waals) which usually exist between polymer molecules. The introduction of hydrogen bonding is therefore one possible way of strengthening the polymer.

Van der Waals bonds

Van der Waals bonds are the weakest of all chemical bonds. The only materials which have only van der Waals bonds are the solid inert gases. They melt at very low temperatures and cannot be considered useful materials.

Van der Waals bonds are more difficult to understand than are hydrogen bonds. They are also the result of electrostatic attraction between polar molecules, but in this case the polarity of the molecules is not permanent or fixed in direction as it is in water. It is always changing or fluctuating. Take the example of neon, an inert gas with 10 electrons (1st shell, 2; 2nd shell, 8), shown below. At any one instant there may be 4 electrons on one side of the atom and 6 on the other. A fraction of a second later the situation may be reversed. This imbalance in the electron distribution gives rise to a **dipole** because the centers of the positive charge in the nucleus and the negative charge of the surrounding electrons do not coincide. However, the dipole is fluctuating.

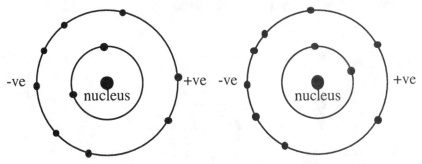

Van der Waals bond formed between two fluctuating dipoles in neon atoms.

These fluctuating dipoles somehow change together so that a bond is formed between the atoms or molecules. The bond is obviously very weak and is non-directional. How could it be anything else, when the dipole is itself always changing direction? Van der Waals bonds are mostly important in polymers and in graphite.

These two bond types - **hydrogen** and **van der Waals -** are known as the **secondary bonds**. They are important in materials because, when present, they are often the weak links in an otherwise strong material.

In closing this discussion of the chemical bonding which holds materials together we shall make a few general important points.

- bonds other than covalent are really caused by positive and negative charges attracting each other.

- only covalent & hydrogen bonds are directed.

- no important engineering material has only hydrogen or van der Waals bonds. Such a material would be too weak to be of use.

Materials with both primary and secondary bonds

There are many important engineering materials which contain both primary *and* secondary bonds. For example graphite contains both covalent and van der Waals bonds. As mentioned earlier (Page 13), it consists of layers of carbon atoms held together by strong covalent bonds in a hexagonal 'chicken-wire' arrangement; these layer planes are held together by weak van der Waals bonds. The weak bonds between the layers allow them to slide over each other easily, hence the lubricating property of graphite.

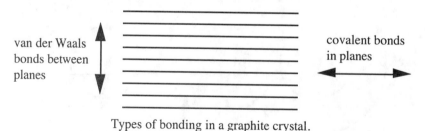

van der Waals bonds between planes

covalent bonds in planes

Types of bonding in a graphite crystal.

Polymers are materials which are based on chains of carbon atoms with strong covalent bonds between the carbon atoms in the chain, but there are usually weak secondary bonds between adjacent chains. For example, polyethylene has the chain shown in the following figure.

$$
\begin{array}{c}
\text{H} \quad \text{H} \quad \text{H} \quad \text{H} \quad \text{H} \quad \text{H} \quad \text{H} \quad \text{H} \quad \text{H} \quad \text{H} \quad \text{H} \\
| \quad | \quad | \quad | \quad | \quad | \quad | \quad | \quad | \quad | \quad | \\
-\text{C}-\text{C}-\text{C}-\text{C}-\text{C}-\text{C}-\text{C}-\text{C}-\text{C}-\text{C}-\text{C}- \\
| \quad | \quad | \quad | \quad | \quad | \quad | \quad | \quad | \quad | \quad | \\
\text{H} \quad \text{H} \quad \text{H} \quad \text{H} \quad \text{H} \quad \text{H} \quad \text{H} \quad \text{H} \quad \text{H} \quad \text{H} \quad \text{H}
\end{array}
$$

A portion of a polyethylene chain molecule.

A piece of solid polyethylene consists of millions of these chains of different lengths, each possibly containing thousands of carbon atoms, held together by weak van der Waals bonds*. In general they are not aligned as shown in the following diagram, but are more convoluted and tangled, however the intention here is to indicate where the two types of bonds are situated.

weak van der Waals bonding

strong covalent bonding

Illustration of a number of polymer chains with covalent bonds along the chains and van der Waals bonds between them.

The following diagram shows what the internal structure of a piece of solid polyethylene may really look like. Sometimes it is likened to a tangled mass of cooked spaghetti. The strands in the spaghetti (polymer chains) are relatively strong, while the bonds between them are quite weak, allowing the strands to slide over each other easily. This easy movement of the chains is what causes many polymers to be plastic, or easily deformed. We shall be reminded several times in this book that deformation of a material involves the motion of atoms. Here this occurs by the sliding of these molecular chains over each other.

---

* Because there are hydrogen atoms on all sides of this long chain polymer molecule there is no dipole production for hydrogen bonding as there is in a water molecule, where there is an oxygen atom on the other side of the molecule. Hydrogen bonds can exist in polymers and, because they are stronger than van der Waals bonds, their introduction provides a means of increasing the strength of the bonds between chains. This is outside the scope of this book.

Diagram of how molecular chains may exist in a piece of polyethylene.

Before we finish this section we should remind ourselves that we have already mentioned another material, not important as a structural solid, which contains two different types of bonds. Ice contains covalent bonds within a molecule and hydrogen bonds between molecules. In a similar manner, dry ice, solid CO_2, also has covalent bonds between the carbon and oxygen atoms in the carbon dioxide molecule, but van der Waals bonds between the molecules. There are many instances where a solid contains two different bonds. We have only mentioned the most important ones.

QUESTIONS: Chapters 1-5

1. Which of the following is true for metallic bonding?
    (a) directional (b) transfer of electrons (c) attraction between cation and anion
    (d) allows for close packing of atoms (e) both c and d

2. Metallic and ionic bonds are similar in what way(s)?
    (a) directional (b) transfer of electrons (c) close packing of ions (d) both a and b
    (e) both a and c

3. Which of the following is not true of ionic bonding?
    (a) non-directional (b) allows for close packing of ions (c) strong (d) bonded atoms
    share an octet (8) of electrons

4. Graphite and diamond both have the same _____ structure.
    (a) atomic (b) electron (c) crystal (d) micro (e) macro

5. A good example of a material that has two different types of bonds is _____.
    (a) diamond (b) silicon (c) sodium chloride (d) iron (e) ice

6. The maximum number of electrons in the 3rd shell of an atom is _____.
    (a) 8 (b) 10 (c) 18 (d) 28 (e) none of these

7. The secondary bonds are _____.
    (a) covalent & hydrogen (b) metallic & ionic (c) hydrogen & ionic (d) hydrogen & van
    der Waals (e) covalent and ionic

8. When buying a diamond, you should look at the "cut", "clarity", "carat", and "color".
    Which level of structure does "cut" relate to?
    (a) electron (b) crystal (c) micro (d) macro (e) electron

9. Graphite has secondary bonds in _____ dimension(s) which makes it a good _____.
    (a) two; conductor (b) one; lubricant (c) three; semiconductor (d) two; superconductor

10. The addition of a small amount of nitrogen to diamond makes it _____.
    (a) brittle (b) yellow (c) stronger (d) blue (e) none of the above

11. The element sulfur has 16 electrons. How many are in its outermost shell?
    (a) 0 (b) 2 (c) 4 (d) 6 (e) 8

12. In diamond, all four valence electrons of a carbon atom are bonded to other carbon atoms
    with _____ bonds.
    (a) covalent (b) ionic (c) metallic (d) van der Waals (e) hydrogen

13. Which is not a primary bond?
    (a) covalent (b) hydrogen (c) ionic (d) metallic

14. Carbon black is important in car tires because it _____.
    (a) reinforces (b) repels water (c) keeps light out (d) both a and b (e) both a and c

15. Which is true of a polymeric material?
    (a) only made from synthetic materials (b) magnetic (c) based on chains of argon atoms
    (d) usually thermal and electrical insulators (e) usually brittle

16. In which of the following would you probably not find the element silicon?
    (a) sand (b) semiconductors (c) glass (d) plastic

17. The intentional addition of foreign atoms to a material is called _____.
    (a) doping (b) smelting (c) refining (d) etching (e) forging

18. An alloy is a mixture of two or more _____.
    (a) ceramics (b) metals (c) polymers (d) metals and ceramics (e) ceramics and polymers

19. Elements desire to have _____ electrons in their outermost shell.
    (a) 0 (b) 4 (c) 6 (d) 8 (e) as many as possible

20. The outermost electrons surrounding an atom are called the _____ electrons.
    (a) orbiting (b) inert (c) free (d) valence (e) none of the above

21. When atoms release electrons they have a net positive charge and are called _____.
    (a) isotopes (b) cations (c) anions (d) inert (e) amorphous

22. Which of the following is not true of covalent bonding?
    (a) directional (b) easy for atoms to move past each other (c) strong (d) bonded atoms share an octet (8) of electrons

23. Which of the following is not an inert gas?
    (a) Hydrogen (b) Neon (c) Xenon (d) Argon (e) Helium

24. Van der Waals bonds are due to a(n) _____ imbalance in an atom or molecule.
    (a) atom (b) anion (c) cation (d) electron

25. Which is the only bond not caused by the attraction of positive and negative charges?
    (a) metallic (b) ionic (c) covalent (d) hydrogen (e) van der Waals

26. Window glass has a slight green tint due to _____ impurities.
    (a) iron (b) carbon (c) sodium (d) aluminum (e) there are no impurities

27. Materials which lack a crystal structure are called _____.
    (a) amorphous (b) crystalline (c) anisotropic (d) nanophasic (e) none of these

28. The majority of elements in the periodic table are _____.
    (a) metals (b) non-metals (c) ceramics (d) semiconductors (e) superconductors

29. An anion is _____.
    (a) an atom which has gained an electron (b) an atom which has lost a proton (c) an atom which has lost an electron (d) an atom which has gained a proton (e) charge neutral

30. Which is the incorrect statement?
    (a) some metals are non-magnetic (b) most metals are ductile (c) no metals are liquid at room temperature (d) most metals can be easily deformed (e) all these are correct

31. The following two bond types lead to close-packed structures.
    (a) covalent, metal (b) covalent, ionic (c) ionic, metallic (d) Van der Waals, covalent (e) hydrogen, ionic

32. After the composition has been selected, changes in the processing of a material may affect the material's _____.
    (a) atomic structure (b) microstructure (c) properties (d) both a and c (e) both b and c

33. Van der Waals bonds are found in _____.
    (a) ceramic materials (b) hydrogen atoms (c) water (d) inert gases (e) semiconductors

34. Which of the following pairs of bonds is directional?
    (a) covalent, ionic (b) ionic, metallic (c) metallic, hydrogen (d) hydrogen, van der Waals (e) none of these combinations is correct

35. Which of the following is not true for most metals?
    (a) they are ductile (b) they are opaque (c) they cannot be oxidized (d) they are not magnetic (e) they conduct electricity

6. CRYSTAL STRUCTURES

Close packed structures

To a large extent the bonding determines the way the atoms pack together in solids. We have already mentioned that the atoms in materials with non-directional bonds can pack more closely than those held together with directed bonds. This means that the easiest to consider are the pure metals (metallic bonding) and solid inert gases (van der Waals bonding). In these cases the atoms are all the same size and the bonds are non-directional so that the atoms can stack very close and efficiently in the same way that the balls are racked up on a pool table for the break.

We call the way they stack **close packing**. A plane of close packed atoms is shown very simply in the following diagram.

A close packed plane of atoms in a metal.

Notice that where atoms touch each other there is a sort of triangular hole or depression into which another atom, placed on top of this plane, will naturally fall and rest. If we were to place another atom there it would form a tetrahedron with the three atoms it touches. We can continue to place atoms in these triangular depressions and so build up a second close packed atom plane. Notice that this second plane can stack on the first plane in one of two positions. It is physically impossible to place atoms in both positions at the same time.

If the first layer is designated A, then the two possibilities for the second layer are B and C, shown by the dashed and dotted circles in the following diagram. The diagram also illustrates the impossibility of filling both sites at the same time.

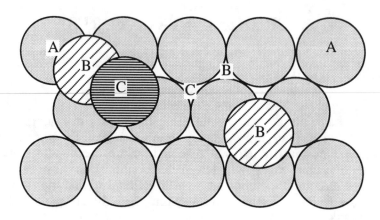

Stacking of two close packed planes in a metal crystal. Note that it is impossible to have atoms in both B and C positions in the same plane.

If we now take a stack of two layers, AB, and build up a third layer it too can occupy one of two positions on top of the B layer. One is directly on top of the original A layer and the other is in the C positions.

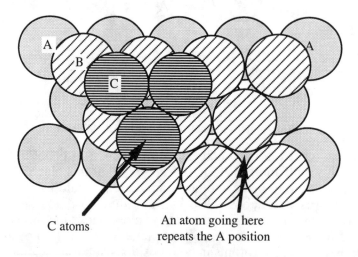

C atoms

An atom going here repeats the A position

Stacking of three close packed planes in the ABC sequence in a metal crystal.

These two stacking sequences, AB and ABC, form the basis of the crystal structures of many of the metals and all the solid inert gases. The latter are of no practical importance to us so we shall be mainly concerned with the metals.

A repetition of the AB sequence produces what we call the **hexagonal close packed (HCP)** arrangement of atoms, whereas by repeating the ABC sequence we produce a **cubic close packed (CCP)** arrangement.

ABCABCABCABCA -- is cubic close packed (CCP)
ABABABABABABA --is hexagonal close packed (HCP)

These arrangements are exhibited by the following solid inert gases and metals. The list is not complete.

HCP - Helium, cadmium, titanium, magnesium, zinc, cobalt, zirconium
CCP - Argon, neon, gold, silver, copper, aluminum, iron, nickel

When we stack atoms in the --ABCABCABCA-- sequence we say that we form a **cubic** close packed structure. Why cubic? Simply because when stacking this way we form a cube. It is not easy to see that this is the case unless one has a three dimensional model, but the following diagram may be a help. Note that the atoms in a close packed plane touch each other as shown in earlier diagrams, but for the three dimensional diagram it is easier to use an 'exploded' view. Remember that the atoms are really in contact as discussed earlier.

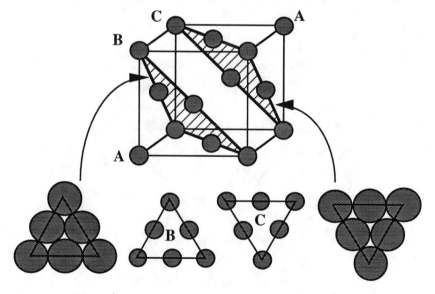

'Exploded' view of a cubic close packed (CCP) crystal showing the close packed planes.

This structure is very important in metals because it is these close packed planes of atoms which slide over each other and allow metals to deform easily. The following diagram illustrates the effect of plane sliding. It is just like shearing a pack of cards.

◀——— shear

produces

shear ——▶

Sliding of close packed planes to produce shear in a crystal.

When this happens between two close packed planes the atoms in one plane sort of zigzag across the adjacent plane as shown in the following diagram. The wavy grooves indicated are the directions in which the atoms can move relatively easily, because they are the directions in which there is the least up and down motion of one plane over the other.

There are three directions in which this slippage can occur and of course it can occur both backwards or forwards.

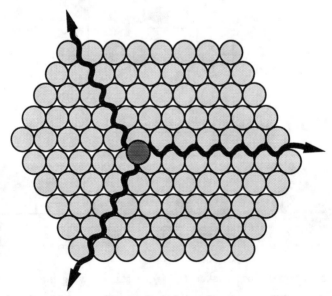

Directions in which one close packed plane of atoms can slide over another.

If you can see that the packing of close packed planes in the ABC sequence produces a cube, you should also be able to see that there are four close packed planes in this crystal structure which are equivalent, and slip is just as likely to occur on any or all of them. Notice that in the diagram of the cube the close packed plane is drawn by joining three corners of the cube to produce a diagonal plane. If you hold the cube by the corners marked A so that these corners are vertically over each other, the close packed planes are horizontal. We could also hold the cube by any of the other three pairs of opposite corners and the arrangement would be identical. These four possibilities correspond to the four close packed planes (**slip planes**) which exist in a CCP crystal and are illustrated below.

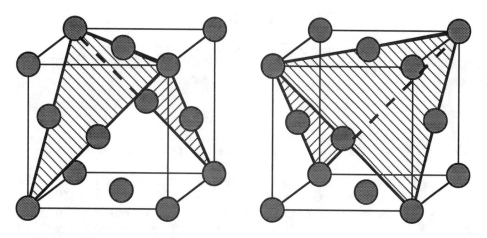

Diagrams illustrating the four completely different non-parallel close packed planes. Slipping can occur on any diagonal plane cutting through three corners of the cube.

Since there are **4** different non-parallel slip planes and each can slide along **3** directions, there are therefore **twelve** (4 x 3) ways close packed planes can slide over each other. When we pull a crystal we are never far from one of these slipping possibilities (called **slip systems**) and the metal deforms.

Imagine that you are looking at a CCP metal single crystal along the diagonal of the top face as shown in the following diagram. The two shaded planes are two planes on which slip can occur and they are both parallel to your viewing direction. Now imagine you pull the crystal in the direction indicated. Slip can take place on these two planes, and the crystal elongates by a combination of these two slip motions as illustrated.

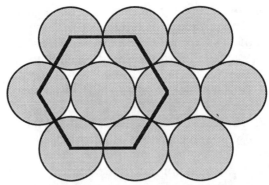

The upper diagram shows a cubic close packed crystal with the two possible slip planes for the direction of pull. The lower diagram illustrates how deformation (stretch) may occur.

This is obviously a much simplified illustration, but it does indicate possibilities which do not exist in HCP metals which have **ABABAB** stacking. (It's called HCP because the plane contains hexagons as indicated in the next diagram.) No new close packed planes at any other angles are formed in this case, and slip can only occur on the parallel stacked close packed planes. This means that HCP metals have only three slip systems and are hence not as ductile.

The hexagon in a close packed plane of atoms. When the layers are stacked in the ABABA sequence no new close packed planes are formed and slip can only occur on this one plane.

If we pull a single crystal of an HCP metal we get slip only on the parallel close packed planes as illustrated in the following figure. The crystal shears like a stack of coins. This might be typical of a zinc crystal, shown in the photograph.

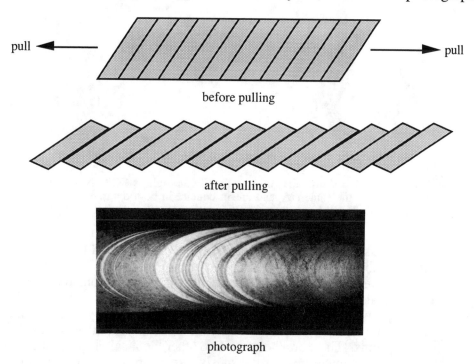

before pulling

after pulling

photograph

Diagrams and photograph of slip in a zinc crystal (HCP), which can only slip on one plane.
(Photo courtesy of Professor Earl Parker, Univ. of California at Berkeley)

Structures of some other crystals

Some metals are what we call body centered cubic (BCC). They also have atoms on the corners of a cube. but there is an additional one in the center of the cube rather than one on the center of each face. These atoms are not 'close packed' although they are close to being so. The atoms in this arrangement occupy 68% of the total volume, compared to 74% for CCP crystals.

The following diagram shows a BCC crystal. It contains more open space than does CCP, but there is one very important difference, the open space in BCC may be more in total volume, but it is divided up into much smaller holes (**interstices**). Of course there are many more interstices in BCC crystals than in

CCP to give the larger total empty volume, but the fact that the interstices are smaller gives the two structures very different properties.

 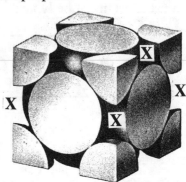

The left diagram shows a BCC crystal while the right is CCP. Note that the atoms are the same size and are in contact in both diagrams. This makes the CCP cell larger than the BCC. It is clear that the interstices at the edges of the CCP cell (X) are larger than any in the BCC cell.

BCC metals can also slip on planes in the crystals, and there are in fact just as many possibilities for slip as there are in CCP crystals. This makes BCC metals as **ductile** as the CCP metals, hence most metals are considered ductile. It is the HCP metals which are somewhat brittle. The following diagram shows one of the planes in the BCC crystal on which slip occurs. Any plane produced by making a diagonal cut perpendicular to a cube face will have the same arrangement of atoms. There are therefore five other identical planes in the crystal on which slip can occur, giving a total of six **slip planes**. See if you can find them.

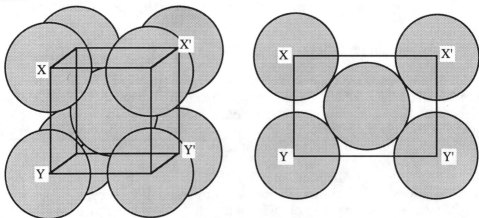

One of the six possible slip planes in a BCC crystal.

Each of the six slip planes in this BCC crystal has two directions in which an atom on an adjacent plane can move, as illustrated below, so that there are again twelve slip systems (**6 planes x 2 directions**) which is the same number as in CCP crystals. We should therefore not be surprised to find that BCC metals are as ductile as are CCP metals.

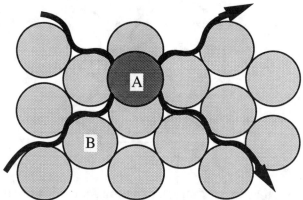

A close packed plane of atoms in a BCC crystal (B) showing the two directions in which an atom in an adjacent plane (A) can move.

NOTES: 1. Up to this point we have referred to the crystal illustrated on page 49 as CCP, cubic close packed. Look at the figure again. You will see that there is an atom on each corner of the cube and one on the center of each cube face. For this reason we usually refer to this arrangement of atoms as face centered cubic (FCC). However, note that FCC merely refers to the *arrangement* of the atoms. It does not indicate that they are in contact with each other, i.e. close packed. Atoms in an FCC arrangement need not be close packed, and are therefore not necessarily CCP. Atoms which are CCP are always FCC, but FCC crystals need not be CCP, and in fact are usually not.

2. The larger CCP (FCC) cube contains 4 atoms and the smaller BCC cube only two atoms. Count the various parts in the diagrams on the previous page. The eight corners each have an eighth of an atom and there are halves of atoms on the faces of the FCC cell. Of course we can't split atoms this way, we are simply showing that an atom is shared between two or more cubes, or cells.

Silicon & Diamond have their atoms bound together by covalent bonds. We have already discussed their crystal structure in chapter 3 but mention it here again to point out that it is in fact an FCC crystal. Remember that each atom forms covalent bonds with four other atoms on the corners of a tetrahedron.

The diagram shows one tetrahedron, and also how several of these units are arranged to form an FCC crystal. Notice that this structure is more complicated than what we have seen so far because there are four extra atoms in the cell.

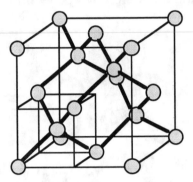

The crystal structure of diamond and silicon. Note the FCC arrangement.

Notice also that these four extra atoms, shown darker in the following diagram, form their own FCC arrangement. We find that this is typical of all complex crystal structures. It's like having two interwoven cubes, both of which are face centered cubic. Perhaps the following diagram will help you see this. Remember that the darker atoms are the same type as the others. .

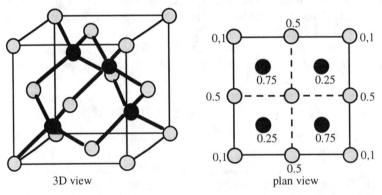

3D view   plan view

The crystal structure of diamond and silicon, showing the two different FCC arrangements it contains (numbers give heights in the cube).

Silicon and diamond are examples of crystals which are FCC but are not CCP, i.e. the atoms are not touching.

Graphite has another crystal structure (Page 13) which we have already discussed. Each carbon atom uses three valence electrons to form covalent bonds in a plane while the fourth electron is allowed to move freely through the crystal between the planes. Note that this electron cannot move across the planes, which gives graphite the property of being able to conduct electricity along its layer planes but not across them. It is therefore an electrical conductor in the planes but an electrical insulator in the perpendicular direction. A material which shows different properties in different directions is called **anisotropic.**

Note that the planes in graphite also stack ABABAB, just as they do in HCP crystals, but there is no atom in the center of the hexagons.

Sodium Chloride has ionic bonds which are non-directed. However in this case it is not simply a matter of stacking atoms of the same size together, as is the case in pure metals, but two sizes of ions are involved. The ions stack as closely as possible, as shown in the following diagram.

The crystal structure of sodium chloride

Note that this is also a face centered cubic crystal. There is an FCC arrangement of Na$^+$ intertwined with an FCC arrangement of Cl$^-$.

As mentioned in the previous chapter, the packing arrangement of ions depends on their relative sizes, which gives rise to different crystal structures. In sodium chloride each sodium cation is surrounded by six chlorine anions, whereas in **cesium chloride**, eight chlorine anions can pack around the larger cesium cation. The arrangement of the ions in cesium chloride is shown below. Notice that it is similar to the BCC atom arrangement in some metals (Page 53). However here the atom in the center of the cube is of a different type and size.

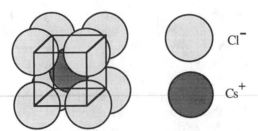

The crystal structure of cesium chloride

Polymers are not often thought of as being crystalline. The long spaghetti-like molecules do not easily lend themselves to the neat orderly arrangements we have come to expect in crystals. However, there are many polymers which contain at least some crystalline regions. The most easily crystallized polymer is **polyethylene** (Page 41), which consists of a chain of carbon atoms with two hydrogen atoms on each carbon atom in the chain. These hydrogen atoms are very small, after all hydrogen is the smallest and lightest atom found in the universe. The 'straight' polyethylene chain actually zigzags as shown in the following diagram. If you can imagine looking at the chain from one end you would see some thing which could fit fairly well inside a rectangular beam, something like a two-by-four. (See also photos on page 130.)

Photographs of a model of a polyethylene chain seen from the side (above) showing the zigzag backbone, and from the end (below) together with diagram used on next page.

Now, continuing to look at the chains from their ends, we can see how they stack when the material is crystalline. Their arrangement is more like a herringbone pattern. Adjacent chains are at an angle to each rather than being stacked parallel as you might usually see two-by-fours stacked in a lumber yard.

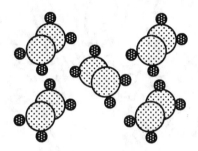

Stacking of polyethylene chains to form a crystal.

Note: Polyethylene is the simplest polymer. It only has small hydrogen atoms attached to the carbon chain, and these don't get in each other's way when the chains try to stack together in an ordered manner, i.e. crystallize. Other polymers do not crystallize so easily because the carbon chains have much larger and more irregular shaped chemical groups attached to them which do get in each others way when the chains try to stack together in a neat arrangement. We call this effect **steric hindrance** because in three dimensions (stereo) these large groups hinder the neat stacking of the chains.

However, even polyethylene never exists in a totally crystalline form. It usually contains both crystalline and amorphous regions. The reason for this is illustrated in the following diagram. A chain folds back on itself repeatedly to form a single crystal so that the 'surfaces' of the crystal are really amorphous because here the chains are not arranged in an ordered parallel manner.

Chain folding to produce a 'single' crystal of polyethylene.

Another model for a polymer material is shown below. Many chains are wandering almost randomly but are occasionally parallel and form crystals. This produces crystalline regions in an amorphous surrounding or matrix.

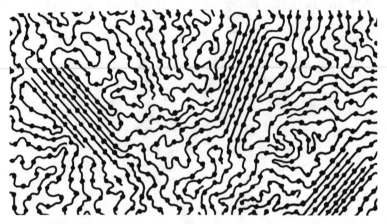

Formation of small polymer crystals in an amorphous matrix.
(K. Easterling, *Tomorrow's Materials*, The Institute of Metals, London, U.K., 1988. Fig. 2)

We shall later see (Page 134) that one way of stiffening a polymer is to increase the fraction of the total volume which is crystalline. This structural feature is therefore an important factor in determining properties.

Apart from glasses and most polymers, materials are generally crystalline. In museums and art galleries you will often see a display of crystals which are found in natural mineral deposits. These are rare and unusually large. Sometimes you can see the crystals in old brass door knobs and handles. This is because acids from hands have etched the material over the years and light reflects differently from adjacent crystals, as already mentioned in the Introduction to this book. These crystals are often several millimeters in size. In most materials, however, the crystals are too small to be seen by the naked eye, and in some special materials the crystals may only contain a few thousand atoms. This is very small indeed. (Note that a crystal cube with 20 atoms along the edge will contain 8000 atoms.) In fact there is a general rule which we shall later encounter which says that the smaller the crystals in a material, the stronger it is.

In all these materials the regular repetitive arrangement of atoms into crystals has a major effect on the properties. We shall encounter a major effect of different crystal structures when we consider metals in Chapter 10.

7. AMORPHOUS MATERIALS

When a crystalline material is heated, energy is being given to the atoms and they begin to vibrate. The crystal arrangements we have discussed in Chapter 6 represent the mean position of the atoms. In reality the atoms are moving around this position and as the material becomes hotter the atom motion becomes more energetic. Eventually this movement (usually somewhat inaccurately called vibration), illustrated in the following figure, becomes so energetic that the atoms are able to break the bonds which hold them together and the material melts. In this liquid form the atoms (or molecules, as in water) are moving quite freely and are usually arranged quite randomly, i.e. the material is **amorphous**. The word amorphous means that there is no **long range** order to the atoms or molecules. There may be a few clusters of atoms which have an ordered arrangement but on the whole there is no order over any longer distance.

increasing temperature →

Illustration of how atoms move around their mean positions as temperature is increased.
(R. Cotterill, *The Cambridge Guide to the Material World,* Cambridge University Press, 1985. p. 41)

Glass

In today's world we are quite familiar with the amorphous material glass, but we have a need for other materials in an amorphous state especially metals. The problem is how to make them. As soon as we begin to cool the liquid, the atoms start to move back into their crystal positions. The only way to stop them is to remove their energy so quickly that they have no time to return to their crystalline arrangement. As a result we can understand that any material can be produced in an amorphous solid state as long as we can cool the liquid quickly enough. This rapid cooling is what we call **quenching**.

The question which we must answer is "how fast is quickly enough?" and this is a very difficult question to answer. It all depends on the speed at which the atoms are moving in the liquid. If the liquid contains very large molecules especially of an irregular shape they tend to move sluggishly with the result that the liquid is very **viscous**. If the liquid contains only small spherical atoms they tend to move easily and rapidly.

A good example of the former is sugar (sucrose). When we buy it, it consists of small crystals. If we heat it carefully until it melts and then cool it by dropping it in cold water we can produce a brittle hard candy, essentially a sugar glass. The large sucrose molecules find it impossible to return to the ordered crystalline state during the cooling process. Different cooling processes can be used to produce toffee and fudge. By warming the toffee we allow the molecules to move around more so that they form very small crystals, i.e. fudge. The technical term for this process is **devitrification** (vitreous means glassy), removing the glassy state.

We do something similar when we make Corning Ware® (Chapter 19), starting with a glass object and then causing some small crystals to form within it. The SiO_2 tetrahedra in glass are quite large and angular and therefore not particularly mobile. The liquid glass is very viscous immediately before it solidifies and therefore an amorphous solid is produced. In fact we can cool glass very, very slowly (1°C per million seconds) and it still remains amorphous. The enormous glass mirrors for some astronomical telescopes had to be cooled very slowly in order to avoid cracking. In Corning Ware® we add some very small nuclei to initiate the forming of crystals. These somehow persuade the SiO_2 tetrahedra to organize into very, very small crystals , i.e. the material devitrifies.

In regular glass, the SiO_2 tetrahedra link up to form a complex random three dimensional network as shown schematically in the following figure. Note that the SiO_2 tetrahedra (only three of the four oxygen atoms are shown) are an example of **short range** order, but there is no long range order.

We can replace some of these strong covalent bonds with weaker ionic bonds by the addition of **fluxing ions** such as sodium to the molten glass. Some of the oxygen atoms are now only bonded to one silicon atom and have weaker bonds with the sodium atoms. These weaker bonds are of course broken more easily than the stronger covalent bonds with the result that the glass softens at a lower temperature.

Diagram illustrating the arrangement of silica (SiO_2) tetrahedra in glass.

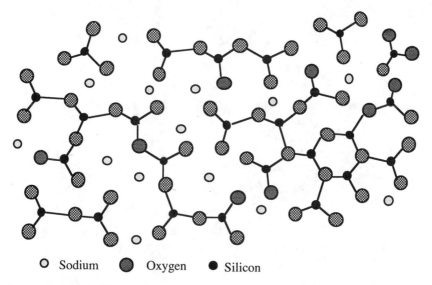

Arrangement of silica (SiO_2) tetrahedra in a sodium glass. The sodium atoms come between the tetrahedra linking them with ionic bonds rather than covalent.

Amorphous metals

The uses of amorphous glass are well known, but why would we want to make amorphous metals? Remember that the atoms are randomly arranged. There are no planes of atoms to slip over each other so an amorphous metal would be very strong, but brittle. You should also be able to see that it would be less dense. However, it is the amorphous magnetic metals which are of special interest. The following illustrations represent the difference between crystalline and amorphous metals. In the latter there some regions with a few atoms in alignment but there are no extensive three dimensional arrangements. There are therefore no crystals and no atom planes.

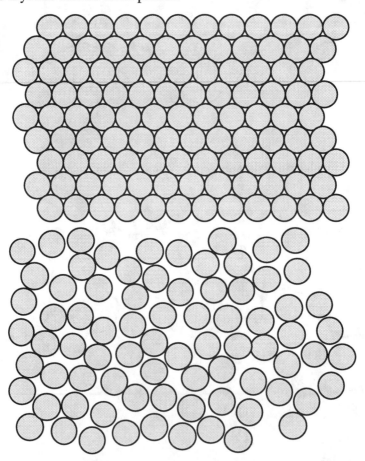

The different arrangements of atoms in crystalline (above) and amorphous metals (below).

Metals like to magnetize in certain directions in the crystal, as a result it is often difficult to change the direction in which a metal is magnetized. Amorphous metals have no crystals and therefore no crystal directions. They can therefore be magnetized equally easily in all directions and the direction of magnetization can be easily changed. This is just what we need to do in an electrical power transformer where we reverse the magnetization direction sixty times in one second. Amorphous magnetic metals have an important application here and are of tremendous interest in today's world.

Now comes the difficult part - cooling the metal quickly enough. The small spherical atoms move very quickly in the liquid and in order to keep them in this amorphous state they must cooled very, very rapidly, as fast as a million degrees a second. This means that if the molten metal is at 1000°C it must be cooled to room temperature in a thousandth of a second. This is a real problem.

If you take a cake from the oven, it can cool so that the outside is cold, but when you cut into it the center is still hot. If you imagine this happening in a metal it means that the center has time to crystallize, something we don't want. To cool something very quickly all the way through it must be very thin. It is impossible to produce amorphous metals except in the form of very thin sheets, because it is only then that we can get the heat out quickly enough. In thick pieces there is no way to stop the atoms in the center from crystallizing.

The following diagram shows one method of doing this. A rapidly rotating copper (good conductor of heat) wheel is chilled with an internal coolant and a stream of molten metal is poured onto it. When the molten metal hits the wheel it is immediately quenched and thrown out into a very thin ribbon. Tens of meters of the thin amorphous metal ribbon are produced in one second!

Process for making an amorphous metal.

Conclusion

Amorphous materials which we encounter in today's world are usually glasses and polymers. Metals are notoriously difficult to obtain in an amorphous state because the bonding allows for easy atom movement. Recent techniques are allowing us to produce amorphous metals, but only in very thin sheets. They are expensive to produce and their major application is in electrical transformers. We shall discuss some of their implications in the chapter on magnetic materials.

8. DEFECTS IN SOLIDS

Properties are determined by structure. For example, we have seen that the crystal and electron structures of graphite make it a good electrical conductor in one direction and an insulator in another, and that the stacking of atoms in metals (crystal structure) affects their ability to move and hence the deformability and ductility of the material. But what more often determines properties are the **imperfections** materials contain.

We have already mentioned that steel is strong because of carbon atoms being dissolved in it during heating, that diamonds are colored by impurities and that the doping of semiconductors with impurity atoms enables us to tailor their electrical properties to our needs. When the first transatlantic telephone cable was laid it was found that its electrical conduction was only 14% of that of the best copper available. We now know that this difference was caused by the presence of impurities. The fact that modern stainless steel cookware does not conduct heat as well as the old cast iron pots is due to the presence of the impurities we add to the iron to make it stainless. We shall later come to understand these different phenomena but our immediate purpose is to understand something about these defects themselves.

We start with a different type of defect from those we have just mentioned. In our discussion of metal crystal structures it was pointed out that metals deform by the closest packed planes of atoms sliding over each other. Early in the 1900's, physicists were able to calculate the force needed to slide these planes of atoms over each other and were puzzled to find that their calculations (theory) gave a value which was one thousand times greater than the measured force (experiment) to deform a metal.

If we find that our theory and experimental results differ by a factor of 2 or 3 we are usually content to think that we have come close to understanding what is going on in our experiments, and we then try to adjust the theory to get better agreement. In fact, in many phenomena we are quite happy to have a theory which agrees so closely with our measurements. However, an error, or discrepancy, of one thousandfold is too large to be due to calculation errors. There must be something wrong with the model, or something which we have overlooked. In this case it turns out that we have overlooked a defect which we call a **dislocation**.

Dislocations

When the scientists formulated their theory of the slip of atom planes over each other in metals they assumed that when two planes slide over each other **all** atoms on the planes are sliding at the same time. It turns out that this does not happen. To make things easier the atoms move a row at a time. This is made possible by the presence of defects known as **dislocations.**

What is a dislocation? The easiest way to think of it is to take a book and imagine the pages to be the planes of atoms in the crystal. Now take a sheet of the same paper and place it between two pages of the book but only half way into the book. You have now inserted an extra 'half-plane' of atoms. Actually it's part of a plane, not precisely half a plane. The termination of the half-plane is a line and is called a **dislocation line**.

The diagram below shows what we have been talking about. The extra partial plane finishes at the line D, which we call the dislocation line. This is the defect. Notice that there is nothing we can call a defect if we go away from this line. Do the book experiment! Just by looking at the edges of the pages you will see nothing wrong or unusual except where the extra page terminates. A quarter of an inch away from this position in any direction you can see no disturbance. Indeed the disturbance is confined to the region where the extra page, or in our case the extra atom plane, terminates. This defect is what causes plane A to slip over plane B a thousand times easier than it could slip without the defect. It does so because it introduces a mechanism for the planes to slide a little at a time.

When plane A slides over plane B it uses the dislocation to move gradually - a little at a time.

Three dimensional diagram of a dislocation in a simple crystal
(W. F. Smith, *Principles of Materials Science and Engineering,* McGraw Hill, New York, 1986. Fig. 4.18.
Reproduced with permission of the publisher)

There are two analogies in your experience which may help you to understand what is happening. One is illustrated below.·

Remember how a caterpillar moves by using one pair of legs at a time rather than by moving them all at the same time. In the same way the crystal slips its atoms one row at a time, rather than moving all the atoms in a plane simultaneously. This means that the force required at any one instant is less.

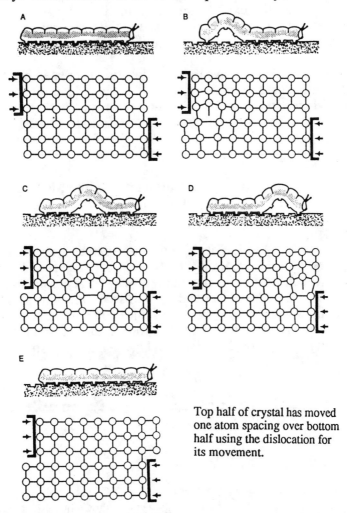

Top half of crystal has moved one atom spacing over bottom half using the dislocation for its movement.

A caterpillar's walk is like a dislocation moving through a crystal.
(R. Cotterill, *The Cambridge Guide to the Material World*, Cambridge University Press, 1985. p.70)

When the top part of the crystal wants to slide over the bottom part, it first moves the first atom plane, thus bunching up the next plane and producing a dislocation. In the same way a caterpillar moves its rear legs and produces a small kink or fold in its body; this fold is analogous to the dislocation. It then moves this fold along the body putting down the feet at the rear of the fold and lifting up those at the front.

In the same way the extra plane of atoms links up with a plane in the lower part of the crystal, forcing the next plane in the top part of the crystal to be the one producing the dislocation. This continues until it reaches the other side.

The previous diagram shows that a dislocation is created by forcing a few planes in the top of the crystal together. The dislocation can then move through the crystal, and when it reaches the other end the result is that one half of the crystal has slipped over the other half by **one** atom spacing. In the same way the caterpillar has progressed one step as a result of the sequence of its leg movements.

The above concept is one we are all familiar with. Moving one item at a time is easier than trying to carry everything at once. Just think how you would transport a pile of bricks!

The second analogy is that of sliding a large carpet over a floor. To move the whole carpet involves overcoming the friction between it and the floor, and this might be too much for you to manage. A way of accomplishing the same thing is to put a wrinkle in the carpet and push this wrinkle across the floor. The end result is that the whole carpet moves a distance equal to the length of material used to make the wrinkle you introduced. The force required is much less because you are only having to overcome the friction between a small strip of carpet and the floor at any instant.

Carpet has moved as shown by dashed line

It is easier to move a carpet on a floor by putting a wrinkle in it and pushing that along.

Now just consider the implications of what we have discussed. A dislocation is a defect which allows atoms to slide over each other, but it only produces a net movement of **one atom spacing**. When it exits the material at the far side, it is gone. We know of course that we can easily make metals move much more than one atom spacing. If you bend a paper clip the atoms on the outside of the bend must have traveled large distances to produce the effect. If this movement is produced by dislocations, each moving the atoms by only one atom spacing, there must be millions of these dislocations to produce the large deformations we have just mentioned.

This is in fact the case. In a one pound block of aluminum there are enough dislocations to circle the equator of the earth over **one thousand times** if they were all straightened out and placed end to end. This may be difficult to imagine, but it is true. We can see these defects in the electron microscope and measure their total length, and these are the values we obtain.

Summary. Dislocations make it a thousand times easier for the planes of atoms in a crystal to slide over each other than would be the case if they were to slide over each other as complete perfect entities. There are hundreds of miles of dislocations in even a very small piece of metal such as a paper clip.

What's more, we saw (Page 51) that in cubic close packed crystals there are four different non-parallel planes which can slide over each other, i.e. there can be dislocations moving on many different planes at the same time. As already mentioned, the four planes, with each able to slip in three directions, produce a system of slip possibilities such that whatever way you apply a force to the crystal it will never be far from one of them. The dislocations simply make such slip one thousand times easier. That's why metals usually deform easily.

Just think for a moment why it is the close packed planes of atoms which slide over each other. Are these the only planes which slip? The answer is 'yes' most of the time, and for our purposes we can assume that it is always the case. The reason is not really difficult to understand. In any given crystal there is a fixed number of atoms in a given volume. We can think of these atoms as lying on planes as shown in the following diagram. There are many possible planes just as there are many different ways of seeing rows of trees in an orchard. As you walk among the trees you can align them in many different ways. In the same way we can look at atoms in a crystal.

Notice from the diagram that different planes have different atom densities (different numbers of atoms per unit area). The closer to each other the atoms are on a plane, the greater the distance to the next plane. If you think about it, this statement is a logical necessity. In a given volume there will be a certain number of parallel planes, and the number of atoms in this volume is given by multiplying the number of atoms on one plane by the number of planes. If we choose a different plane with fewer atoms on it then there must be more of these planes in the volume because the number of atoms in the volume has not changed. Also if there are more of these new planes they must be closer together. This is also clear in the following diagram.

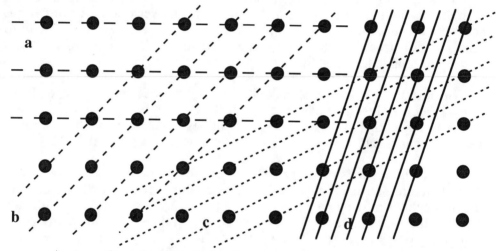

As you go from planes a to d, the planes get closer together and the atoms in
the planes become further apart.

It should be easy to see that the planes with the highest atom density are those that are the furthest apart and thus are most easily able to move over each other. This is why the planes which have the largest number of atoms per unit area are the ones which slip. In the CCP crystal these planes are, of course, the close packed planes. It's just impossible to have a higher atom density than they have. In the BCC crystal the plane with the highest density of atoms is the one shown in the diagram on page 54. This is the plane on which slip occurs in metals with this crystal structure and there are six identical non-parallel planes on which such slip can occur.

Another way of thinking of this fact is to consider the smoothness of two planes with different atom densities. The plane with the higher atom density is 'smoother' than the other, and it is therefore easier for an atom to move on this plane than on any other. This is illustrated in the following diagram.

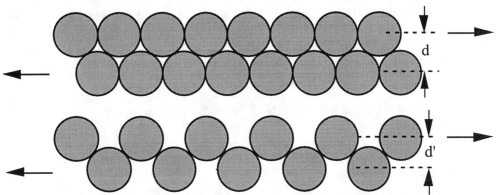

In the upper diagram the planes are smoother (closer packed) and an atom makes less up-and-down movement as it moves across, so that less force is required to move it. In the lower diagram the atoms make much more vertical movement requiring a much larger force for their movement (d greater than d').

One final note on dislocations. Once a dislocation has moved in one direction it would require an equal and opposite force to move it back. The atoms do not return to their original positions when the force is removed. Dislocations are therefore responsible for **plastic deformation** in a material.

Let's pause and consider what we mean by this. The easiest model is to once again consider an atom moving over a plane of atoms as shown in the previous diagram. In order to move, the atom has to climb over the atom in the plane underneath. If pushed hard enough it will go all the way over and fall down the other side. The atom will then stay there when the force is removed. The motion is permanent until a force is applied in the opposite direction. This is what we mean by plastic deformation. A force deforms a material and the material stays deformed when the force is removed. We say that the deformation is permanent (**plastic deformation**). However, if the force is less, and the atom is only pushed part way over the underlying atom (or part way up the hill) there is a deformation as a result of the atom displacement, but the atom returns to its original position when the force is removed. We call this **elastic deformation**. Just like a piece of elastic, the atoms and the material return to their original state when the force is removed.

Point defects

Because dislocations are essentially **lines** which wander through the crystal, we call them **line** defects. Other major defects are **point** defects - they involve only one or two atoms. Point defects are relatively simple to understand. They are often divided into two categories; those which come from the material itself (**intrinsic** defects) and those which come from outside impurities (**extrinsic**).

As far as we are concerned there are two extrinsic and two intrinsic point defects of importance.

Intrinsic point defects.

Just as we have seen that there can be some imperfections in the way planes are arranged (thus forming dislocations) there can be imperfections in the way the atoms are arranged in the planes. The two common ones which occur in pure crystals are the **vacancy** and the **interstitial**.

A **vacancy** is quite simply a missing atom or group of two or three atoms. It is important because it produces a distortion in the neat orderly arrangement of the surrounding atoms which move slightly to partially fill the hole left by the missing atom.

An intrinsic **interstitial** is a defect caused by an extra atom pushing its way into the ordered arrangement. The extra atom is of the same type, and hence the same size, as the rest of the atoms in the crystal. It simply elbows the surrounding atoms out of the way to make room for itself. Once again there is a distortion (strain) around the defect.

Because it takes a lot of energy to push atoms apart to allow an extra atom to enter the arrangement, there are usually only a few of these interstitial defects. However, there are many more vacancies, and these are really important.

The number of vacancies increases with temperature until, at the melting point about 0.01% of the atoms are missing. This means that one out of every 10,000 atom places in the crystal is vacant. (Note: they have not evaporated, they have just gone to positions on the edges of the crystals. This causes a large expansion of the material as it reaches the melting point).

Why are these defects so important? For two reasons. First, as already mentioned, they distort the arrangement of the atoms (the lattice). This makes it more difficult for electrons and dislocations to move around. Second, these defects provide a mechanism for atoms to move around in the crystal.

Atoms move in a crystal by means of these point defects. The most usual means is by using the vacancies because there are many more of them than there are interstitials. The situation is similar to moving tiles in the 4 x 4 arrangement shown below. We can rearrange the tiles in any way we wish because one tile (the vacancy) is missing. If there were no vacancy the only way to rearrange things would be to take everything apart. We do the latter in materials when we melt them and resolidify them, but vacancies allow materials to rearrange their atoms while still in the solid state. This means that we can fuse particles together while they are still solid. When we fire (bake) a piece of formed clay, the crystals join (**sinter** is the technical term) because the vacancies allow the atoms to move around. Remember, there are more vacancies at higher temperatures, that's why we apply heat. Not only does this give the atoms more energy but it also creates more vacancies for them to move through.

Arrangement of tiles as in the common game. Because they are all identical, there are many ways of going from the situation shown on the left to the one on the right. It would be impossible to say which tiles had moved - only that the hole had gone from A to B.

The empty space allows the tiles to move around in the same way that atom vacancies allow atoms to move around and rearrange themselves in a crystal. By following the sequence of diagrams you can tell which tile has been moved in each case. However if you compare the first and last diagrams you cannot tell which tiles have been moved to achieve the new arrangement. All you can say is that the empty space has moved from one position to another. The same thing happens in crystals, we can only tell that the vacancy has moved from one position to another. We therefore say that the rearrangement has occurred by **vacancy motion**.

Extrinsic point defects

The two defects in this category are both related to impurities. When an atom of an impurity is added to a material it can enter the atomic arrangement in two different positions, **interstitial** or **substitutional.** It is difficult to predict which one will occur, but it usually depends on the size of the impurity atom.

An extrinsic **interstitial** impurity atom sits in the spaces (**interstices**) between the original atoms. Because of this it is usually quite a small atom (carbon, nitrogen, boron). Even though there is a space between the atoms, there is almost never quite enough room for the impurity atom, so that once again there is a distortion as the surrounding atoms are pushed back. This also squeezes the surrounding interstices so that they cannot accommodate an impurity atom. As a result there is a limit to the number of interstitial impurity atoms we can put into the crystal without them forming their own little crystals or precipitates.

Iron can exist in two crystal forms, CCP (FCC) and BCC. Note that the diagrams shown on page 54 indicate that even though the BCC arrangement has more empty space within it, it cannot accept as much interstitial carbon as can the FCC form because the space is divided up more, i.e. the empty space is split into a much larger number of smaller interstices.

A **substitutional** impurity atom is usually about the same size as the atoms of the host material. The foreign atom simply replaces one of the original atoms of the pure material. However even in this case there is always a distortion of the surrounding lattice because the impurity atom is never exactly the same size as the atom it replaces. In stainless steel the chromium, which makes it stainless, is a substitutional impurity in the iron, and the carbon, which makes it a steel, is an interstitial impurity.

In some cases the distortion produced by the impurity atoms is so small that we can replace the original atoms *ad infinitum* until we have only atoms of what was the original impurity, but such cases are not common. When this occurs we say that the two materials are completely soluble in each other - or that they show complete mutual **solid solubility**.

If we try to put more impurity in the material than it can accept, the impurity forms its own little crystals within the host material. In this case we say that we have formed precipitates of the impurity within the original material. We shall see an important example of substitutional impurity atoms and the formation of precipitates in the case of aluminum-lithium alloys in one of our case studies.

NOTE: Impurity atoms change the atomic structure of the material; precipitates change the microstructure of the material.

The following diagrams illustrate these common point defects in materials. The strains (distortions) produced will depend on the relative sizes of the atoms involved.

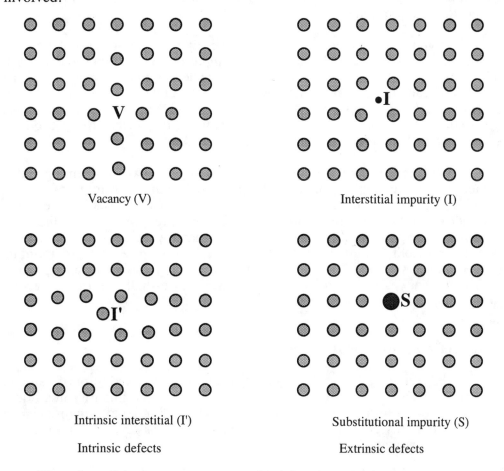

Vacancy (V)   Interstitial impurity (I)

Intrinsic interstitial (I')   Substitutional impurity (S)

Intrinsic defects   Extrinsic defects

Illustrations of the four most common point defects in materials. In the vacancy (upper left) the atoms tend to collapse into the space left by the missing atom. A much smaller impurity atom (upper right) tends to push its way into an interstice, while a larger impurity atom (lower right) will substitute for one of the original atoms. Sometimes an extra atom of the original material forces itself into an interstitial position (lower left). See important notes at end of this chapter.

How to purify materials

While we have seen that impurities can be added to change the atomic structure (doping) and hence the properties of materials, we are often faced with the problem of getting them out. Such was the problem with obtaining useful silicon for semiconductors. We needed to get unwanted impurities out before adding the ones we wanted.

As you may imagine, it is far more difficult to get impurities out than it is to add them, and the methods for removing impurities are difficult to explain at this level. It should be obvious that it is impossible to remove impurities from a solid. You can't just pluck them out with fine tweezers! There really is no way to do it. We therefore have to have our material in either a liquid or a vapor state. We shall discuss one example of each possibility, the former being used for silicon and the latter for chromium.

NOTE: Before we begin our discussion it is worth pointing out a sometimes confusing language problem. We often refer to purifying as 'refining'. A place where gasoline is produced from crude oil is called a refinery, and we earlier referred to the expression "refined by fire." We also use the word 'fine' to denote good or all right. On the other hand we use 'fine' to describe a powder or a cloth, i.e. the opposite of 'coarse'. In this sense the word 'refining' means making smaller. We shall now use the word in its first meaning, while later in the book when talking about HSLA steels, we shall use it in its second meaning.

Zone refining of silicon

The technique known as **zone refining** has been used to purify silicon and takes advantage of the fact that one can dissolve more impurity in a liquid than in a solid. It turns out that by melting a solid and re-solidifying it one can reduce its impurity content, and by repeating the process several times one can obtain very pure materials.

The name zone refining comes from the practical way this is accomplished (see following diagram). A rod of the impure material is held in a container which will not react with, or dissolve in, the silicon. A small furnace is placed around the bottom of the rod which is slowly passed through it. The material entering the furnace at the top is melted and the liquid leaving the furnace at the

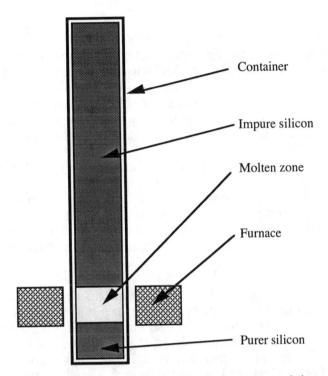

The zone refining of silicon. By repeating the process several times one can
obtain very pure silicon at the bottom of the rod, which is cut off and used.

bottom solidifies. At this stage the impurities in the liquid have a choice of
staying in the liquid or going into the solid which is formed. Because they prefer
to stay in the liquid, the newly formed solid material is purer than the material that
was originally melted. When the rod has passed through the furnace it's as if the
impurities have been pushed to one end. By repeating the process the impurities
are pushed more and more to the top end and eventually the bottom of the rod is
pure enough to be useful.

Chemical vapor deposition of chromium

Another technique used for some metals takes advantage of the fact that it
is quite easy to separate a mixture of liquids using a process called fractionation or
distillation. If we boil a mixture of liquids by gradually increasing the
temperature, we find that each liquid boils and evaporates at a different
temperature. The process is used in the distillation of whiskey and brandy.

In this case we start with impure chromium metal and react it with iodine to form metal iodides. The chromium becomes chromium iodide, any nickel impurity becomes nickel iodide, etc. Metal iodides can often be easily melted and boiled, so the mixture of metal iodides is gradually heated until something begins to evaporate. Each metal iodide boils at a different temperature, and we know what this temperature is for chromium iodide. So as soon this temperature is reached we begin to collect what is evaporating, i.e. pure chromium iodide vapor.

The vapor is then passed through a furnace at a much higher temperature where it decomposes into pure chromium and iodine. The chromium metal, which is a solid at this temperature, falls from the decomposing vapor and deposits in the container in which it is heated, while the iodine vapor passes through the furnace and is collected for reuse. The pure chromium produced in this way is important for electrical contacts in modern semiconductor microchip technology.

The cover photograph shows a piece of this deposited chromium. You can see that some rather nice large crystals (up to 5 millimeters across) are formed which are based on cubes (remember that chromium has a body centered cubic crystal structure). The beautiful ordered atomic arrangement arise because the atoms are released from the vapor and added to the deposit one at a time, giving them plenty of opportunity to fit correctly into any existing arrangement. This is quite the opposite of what we do in attempting to produce amorphous metals (Page 64) where we try to freeze the motion of all atoms at the same time and give them no opportunity to arrange themselves into any order.

Note that we have had to take a rather roundabout route to accomplish our goal of purifying the chromium. First we made another compound (the iodide), purified that, and then re-formed the solid chromium.

The process of producing pure solids by decomposing a pure gas is one we shall encounter in our case study of optical fibers. The process is known as **chemical vapor deposition** (CVD). A chemical vapor of the desired material is decomposed by heat so that the solid deposits in the furnace.

Impurities are still there!

Silicon has an atomic weight of 28.09, which means that this is the weight in grams of 6.02×10^{23} atoms (Page 11). To put it another way, 28 grams of silicon, which incidentally is almost exactly an ounce, contain 6.02×10^{23} atoms. If we manage to obtain silicon by zone refining which is 99.9999999% pure, the best purity level currently achieved, which means one impurity atom for every ten billion (10^{10}) silicon atoms, the ounce of silicon will still contain around 10^{13} (ten trillion) impurity atoms!

The point to be made is that there are still many impurity atoms present. Whether they are important is perhaps still a question we cannot answer.

IMPORTANT NOTE

In most of the diagrams shown in this and all other books about materials there are three important differences between diagrams involving atom arrangements and the real situation.

1. Atom arrangements are three dimensional. This is illustrated in the figure on page 68. The dislocation line extends from one end of the crystal to the other. This is also true of other diagrams, but trying to show three dimensions makes things confusing.

2. The defects involve many more atoms than shown. On page 100 we show a dislocation stopping three atoms short of a precipitate. In reality the dislocation would be stopped tens of atoms short of the precipitate, perhaps even hundreds. The diagrams of a dislocation on pages 68 - 69 use around a hundred atoms. A real dislocation involves many more atoms than this. The stacking of atoms is not back to normal just five or six atoms away from the dislocation, you would need to go at least a hundred atoms for this to happen. This is why metal whiskers (Page 97) cannot contain dislocations.

3. Atoms are close-packed, as in CCP, or quite close to it, as in BCC. They are not separated as illustrated in this chapter, but are much like those shown on page 101. This means that interstices, for example, are not as large as you might expect from the diagrams on page 77.

QUESTIONS: Chapters 6-8

1. Carbon in iron is an example of _____.
   (a) a point defect (b) an substitutional impurity atom (c) an interstitial impurity atom (d) both a and b (e) both a and c

2. In order to form amorphous metals, we have to cool liquid metals at a rate of _____.
   (a) 100°C per second (b) 1,000,000°C per hour (c) 10,000°C per second (d) 1,000,000°C per second

3. Zinc has a _____ crystal structure.
   (a) hexagonal close packed (b) cubic close packed (c) body centered cubic (d) face centered cubic (e) both b and d

4. The main defects responsible for plastic deformation in a metal are _____.
   (a) dislocations (b) vacancies (c) extrinsic interstitials (d) substitutional atoms

5. The defect associated with a dislocation is a(n) _____ atom(s) which disturbs the perfect crystalline order.
   (a) cluster of (b) extra half plane of (c) single (d) tetrahedron of (e) crystal of

6. A small space which exists between atoms in a perfect crystal is a(n) _____.
   (a) vacancy (b) hole (c) interstice (d) mer (e) interstitial

7. When atoms in a material are arranged in a regular repeating order the material is _____.
   (a) amorphous (b) anisotropic (c) crystalline (d) glassy

8. Crystalline silicon and diamond both have the same _____ structure.
   (a) atomic (b) electron (c) crystal (d) micro (e) macro

9. Which of the following does not describe an interstitial?
   (a) a point defect (b) occurs between lattice sites (c) intrinsic or extrinsic (d) a missing atom (e) takes more energy to produce than a vacancy

10. In a cubic close packed (CCP) crystal there are _____ equivalent slip planes.
    (a) 1 (b) 2 (c) 3 (d) 4 (e) none of these

11. A repetition of the AB sequence of close packed planes in metals is called _____.
    (a) HCP (b) CCP (c) FCC (d) BCC

12. A material which shows different properties in different directions is called _____.
    (a) anisotropic (b) amorphous (c) crystalline (d) annealed (e) inert

13. At the melting point of a material there are approximately _____% of the atoms missing due to vacancies.
    (a) 0.01 (b) 0.1 (c) 1 (d) 10 (e) 100

14. The process used to purify silicon is called _____.
    (a) grain refining (b) precipitation hardening (c) chemical vapor deposition (d) annealing (e) zone refining

15. Face centered cubic (FCC) crystals are _____ cubic close packed (CCP).
    (a) always (b) sometimes (c) never

16. Dislocations allow planes of atoms to move approximately _____ times easier than in a perfect crystal.
    (a) 0 (b) 10 (c) 100 (d) 1000 (e) none of these

17. Select the false statement from the following:
    (a) FCC and BCC metals both have twelve ways for close-packed planes to slip
    (b) HCP metals have a more efficient atom packing than do BCC metals
    (c) there are four different non-parallel slip planes in FCC metal crystals
    (d) FCC metals are more ductile than BCC metal
    (e) all CCP metals are also FCC

18. Dislocations in a solid are responsible for _____.
    (a) thermal conduction (b) electrical conduction (c) color (d) elastic deformation (e) none of these

19. Amorphous materials lack _____.
    (a) long range order (b) strong bonding (c) molecules (d) short range order (e) stiffness

20. The addition of sodium to silica glass replaces some of the _____ bonds with _____ bonds.
    (a) covalent; ionic (b) covalent; metallic (c) ionic; covalent (d) metallic; hydrogen (e) ionic; metallic

21. The planar stacking sequence ABCABC is found in _____ materials.
    (a) BCC (b) HCP (c) CCP (d) all (e) both a and b

22. Close packed planes in crystals _____.
    (a) are planes which are closest to each other (b) are planes which are farthest apart (c) cannot slip over each other (d) are imperfections (e) none of these is correct

23. Which of these materials is the easiest to deform?
    (a) silicon (b) silica (c) aluminum (d) diamond (e) glass

24-26   The process during which molten metal iodides with different boiling points are separated is known as ___24___. This process is used to purify ___25___ for electronic applications. The pure ___25___ iodide gas is then reduced to a pure metal by a process known as ___26___.

24. (a) distillation (b) chemical vapor deposition (c) zone refining (d) vitrification (e) sintering
25. (a) iron (b) gold (c) chromium (d) nickel (e) aluminum
26. (a) distillation (b) chemical vapor deposition (c) zone refining (d) vitrification (e) sintering

9. WHAT DO WE MEAN BY 'STRONG'?

Strength and stress

'Strong' is a word we use frequently without stopping to ask ourselves what it really means. The dictionary defines it as meaning "having power of resistance, not easily broken or torn, or worn, firm, solid." Quite often we use the word 'strong' when we really mean 'rigid' and as we shall see, they are not the same. From a scientific standpoint, none of these definitions is really satisfactory. It's one of those words that you would probably define by using the well worn phrase "you know what I mean", meaning that you really are not sure! Even scientists sometimes use the word rather loosely because there is no one meaning for the term.

If you were given a piece of blackboard chalk and asked to break it you would almost certainly do so by bending it between your two thumbs and two forefingers. From a scientific standpoint you would be performing a four point bend test. The following diagram illustrates what happens. At the center you push up, usually with your thumbs, while at the ends you press down with your fingers. In the laboratory this would be one way of measuring the strength of a material. This is called the **bend strength**.

The four point bend test for a material. There are two central points where a force is applied upwards, and two end points where the force is downwards.

You could also hold one end of the chalk tightly in your fist while grabbing the other end and twisting it. If you try it, you will find that this method of breaking is more difficult, although you will probably succeed. You should also notice that fracture has occurred at an oblique angle to the length of the chalk rather than almost perpendicular to the chalk as was the case with the bend test.

In this case you will have tested the **shear strength** of the material. Shear strength is important for rods of material which are rotating. You may have been driving a screw into a hard material only to have it break, or shear off. This is because you have exceeded the shear strength. Rotating axles in machinery sometime fail in this way.

If we take the piece of chalk and hold one end while pulling on the other until it breaks we are testing its **tensile strength**. If we hang a weight on a wire we are putting it into tension. The same occurs when we stretch a guitar string to tune the instrument. Too much tension and it breaks. We apply what we call a **tensile load** to the material; we are pulling it. As we increase the load the string stretches and then breaks. The same happens with our piece of chalk although we need special equipment to see the stretch because it is so small.

Materials such as the piece of chalk, notably ceramics, break in a brittle manner, showing very little stretch before they fail. Others, such as some plastics and rubber, will stretch to several times their original length before they break. When the material breaks we say that is has reached its breaking strength, or to use the correct scientific jargon, it has reached its **ultimate tensile strength (UTS)**. This is the maximum load the material can carry without breaking.

The following diagram illustrates a simple way of measuring the UTS. A rod of material is held tightly at one end while a weight, or load, is applied to the other. The weight is increased until the material can take no more and breaks.

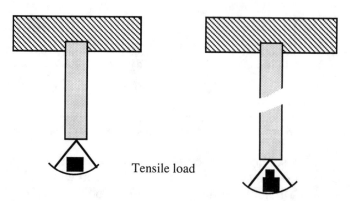

Tensile load

A material breaks in tension when its tensile strength is exceeded.

If we are building something, be it a building or a piece of equipment, we are always aware that we don't want components to break. If we think this may happen we have two alternatives: either use a stronger material or use a thicker piece of the same material, something we sometimes call "beefing it up." We are all aware that thicker things are more difficult to break. The simple reason in that there are more bonds to break. Never lose sight of the fact that in nearly all cases, breaking a material means breaking bonds between atoms.

Now while it may be good to know how much weight a material can bear before breaking, we are often not interested in approaching this value. What is of more concern, especially for a metal, is how much weight it can bear before it really begins to stretch. This means that the dislocations are now beginning to move freely in the material so that there is a lot of movement of **slip planes** over each other. But there is no definite point at which we can say this motion starts to be important so we need a more precise criterion. For engineering design we arbitrarily adopt the criterion of the material having permanently stretched by 0.2 percent of its original length. This means that a 100 cm long rod of the material is loaded so that it has a permanent stretch of 0.2% when the load is taken off. The rod has therefore been permanently lengthened to 100.2 cm. As you can well imagine, ceramics do not usually stretch by these amounts.

The load required to permanently stretch the rod by this amount is known as the **yield strength (YS)**. We say that the rod has suffered a 0.2% **plastic strain** deformation. As far as we are concerned we shall loosely say that the yield strength defines when the metal material begins to deform permanently. We shall come back to a definition of strain later.

For ceramic materials especially we define a fifth strength, called the **compressive strength**. If we take a short thick rod of this material, place one end on a rigid, strong surface and pile weights on top, the material will again eventually fail. The weight required to produce this break defines the compressive strength of the material. For ceramics the compressive strength is much larger than its tensile strength and bend strength. This is why we can use concrete foundations to support large buildings. We shall later see why this is, and how we can use it to make ceramics more serviceable. Just try crushing a stick of chalk between your hand and a table: you will probably hurt your hand before the chalk breaks.

The following diagram illustrates how we measure the compressive strength of a material. Here again, fracture occurs at an oblique angle to the length of the piece although it is unlikely to be as clean a break as is depicted. Because we are really crushing the material there will usually be several pieces resulting from this test rather than just the two pieces shown.

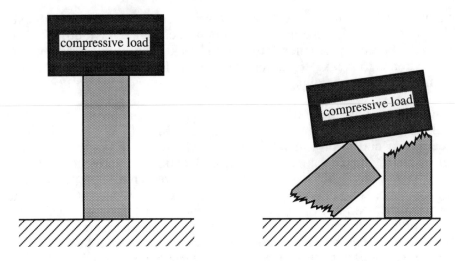

Testing the compressive strength of a material.

In the following discussion we shall only consider tensile, yield and compressive strengths, but do not forget that the others are very important.

We measure ultimate tensile strength using units of **pounds per square inch (psi)**. If our rod has a rectangular cross section one inch by two inches (1" x 2") the cross section area is two (1 x 2) square inches. If the rod breaks when a load of seventy pounds is hung on it, its ultimate tensile strength is 35 psi (70 pounds/2 square inches). The strength is therefore obtained by dividing the weight or load by the cross sectional area.

$$\textbf{UTS (psi)} = \frac{\text{weight at which rod breaks (pounds)}}{\text{cross sectional area (square inches)}}$$

You should now be able to see that by making our rod twice as thick (2" x 2") it can withstand twice the load without breaking (i.e. 140 pounds)

When we put a load on a material we rarely talk about the weight in pounds, we refer to the number of pounds per square inch applied to the material, a quantity we call the **stress**. Stresses can be tensile or compressive. When pulled, a material breaks at a constant stress which is what we call its ultimate tensile strength, or quite often just 'strength'. The load can vary depending on the size of the rod but the stress (UTS) at which it breaks is constant.

We similarly measure **yield strength** in terms of a stress and for a metal it is usually much less than the UTS.

$$\textbf{Stress (psi)} = \frac{\text{Force or Load (pounds)}}{\text{Area (square inches)}}$$

Note: Today's scientists refer to strength and stress using units known as Pascals. We shall not use these units because you are more familiar with a pound and a square inch. If you ever come across them you will need to know that **one** psi is equal to 6890 Pascals.

Examples.

1. A person weighs 170 pounds and wears a size 8 shoe with an area of 35 square inches per shoe sole, he/she exerts a compressive stress on the floor of:

$$\frac{170 \text{ pounds}}{2(\text{shoes}) \times 35 \text{ sq.in.}} = 2.43 \text{ psi}$$

when standing on both feet. When standing on one foot the stress is doubled.

2. A metal rod with a square cross section 0.5 x 0.5 inches bears a tensile load which is increased until the rod breaks with a load of 350 pounds. The ultimate tensile stress is given by:

$$\text{UTS (psi)} = \frac{350 \text{ pounds}}{0.5 \times 0.5 \text{ square inches}} = 1400 \text{ psi}$$

3. What size rod of this last material is needed to support a one ton (2000 pounds) weight? Since the UTS is a constant, we can set:

$$1400 \text{ psi} = \frac{2000 \text{ pounds}}{\text{cross sectional area (square inches)}}$$

$$\text{so the required area of rod} = \frac{2000 \text{ pounds}}{1400 \text{ psi}} = 1.43 \text{ square inches}$$

Thus a rod 1 inch by 1.5 inches (1.5 square inches) would be adequate, although you would probably make it larger to give a safety margin. We also haven't considered whether it will stretch too much to serve its purpose.

Strain

This quantity has a very simple definition for our purposes. It is the extension (or contraction) of a material divided by its original length. Because it is the ratio of two lengths it has no units - we say it is a **dimensionless quantity**. We can therefore measure lengths in inches, centimeters, yards, etc. as long as both original length and amount of stretch, or contraction, are in the same units. We usually express it as a percentage, and therefore multiply the fraction by one hundred.

$$\textbf{Strain} = \frac{\text{Extension}}{\text{Original length}} \quad \text{OR} \quad \frac{\text{Extension}}{\text{Original length}} \text{ x } 100\%$$

Examples.

1. The yield strength occurs at a strain of 0.2% so:

$$\text{Strain} = 0.2\% = \frac{\text{Extension}}{\text{Original length}} \text{ x } 100\%$$

Hence: Extension = 0.002 x Original length

Therefore, if we started with a piece of wire 12 feet long (144 inches), it will now have stretched by 144 x 0.002 inches, i.e. 0.288 inches, or a little over a quarter of an inch.

2. If we take a rubber band and stretch it to three times its original length, the extension is 2 lengths, the original length is 1 length and the strain is therefore 200% or 2. Notice here that we haven't even said how long the elastic band was originally. A strain of two means that the length has been trebled.

It is worth pointing out as a follow-up to the previous example that a strain of 'one' means that the length has doubled. A strain of 'six' means that the band is seven times its original length.

Of course, your experience tells you that there are few materials which will exhibit such large strains. These materials are usually polymers which we call elastomers, and rubber is one of them.

Stiffness

Stiffness is what we often refer to in normal speech when we use the word 'strong'. If you ask many people whether a piece of plastic film is strong, they will say "no". They see it as not being stiff, which often implies weakness. In fact the film is quite strong. Try breaking a piece by pulling it in tension. It is not easy to do. Boxes of plastic film usually come with a cutting edge.

If we compare two materials by putting the same tensile stress on them, the stiffer of the two will stretch less. In any application we usually wish to know what strain (stretch) will be produced by a certain stress (force/area) and it is the stiffness which tells us this. We define stiffness using a quantity known as **Young's Modulus (YM)** which is defined by:

$$\text{Young's Modulus} = \frac{\text{Stress applied}}{\text{Strain it produces}}$$

(NOTE: strain is **not** a percentage here)

This equation satisfies the requirement that the smaller the strain (amount of stretch) the greater the stiffness. You may also notice that if the strain is 'one' the Young's modulus is equal to the stress, in other words you can think of the Young's modulus as the stress required to double the length of the material.

The Young's modulus is also measured in psi, and values are typically around a million (1,000,000 or 10^6) psi.

Examples.

1. If a piece of wire, 50 inches long, is pulled with a tensile stress of 2000 psi and stretches to 50.1 inches, the stiffness (Young's modulus) is calculated as follows:

Strain = 0.1 inches (extension)/50 inches (original length) = 0.002

$$\text{so Young's Modulus} = \frac{2000 \text{ psi (stress)}}{0.002 \text{ (strain)}}$$

$$= 1,000,000 \text{ psi}$$

2. If we have a three feet long metal rod with a Young's modulus of 6×10^6 psi and apply a tensile stress of 5,000 psi we can calculate the strain as follows:

$$YM = 6 \times 10^6 \, psi = \frac{stress}{strain} = \frac{5000 \, psi}{strain}$$

$$so \; strain = \frac{5000 \, psi}{6 \times 10^6 \, psi} = 0.00083 \; or \; 0.083\%$$

$$now \; strain = \frac{extension}{length} = \frac{extension}{36 \; inches}$$

$$therefore \; extension = 0.00083 \times 36 \; inches = 0.03 \; inches$$

This means that if we hang a weight of 5000 pounds (two and a half tons) on a rod which is three feet long and has a cross section of 1" x 1", it will stretch only 0.03 inches (three hundredths of an inch).

3. If a 3 feet long plastic rod has a Young's modulus of 5×10^4 psi, what stress is needed to stretch it one inch?

$$the \; strain \; is \; 1 \; inch/36 \; inches = 0.028$$

$$stress = YM \times strain = 5 \times 10^4 \times 0.028 = 1389 \; psi$$

If this material were a 3 feet long circular filament, a tenth of an inch in diameter (radius = 0.05 inches), what weight would you need to hang on it to produce the one inch stretch?

$$cross \; section \; area \; of \; filament = \pi r^2 = \pi \times 0.05^2 \; square \; inches$$
$$= 0.0079 \; square \; inches \; (in^2)$$

$$weight \; required = 0.0079 \; in^2 \times 1389 \; psi = 10.97 \; pounds$$

4. If you pull a 50 inch piece of material with a UTS of 5000 psi and a YM of 5×10^6 psi, how much will it have stretched when it breaks?

$$Using \; YM = stress/strain, \; we \; have \; 5 \times 10^6 \, psi = 5000 \, psi/strain$$
$$which \; gives \; a \; strain \; of \; 5000/5 \times 10^6 = 0.001$$

The extension (stretch) is therefore 50 inches x 0.001 = 0.05 inches, or a twentieth of an inch.

Remember that the larger the Young's modulus the stiffer the material. Here are some typical values:

ceramics have high values   -   100 million psi $(100 \times 10^6 \text{ psi})$

metals have medium values   -   10 million psi $(10 \times 10^6 \text{ psi})$

polymers have low values   -   100 thousand psi $(0.1 \times 10^6 \text{ psi})$

But there are many exceptions to this trend.

If two materials have the same strengths (UTS) but different stiffnesses it means that they will both break under the same load but the one with the lower Young's modulus will stretch more than the other. Some plastics are very strong (high UTS) but we would not use them for an aircraft wing because they lack rigidity (stiffness), i.e. have a low Young's modulus.

We are now in a position to more intelligently examine some of the mechanical properties of materials. Remember the definitions! We shall use them later, especially in our case studies.

QUESTIONS: Chapter 9

1. The Young's Modulus is also known as the _____.
   (a) strength (b) stiffness (c) stress (d) strain (e) extension

2. A ceramic usually is strongest in _____.
   (a) tension (b) shear (c) bending (d) compression

3. If a 50 foot long piece of fishing line extends 6 inches then the strain is _____.
   (a) 6/50 inches (b) 6/600 inches (c) 1 % (d) 10 % (e) 0.1

4. If a 1000 pound weight is suspended from an iron bar of cross-section 2 inches by 5 inches
   the stress on the rod is:
   (a) 1000 p.s.i. (b) 10 pounds (c) 10 p.s.i. (d) 100 p.s.i. (e) 100 pounds

5-9.   A bar of material is 100 inches long and has an cross sectional area of 50 square
   inches. If a weight of 50,000 pounds is placed on the rod it will feel a stress of __5__.
   If under this weight the rod extends 0.001 inches then the rod is experiencing a strain of
   __6__. Therefore, the Young's modulus of the rod is __7__. This value for
   Young's modulus would most likely correspond to a __8__. If we keep adding weight
   to the rod until at 1,000,000 pounds the bar finally breaks its ultimate tensile stress will be
   __9__.

   5. (a) 10 psi (b) 100 psi (c) 100 pounds (d) 1,000 psi (e) 10,000 psi
   6. (a) 0.1 % (b) 0.001 % (c) 0.001 (d) 10 % (e) 10,000,000 %
   7. (a) 10,000 psi (b) 100,000 psi (c) 1,000,000 pounds (d) 1,000,000 psi
       (e) 100,000,000 psi
   8. (a) polymer (b) metal (c) ceramic (d) semiconductor (e) not enough information
   9. (a) 20 psi (b) 5,000 psi (c) 20,000 psi (d) 200,000 psi (e) 5,000,000 psi

10. What type of material would likely have a Young's Modulus of 100,000 psi?
    (a) metal (b) ceramic (c) polymer (d) semiconductor (e) not enough information given

11. If a weight of 800 pounds is hung from the end of a 30 inch long rectangular bar of material
    (4 inches by 2 inches) the bar extends by 0.03 inches.

    Calculate the (a) stress, (b) strain (in percentage) and (c) Young's Modulus of the bar.

    We continue to add weight to the bar until at a total weight of 2400 pounds the bar breaks.

    (d) What is the ultimate tensile strength of this material?
    (e) Knowing this, could a bar of the same material with sides 2 inches by 2 inch hold the
    original weight of 800 pounds?

10. MAKING METALS STRONGER
or
HOW TO STOP THOSE DISLOCATIONS MOVING

We have now learned that metals deform by the movement of the closest packed planes of atoms in the structure as they slide over each other. We have also seen how dislocations facilitate this movement, making it a thousand times easier than would be the case if the planes slipped as complete entities. The dislocations allow these planes to slide one row of atoms at a time which is much easier.

The idea of dislocations started as just that, an idea or theory. Nowadays we have millions of pictures of the defects taken with an electron microscope. For reasons which are too complex to go into here, the dislocation (termination of the extra part plane, see Page 68) shows up in these photos as continuous or spotty black lines. You must appreciate that in an electron microscope we are looking *through* the sample, just as you might be looking through a piece of glass. In the photograph on the next page the slip planes are at an angle to the specimen surface as shown below. The dislocations are effectively lines on these planes and they therefore appear as short line segments, one end of which intersects the top of the specimen and the other the bottom. The following diagram attempts to illustrate this.

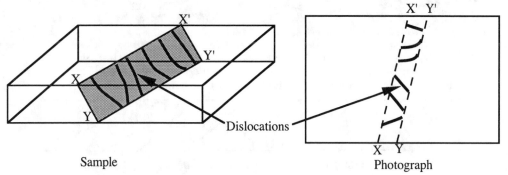

Sample   Photograph

The diagram on the left shows a thin piece of metal (specimen) containing one slip plane XX'YY' on which there are six dislocations. When viewed from above, as in an electron microscope, one sees the dislocations as shown in the diagram on the right. Note that the lines XX' and YY' are not seen in the photograph.

In the photograph shown below you can see dislocations on seven different parallel slip planes. You can also see that there are sometimes as many as ten dislocations in one micron (10^{-6} meters or 10^{-4} cm) so that they are as close as ten millionths of a centimeter (10^{-5} cm) to each other. This means that there are only around 500 atom spacings between dislocations. This should not be surprising bearing in mind that each only produces a movement of one atom spacing, and we need millions of these movements to produce something we can see with the naked eye.

Photograph showing seven parallel slip planes in a metal crystal. The dislocations appear to lie and move on 'tram lines' which would be parallel and all the same width if the specimen were uniformly thick. This is obviously not the case.

The seven parallel slip planes in section DD of the above photograph.

If indeed dislocations are the points of weakness in a metal, allowing it to deform at much lower stresses, to strengthen and stiffen the material we must either eliminate the dislocations or stop them from moving. There is only one way to accomplish the former and several approaches to the latter.

Metal whiskers

Although we have talked of dislocations as lines, and a line has length but no other dimensions, the dislocations do have a width. They affect atoms for quite a distance away. The diagram on page 68 is really showing only maybe one atom in fifty. You must imagine that there are fifty atom planes for every one shown. If we were to show every atom, the diagram would fill a room rather than a page in a book! The reason for mentioning this is that dislocations affect quite a large volume of material as far as atomic dimensions are concerned. If there is not enough room it is impossible to form dislocations.

We find that this is the case with a class of materials known as metal whiskers which have strengths close to the theoretical value (i.e. 1000X larger than the usually measured value). These whiskers are no more than a thousandth of a millimeter wide and a few millimeters long. They are of theoretical interest but are not really of much practical value. We want to use metals in the form of steel girders, not in such small particles. These are the only metals which are known to not contain dislocations. It is therefore logical that our only approach to strengthening metals is to stop the dislocations moving, or **pin** them.

Work hardening

One method of stopping dislocations with which you are probably familiar, although you may be unaware of what you are doing, or of what the effect is called, is **work hardening**.

In a CCP (FCC) metal there are four possible non-parallel slip planes, and in a BCC metal there are six. Dislocations can move on many of these at once and of course the planes on which they are moving will often intersect each other, as shown below.

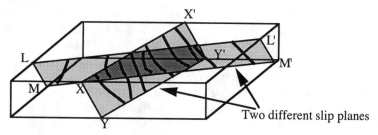

Diagram showing the previous XX'YY' slip plane together with another non-parallel slip plane, LL'MM'. When two moving dislocations intersect they pin each other.

It is easy to think of a dislocation line (the termination of the extra partial plane) as a short length of twine. When two are moving on different non-parallel planes, as shown in the previous diagram, and meet, they form a kind of dislocation knot at the intersection. Each pushes the atoms in a different direction with the result that they are no longer being pushed in a direction of easy movement (slip direction). As the metal is deformed more, there are more and more of these knots or tangles formed and the dislocations are eventually unable to move. Here again we turn to the electron microscope to support this. The left hand photograph of the sequence shown below is just one mess of dislocation tangles. The metal (aluminum) has been deformed a great deal and the tangles are the result. Now that the dislocations are immobile the material is quite brittle. We call this method of strengthening **work hardening**.

Sequence showing loss of dislocation tangles as a piece of deformed aluminum is annealed.

If you bend a piece of wireback and forth until it breaks you may notice that the wire gets hot and stiffer. In fact unless you force the bend to keep happening at the same place you will find the wire starts to bend at another location. The former effect is simply due to the friction as the atom planes rub over each other, just as you warm your hands on a cold winter's day. The stiffening happens because you are creating so many dislocations that they literally lock each other in knots so that no further yielding is possible and the material becomes brittle and breaks. This is usually not a very practical way of hardening a material but it is used in some cases. A metalsmith may sometimes decorate the surface of an article by using a ball peen hammer, one which has a ball-like hitting surface on one end. Not only does this produce a decorative finish but it also hardens the surface of the metal. Sometimes we fire small hard metal shot at the surface in a process called shot-peening. Railroad lines are often shaped by passing through rollers when cold. The deformation produces a multitude of dislocations which become tangled, and the metal is hardened.

When a metalsmith forms a piece of metal by hammering or bending, it becomes hard and brittle and has to be periodically **annealed**. To anneal a material means to heat it, but there is more to it than that. Dislocations move atoms in certain directions on slip planes, and dislocation tangles are regions where the atoms have been forced in two or more directions at the same time and are therefore not in their correct positions in the crystals. The material therefore has to be made hot enough for the atoms to become very mobile, which needs vacancies, so that they can rearrange themselves into more perfect crystals with fewer of these defects. The temperature needed depends on the metal being used.

The previous sequence of photos shows how annealing removes the dislocation tangles in aluminum. If the metalsmith fails to notice that the metal is getting hard and continues to beat it, the result is the formation of cracks and the piece is ruined.

Precipitation hardening

The method which is perhaps most frequently used for strengthening metals is to introduce something in the material which blocks the movement of the dislocations, and the most usual way of doing this is to somehow treat the material so that small precipitates of a different substance are produced within it. When we discussed point defects (Page 74) we mentioned that if we add too much impurity to a material there is a chance of producing small precipitates, and it is these precipitates which can pin the dislocations.

The reason for this effect is not difficult to understand. Remember that a dislocation moves along between the two planes which are slipping over each other (Pages 68-69). The planes slip one row of atoms at a time. If the precipitate cannot slip and get out of the way of the advancing row of atoms, it presents an obstacle to their motion.

Often the atoms in the precipitate are of a different type and of a different crystal structure, i.e. they are arranged quite differently. They may also be held together with either covalent or ionic bonds. The dislocation can only proceed if the precipitate gives way and allows the dislocation to pass through to the main body of the material (usually referred to as the **matrix**). Refer to the diagram on page 69 and you can see that the top half of the crystal moves out one atom spacing because there is no obstacle to its motion; the precipitate provides such an obstacle. Precipitates in steels are usually combinations of carbon with some of the metal elements (iron or one of the alloying elements). These carbides are not bonded by metallic bonds and therefore do not slip as do pure metals.

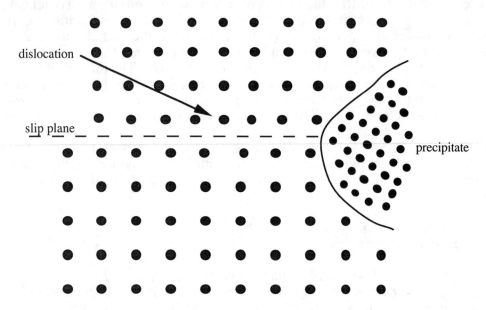

Dislocation held up (pinned) by precipitate particle.

Because there are millions of dislocations in the material what we really need are millions of very, very small precipitates rather than a few large ones so that there is always likely to be a precipitate in the way of the moving dislocation. This is where Materials Science comes in, providing the information of which atoms to introduce to form the precipitates, and how to process the metal by heating, cooling etc., to produce the required precipitate distribution. This phenomenon is known as **precipitation hardening**.

In the following case study we shall discuss how this is done in the new aluminum-lithium alloys. Lithium is the lightest metal, so that not only does it make the aluminum stronger, it also makes the aluminum even lighter than it already is. Such a material is of great importance in aircraft manufacture where lighter, stronger materials reduce the operating costs of the planes.

Sometimes the precipitates take a long time to form in the metal, just as sugar precipitates may form in a bottle of syrup or honey, or tartrate crystals in a bottle of wine over a period of months or years. A good example of this is seen in sterling silver which is an alloy of 92.5% silver, 7.5% copper. When left at room temperature for long periods of time the metal hardens because the copper forms precipitates. If a silversmith leaves a piece unfinished for a few weeks, the metal first has to be annealed to cause these precipitates to redissolve in the metal so that the dislocations can continue to move, and the metal may be worked to its desired shape. This is in addition to the periodic annealing necessary to eliminate the dislocation tangles produced by the hammering of the material, which we have already mentioned (Page 98).

Just having isolated impurity atoms in the metal can also produce some inhibition of dislocation motion. Look at the diagram below. Where the extra half plane of atoms finishes there is a large interstice. It is natural that an impurity atom should lodge there, and when it does so, it needs the dislocation to stay there to provide it with the needed space. There is therefore a kind of attraction between the two and as a result the dislocation is reluctant to move.

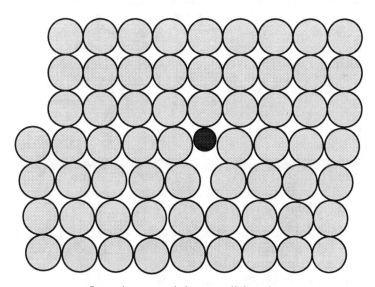

Impurity atom sitting at a dislocation.

Grain Refining

One final way of strengthening a metal is make the grains, or crystallites, smaller. In this case we are not concerned about dislocations being stopped by small crystals of a different material (precipitates) but by another crystal of the same material. However, the next crystal will have a different orientation and the plane on which the dislocation is moving does not continue across the boundary. The dislocation stops moving when it is close to the boundary because if it were to go right through the crystal it would create an atomic ledge (see diagram on page 69). There is no room for this unless the next crystal also slips and so the dislocation stops. The next dislocation stops behind the first etc., and soon a sort of traffic jam is produced. We call this a **pile-up** (one is visible in the photo on page 96). The consequence is that dislocation motion is limited. Obviously the smaller the crystal the less distance the dislocations move, and hence there is some improvement in the material's strength.

You may well be asking why the next crystal, which is of the same material and therefore can also slip, does not just slip out of the way and allow deformation to proceed? We shall leave this question until we discuss HSLA steels which provide us with a practical application of this strengthening method in our second case study. These materials are used in automobile bodies where their higher strength allows thinner metal to be used. This reduces weight and improves fuel efficiency. This is one reason why modern cars sometimes appear flimsy compared to the tank-like vehicles produced 35 to 40 years ago.

Conclusion

To summarize: the weaknesses in a metal are the dislocations. They allow the closest packed planes to slide over each other 1000X more easily than if there were no dislocations. Because of the dislocations the atoms move a row at a time. To strengthen the material we have two options:

eliminate dislocations: only possible if crystals are so small (whiskers) that they cannot accommodate a dislocation: this is not really a practical method.
pin dislocations: three possibilities:-
work harden - much deformation causes dislocation tangles so that the dislocations effectively pin each other.
precipitation harden - introduce small impurity precipitates to hinder dislocation motion.
grain refining - dislocation motion is limited : dislocation pile-ups are produced at crystal boundaries.

11. CASE STUDY: ALUMINUM-LITHIUM ALLOYS FOR AEROSPACE

A brief history

Today aircraft are so much a part of our everyday lives that we scarcely give a thought to the materials which go into them, but the fact that they fly should tell us that the lighter we can build them, the better. Every aircraft has a maximum takeoff weight which depends on air temperature, weather, the altitude of the airport, etc. The lighter the aircraft itself, the more the weight of passengers and freight which can be carried, hence the greater the potential for profits.

Early aircraft had their frames made of wood and their wings covered with fabric. Indeed wood has much to commend it for its combination of lightness and strength. However, it is clear that lightweight metals would be more durable. The first world war (1914-18) saw the development of all-metal aircraft, with the German Dornier RS1 flying boat being the first example. In 1930 lightweight aluminum alloys became the major structural materials used in airframes. Replacing steel with aluminum alloys produced tremendous weight savings[*].

The theoretical weight saving of around 65% assumes that a given volume of steel would be replaced by the same volume of aluminum. Even if the aluminum struts in the airframe needed to be 25% thicker, the weight savings would still exceed 50%.

In today's aircraft, aluminum is still the major material for the main body and airframe although specialty steels are used for the landing gear which suffers severe stresses during take-off and especially on landing. However in some aircraft, mostly military, aluminum is being replaced by even lighter composite materials based, for example, on carbon fibers. These are also used extensively on the executive Learjets and are being introduced into some larger commercial

---

[*] NOTE: The density of a material is a measure of the weight of a certain volume. Scientists usually use the weight in grams (gm) of one cubic centimeter (cm^3) of material, i.e. a cube with an edge length of one centimeter. By comparing densities we are looking at the relative weights of the same volume of material. Whereas iron-based materials (steels) have a density of around 7.8 gm/cm^3, aluminum-based materials have a density of around 2.8 gm/cm^3, so that if the same volume of material were used, the weight saving would be around 65% [(7.8-2.8)/7.8 x 100% = 500/7.8% = 64.1%]

passenger aircraft. The pie charts shown below indicate the percentages of different materials used in two current aircraft, one a commercial passenger plane and the other a military fighter plane. Notice that both planes contain over 70% aluminum.

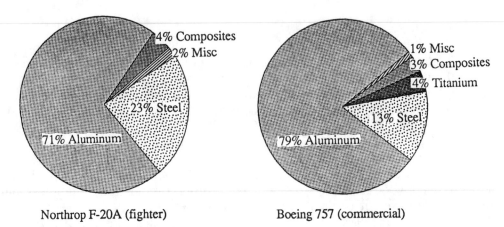

Northrop F-20A (fighter)   Boeing 757 (commercial)

Materials used in aircraft structures.

The reason for making the airframes lighter lies in the statement made earlier. The less the weight of the plane, the more cargo weight which can be carried. The following pie chart shows the weight distribution for a typical passenger aircraft about to take off on a 1,000 mile journey.

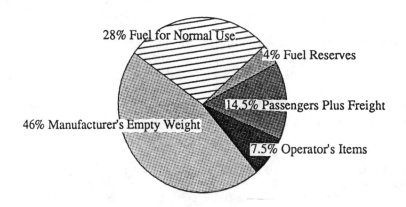

Various contributions to an aircraft's take-off weight.

Notice that the manufactured empty plane accounts for only 46% of the total weight and the passengers and freight for only 14.5%. Now if we could reduce the weight of the empty plane by one tenth (10% or 0.1) and keep the take-off weight the same, we could transfer 4.6% of the total weight (46% x 0.1) to passengers & freight. The load carried would increase from 14.5% of total weight to 19.1%. This means that the weight carried for profit (passengers & cargo) has gone up by nearly a third. Such a substantial increase is well worth striving for!

Another way of taking advantage of this weight saving is to reduce the take-off weight which in turn saves fuel, just as reducing the weight of an automobile increases miles per gallon. The lower fuel requirements also reduce take-off weight and the much lighter plane now needs less engine power so that the engines can also be made smaller and lighter. What started out as a reduction in the airframe weight has resulted in other weight savings which add up to be far more significant.

One way of producing these significant weight savings, as already mentioned, is to replace metals with composite materials made of carbon fibers in an epoxy resin matrix. These materials have a density of less than 1.8 gm/cm^3, more than 30% less than aluminum. They are also very stiff and quite strong so could well replace much of the aluminum which is currently used in airframes and other aerospace vehicles.

The threat to metals by composites

Data published by British Aerospace in 1983, which predicted materials use in aircraft in 1995, showed carbon fiber reinforced composites accounting for 25 - 40% of the weight, and the aluminum content down to 35 - 50%. This second edition of the book is being written in 1995 and these predictions have not been met, but some steps have been made in that direction.

This threat to the aluminum industry of being replaced by lightweight composite materials spurred scientists into a search for newer lightweight alloys of aluminum. This is where lithium comes in. Look at your periodic table (Page 7) and you will see that lithium is element number 3. It is a metal which is the lightest existing solid element at room temperature. If we can replace some of the aluminum atoms with lithium, we can obviously produce a weight saving. It turns out that by suitable manufacturing processes we can also increase strength

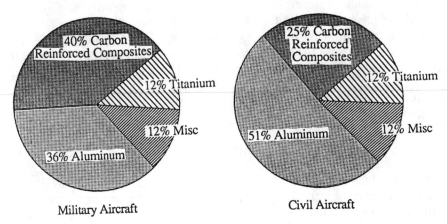

Military Aircraft   Civil Aircraft

Predictions made in 1983 for aircraft materials use in 1995 These have not been met.

and stiffness. This leads to even further weight savings because the load bearing parts can also be reduced in size.

The metallurgy of aluminum-lithium alloys

We have earlier mentioned (Page 76) that impurities (extrinsic defects) can occupy one of two different positions in a metal, interstitial or substitutional. At that time we said that smaller atoms were likely to be interstitial and atoms of comparable size to be substitutional. As an example of the former we mentioned interstitial carbon (atomic number 6) in FCC iron (atomic number 26). Here we are thinking of putting lithium (atomic number 3) into aluminum (atomic number 13) which is also FCC. If you note that these numbers are in the same ratios you might expect lithium to be an interstitial impurity in aluminum. Fortunately you would be wrong!

If we add an extra atom in an interstitial position we are obviously adding more weight, and the material will be denser. If we replace an atom with a lighter one the density is decreased.

Aluminum is one of the many metals which have the cubic close packed (CCP) crystal structure which results in a cube with atoms on the corners of the cube and in the centers of the cube faces. We add lithium to the aluminum in the molten state and when the mix solidifies the lithium atoms are found to have replaced some of the aluminum atoms in this CCP arrangement. The lithium atoms are what we have previously called substitutional impurity atoms. They occupy the positions normally occupied by the aluminum atoms and form what we call a **substitutional solid solution**. In the following two-dimensional diagram there are 75 atoms, 5 of which are lithium, i.e. there is an atom concentration of 5/75 x 100%, or 6.67%, of lithium in the aluminum.

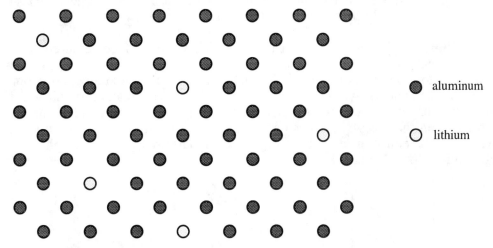

Diagram illustrating the substitutional solid solubility of lithium in aluminum.

When we make solutions of, for example, salt in water, we know that we can dissolve only a certain amount. If we put too much salt in the water there is some which refuses to dissolve. If we heat the water we can dissolve more salt but when we allow it to cool, the salt precipitates out from the solution again. The maximum amount which can be dissolved is called the **solubility limit**. In reality what we have is a saturated salt solution (brine) and also some precipitated salt which in fact contains some water, i.e. we have salt in the water and water in the salt. We call this a **two-phase mixture**. The word **phase** is scientific jargon and is a word which is difficult for even scientists to define. For our purposes we shall define it as meaning a distinguishable portion of matter. Fruit in jello would be a good example. The jello would be one phase, the pineapple chunks another, the bananas yet another, etc. In the case of salt in water we can distinguish the liquid (brine) from the solid (salt containing water). The solid is one phase and the liquid is the other.

When we add lithium to aluminum there is also a solubility limit and we take advantage of this fact. For some metal mixtures (e.g. copper and nickel) there is no solubility limit so that you can keep replacing the copper atoms with nickel atoms until you have 100% nickel. For lithium-aluminum this is not the case. If we add lithium so that we exceed the solubility limit we produce two phases, but in this case they are both solid. On the one hand we have an aluminum-lithium solid solution as described earlier and on the other we have precipitates of lithium which contain aluminum (we must be careful here because these precipitates really contain more aluminum than lithium).

These precipitates are rather unusual. They have a face centered cubic atom arrangement with lithium atoms on the corners of the cube but with aluminum atoms at the face centers. If you carefully count the numbers of atoms in this arrangement you will see that a precipitate has the chemical formula Al_3Li, (remember that only an eighth of each corner atom is in the cube, and only half of each atom on the faces). Because of its exact composition it is known as an **intermetallic compound**. Metallurgists designate this precipitate phase as **delta prime (δ')**. Don't ask why!

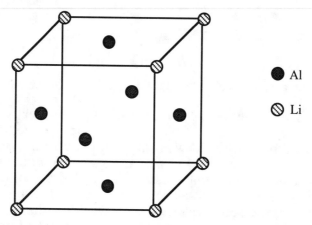

● Al

⊗ Li

The crystal structure of Al_3Li precipitates (δ').

Note that we cannot control whether or not one thing is soluble in another, neither can we control the amount which is soluble. In this case we know that there is a solubility limit (the solid aluminum will only accept so many lithium atoms) and that if we add too much there will be delta-prime precipitates (regions containing 25% lithium atoms) formed. What we can do by suitable processing (controlling cooling rates, heating treatments, etc.) is to ensure that we get a lot of small precipitates rather than a few large ones. Knowing what we can and cannot control in a material is perhaps the most important aspect of Materials Science.

The following photograph is taken in an electron microscope. It is a view through a sample about 3000 Å thick. The bright regions are discrete spheres of δ' and the black background is the aluminum-rich Al/Li solid solution (meaning that this solid solution is mostly aluminum). Notice that the small δ' precipitates are only around 200 Å in diameter (200 Å = 20 nm = 20 x 10^{-9} meters), i.e. about 100 atoms across. This is about a tenth of the specimen thickness.

Photograph of an aluminum-lithium alloy taken in an electron microscope. Remember that you are looking through a thin piece of material and precipitates, the small white regions which are adjacent in the photograph may be far apart in the material - one at the top and the other at the bottom.

This microstructure is just what we need for precipitation hardening. Lots of small precipitates will pin dislocations wherever they are moving. Just imagine these obstacles to dislocation motion dispersed throughout the specimen, each one being about a tenth of the specimen thickness. The next diagram may help you to visualize that the dislocation has little chance of moving more than a micron (10,000 Å) before it encounters an obstacle! Remember the precipitates you see in the previous photograph are distributed throughout a three-dimensional sample.

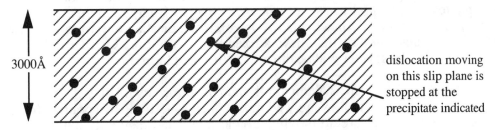

3000Å

dislocation moving on this slip plane is stopped at the precipitate indicated

Side view of the specimen in the previous photograph.

The one remaining question is how we manage to get such a distribution of precipitates. How can we ensure that we don't just get a few large precipitates? For the moment we shall defer the answer while we consider how ineffective a few large precipitates would be. Imagine that all precipitates in the above diagram were combined to form one large precipitate. Only a few dislocations would have their motion stopped. If we now form two smaller precipitates of the same size from this large one (remember that they would have the same volume), each would have a diameter about 80% of the large single precipitate. Placing these two side by side produces a barrier which is 1.6 times taller than the one large precipitate and 0.8 times the width. The obstacles are now 1.6 x 0.8 = 1.28 of the original area. These two smaller precipitates can therefore stop the motion of more dislocations than could the single one. The following illustrations may help to explain this.

In the left diagram there is one large precipitate which can block the motion of dislocations moving on slip planes between the two shown by the dashed lines. The second diagram shows two precipitates with the same combined volume. They can block dislocations moving in a larger fraction of the crystal, again on all slip planes between the two indicated.

For the mathematically inclined, this is a consequence of the fact that volume is proportional to the cube of the linear dimension. For each precipitate to have half the volume of the original it must have a diameter equal to:

(the cube root of 0.5) x the diameter of the original.

The cube root of 0.5 is almost exactly 0.8.

Returning to the original question about the formation of many small precipitates, it is helpful to use an analogy. Imagine a large number of people moving around randomly in a big hall. On command they are to form themselves into large groups, but they only have a fixed time to do it in. Of course the less time they have the smaller will be the groups they can form.

A metal alloy such as aluminum-lithium is formed by melting the elements together and making sure they are well mixed, then solidifying by cooling. In the molten state the atoms are all moving around freely and randomly but we have intentionally added so much lithium that the solubility limit at room temperature is exceeded. We therefore know that Al_3Li precipitates will form, and we can even tell how much. By controlling the cooling we can ensure that the atoms don't have enough time to form large clusters, or precipitates. In other words we want to cool quickly rather than slowly. We saw earlier that atoms have less mobility at lower temperatures.

The cooling procedures necessary have to be determined in the laboratory and can be quite complex, possibly involving letting the material sit at certain intermediate temperatures for some time.

What is the effect on properties?

Stopping dislocation motion by precipitates is what we call **precipitation hardening**. The aluminum has been stiffened by precipitates produced by the addition of lighter lithium atoms. Every 1% of the original weight replaced by lithium produces about a 3.5% decrease in density. The table shows some of the property changes produced by adding about 3% lithium to aluminum. You can see that we have made a material which is lighter, stiffer and stronger.

Property	Conventional Aluminum Alloys	Al - Li Alloys	Change
Density (g/cm^3)	2.8	2.52	10% lighter
Young's Modulus (psi)	11×10^6	12×10^6	9% stiffer
*Ultimate Tensile Strength (psi)	77×10^3	80×10^3	4% stronger
*Yield Strength (psi)	62×10^3	67×10^3	8% stronger

*__Yield strength__ - the stress at which a material begins to deform permanently.

   Ultimate tensile strength - the stress at which a material fails or breaks.

Alcoa has developed an aluminum-lithium alloy for use in the vertical stabilizer and tailplanes of the Boeing 777 and Airbus A330/340. Tests show that it produces a weight savings of 650 pounds over conventional aluminum alloys at a cost of about $220 per pound of weight saved. Thus the cost is a one time expense of under $150,000. If 650 pounds translates into three extra passengers with luggage the cost is therefore around $50,000 per passenger. Using an average ticket price of $250 and two flights a day, you should be able to appreciate that the investment is repaid in just 100 days. Not bad!

Aluminum-lithium alloys are therefore one answer the metallurgist has to the threat of composite materials. They are new materials which have resulted from learning about how properties can be changed by modifying the structure.

Conclusion

In closing, let's give some thought to how science has aided in the development of this material.

First, consider that there are two facts which we have learned but really have no control over. We cannot control whether lithium is a substitutional or interstitial impurity in aluminum, and we cannot control the solubility limit beyond which precipitates will form. What is important is that, armed with these facts, we can design a materials system which can be precipitation hardened and also be of lighter weight.

Second, our control comes in (a) choosing a composition which is above the solid solubility limit, thus ensuring that precipitates form, and (b) making sure the material's cooling pattern produces a large number of small precipitates.

There is still much research work to be done with these materials, and their current use is not as great as predicted a few years ago. However, there is little doubt that they will see more and more use in the years ahead.

12. CASE STUDY: MAGNESIUM ALLOYS, POTENTIAL LIGHTWEIGHT AEROSPACE MATERIALS

Many people's memories of high school chemistry classes may include the time a piece of magnesium ribbon was held in a pair of tongs and then placed in a flame. The spectacular immediate combustion which ensued, in the form of a dazzling white flame, almost certainly gave the impression that here is a metal we want to avoid using. This is perhaps an example of a case where first impressions are misleading.

Magnesium is the eighth most abundant element in the earth's crust, although it is not known to occur in a metallic state. Magnesite and dolomite are minerals from which it can be obtained, although it is more common to obtain it from salt water, which contains magnesium chloride in addition to sodium chloride. This, in itself, is attractive because it does not leave behind large holes in the ground or slag heaps.

This short chapter should make you aware of some exciting new developments in the metallurgy of magnesium. Before we do this we must dispel the fire hazard myth. It is true that thin ribbons and fine powders of magnesium burn vigorously in air, but larger pieces do not burn, mainly because magnesium is such a good conductor of heat that it is difficult to heat one spot so that it bursts into flames. The heat flows away from the spot so that it never reaches a high enough temperature.

Magnesium's principal attraction is its low density, which at 1.74 gm/cm^3 is considerably lower than that of aluminum (2.7 gm/cm^3). This means that changing from aluminum to pure magnesium would result in weight savings of a third. As in the case of most metals, however, an alloy is used rather than the pure form. Magnesium alloys have been used extensively in car wheels ('mag wheels'), frames for soft-sided luggage, lawnmower housings, and in many items of machinery where light weight is a priority. Volkswagen used quite a lot of magnesium on the 'Beetle', and Mercedes sports cars now have magnesium alloy seat frames. More recently Chevrolet has been experimenting with the possibility of a magnesium engine block for the Corvette, which would be more than 100 pounds lighter than the cast-iron one now used.

The metallurgy of magnesium and its alloys

We mentioned earlier (Chapter 6) that magnesium has a hexagonal close packed crystal structure. Because of this there is only one possible slip plane, and deformation is limited in the same way as mentioned earlier for zinc (Page 53). Atoms have three directions of easy motion on this one slip plane but that is all. As a consequence magnesium is quite a brittle metal. In the uses mentioned earlier the items are not hammered or pressed into shape but are formed by melting the magnesium alloy and pouring it into a mold of the required part, a process we call **casting**. Molten magnesium is very runny (has a low viscosity) and therefore can flow into even very small and complex areas of the mold. It is this property which has allowed Audi to use magnesium for a complex dashboard support which is only a millimeter thick in places.

How then can we make magnesium ductile? An answer has recently been provided by some Japanese researchers - mix it with lithium to form a solid solution, just as we did with lithium and aluminum in the previous chapter. What happens is something which is probably most unexpected, adding lithium to magnesium changes the crystal structure from hexagonal close packed to body centered cubic (BCC), and we have already pointed out that BCC metals have six possible non-parallel slip panes with two slip directions in each, giving them twelve slip systems.

This change in crystal structure makes a dramatic change in the properties. An alloy of 57.4% magnesium, 37.6% lithium and 5% aluminum can be stretched 100% (a strain of 1), while another alloy of 56.5% magnesium, 38.5% lithium and 5% zinc can be stretched more than 200% (a strain greater than 2).

The fact that these alloys can be deformed so much should lead you to expect two things about the structure of the alloy. (Yes, you now have the necessary background to anticipate this!) The lithium causes no precipitation hardening, and it also is a substitutional impurity. If these were not true it would be extremely difficult to achieve the dislocation motion necessary for ductility, because interstitial atoms and precipitates impede dislocation motion.

Greatly increased ductility is not the only benefit, however. The density of pure lithium is just a little over half that of water, and as in the case of aluminum-lithium alloys we would expect its presence as a substitutional impurity in magnesium to produce a density reduction. This actually happens and the two alloys mentioned above are even lighter than water, with densities around 0.95 gm/cm^3. Applications for such materials in the aerospace industry are obvious.

Because magnesium and lithium powders and their molten liquids have to be handled very carefully, special care is needed in the manufacture of these alloys. This involves making sure that they do not come into contact with air, and the melting and mixing has to be performed in an inert atmosphere of argon. Manufacturing and handling costs are therefore expected to be quite high and it not likely that we shall see these alloys used in everyday articles. The economics of use in aerospace applications are quite different, as we mentioned in the previous chapter.

Conclusion

While much of what we have said above is reminiscent of aluminum alloys, there is an important difference, namely the crystal structure change. This is again something we have no control over, but once we discover that it happens we can turn it to tremendous advantage.

13. CASE STUDY: HSLA STEELS FOR CAR BODIES

Background

Steel is the traditional material of choice for car bodies, but, as we have seen in our earlier discussion of aluminum-lithium alloys, steels are quite heavy. Replacing them with aluminum and eventually by aluminum-lithium alloys is all very good where the economics can justify it, as in aircraft, but for an automobile body this is not the case. However, there is an incentive to reduce car body weight because of regulations requiring manufacturers to meet a minimum corporate fleet average fuel economy. Another approach to the problem is to produce a steel which is stronger than traditional materials so that less is required. This is the thrust of the research which led to the development of **high strength low alloy steels (HSLA steels)**.

A current (1995) advertisement for the Mercedes-Benz C-class automobile introduced in 1994 says "Take the passenger cabin. The same high-strength low-alloy steel used in all of our cars accounts for one third of its structural weight." One wonders how many readers know what this means? During the past two decades (1975 - 95) the weight of the typical U.S. passenger car has been reduced by about 600 pounds, much of this as a result of the use of these high strength steels. The steel in the Chrysler Neon is about 25% high strength, while at the time of writing the Mazda Millenia has perhaps the largest high strength steel usage (43%). A recent study has shown that the use of these materials can cut vehicle weight by 140 pounds while at the same time *saving* $40. To achieve the same weight saving using aluminum would add $460 to the cost.

The term 'high strength' is well understood, but 'low alloy' needs a little explanation because once again we are confronted with some metallurgical jargon. We call an impurity atom which we add intentionally to the steel an **alloying element**, and a steel with a *small* amount of these impurities is called **low alloy**. In this chapter we shall discuss one of many high-strength low alloy steels which has niobium as one of the important alloying elements. The niobium forms niobium carbide precipitates, but unlike aluminum-lithium alloys where precipitates form within the crystallites to pin dislocations, they are here formed at grain boundaries, i.e. between the crystallites, and it is these boundaries whose motion they stop.

The metallurgy of HSLA steels

We know that metals deform by the motion of dislocations which move on specific planes (close-packed planes) in the crystal. We call these planes **slip planes**. One of the major advantages of most metals is that they are ductile, i.e. they can be quite easily shaped to whatever object we require. On the other hand there are cases (bridges, buildings etc.) when we want them to be stiff and able to carry large loads without bending. We know that the way to accomplish this is by stopping dislocation motion. In aluminum-lithium alloys we have seen how we do this by precipitation hardening. HSLA steels are an example of another way of impeding dislocation motion.

When a metal solidifies it produces a polycrystalline structure, unless cooled very, very rapidly. A metal or alloy is therefore composed of many crystals or grains which can be several millimeters across or as small as 0.1 μm (1 μm = 10^{-6} meters or a millionth of a meter), corresponding to only about 500 atoms across. Two adjacent grains meet at a grain boundary, a planar defect, which can halt the passage of dislocations.

As we just mentioned, the dislocations move on specific slip planes in a crystal. However there is very little chance that this plane will continue across the grain boundary because the crystals on either side of the boundary have different orientations. Thus when the dislocation comes up to, and pushes on a grain boundary, the boundary stays put.

Notice that the dislocation is effectively pushing on the boundary. It wants to shift those atoms which are in front of it, but can only do so if the atoms across the boundary move also. The dislocation cannot therefore cross the boundary. A second dislocation comes along and stops behind the first, etc. However as more dislocations move along the slip plane and approach the boundary they add their force to that of the first dislocation and eventually the grain boundary might move. Of course each successive dislocation in the stoppage is further from the boundary and therefore contributes less and less to the force, but it is adding something. The atoms in the adjacent crystal or grain also move by means of dislocations. This means that dislocations in the first crystal are pushing on the adjacent crystal, trying to form and move dislocations there. If they are successful, the dislocations in the second crystal move on their slip plane until they are stopped by the next grain boundary, where there will be another dislocation pile-up and the process repeats until eventually the whole material may deform.

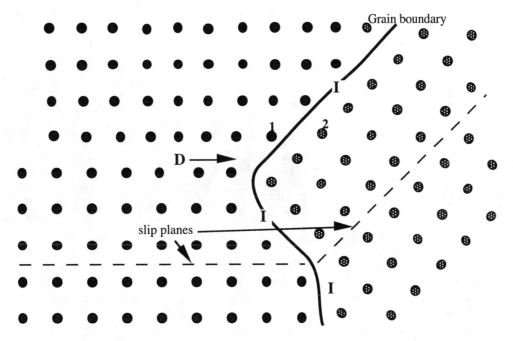

Illustration of a dislocation, moving in the direction of the arrow, stopped at a grain boundary. For further movement, atom 1 would have to move to the right where it is blocked by atom 2. Atom 2 has its slip plane going upward as shown (parallel to dashed line), and there is not enough force to move it in that direction. Also note that there are interstices (I) along the boundaries where impurity atoms could rest, precipitates start to form, or where atoms could start to rearrange into new crystals.

When the dislocations come to a boundary and are stopped they produce what we call a **pile-up**, a kind of traffic jam for dislocations (one was visible in the electron microscope photograph shown on page 96). In the following diagram of a pile-up a dislocation is represented by the symbol ⊥. The accompanying photograph shows such a pile-up in a thin (1000 Å) sample of stainless steel when viewed in a transmission electron microscope. Remember that you are effectively looking through the sample and the slip plane is at an angle to the sample surface, as was the case when we looked at the photograph on page 96. The dislocations appear as dark spotty lines with one end at the top surface of the specimen and the other at the bottom.

Diagram (left) and photograph (right) of a dislocation pile-up at a crystal boundary.

Each dislocation is pushing on the grain boundary and the more dislocations the greater the combined force they exert. Think of the following analogy. People are lined up behind each other in single file trying to push down the dividing partition between two rooms. The more people pushing, the larger the force and the greater the chance of the partition collapsing (forget about the poor person in front getting crushed - it's only an analogy!). Now make the room smaller so that we can only line up three or four people behind each other. The chances of their being able to push the wall down are much reduced. The same thing happens in metal crystals. If we can make the grains so small that only a few dislocations can pile up in the grain, there is little likelihood that the grain boundary will move. Hence there is no overall deformation of the piece. Remember that even though each additional dislocation makes a smaller contribution to the total force, every little bit helps. The fewer dislocations there are, the greater the chance of the crystallite boundary holding and keeping the dislocations from advancing.

This gives us the clue to one further method of making a metal stronger: limit the dislocation motion by making the grains small. We call this process **grain-refining**. Note that by **refining** we here mean making finer or smaller. When we refine precious metals we usually mean that we are making them purer.

The main question now is how can we do it, i.e. refine the grains? The answer lies in taking advantage of the fact that iron changes from a BCC crystal to an FCC crystal when heated above 912 °C and reverses the change when cooled again below this temperature. The temperature is somewhat different for a steel (alloyed iron) but the principal is the same.

We first take a bar of the BCC iron, or in this case steel, (something metallurgists call **ferrite**, or the **alpha phase**) and heat it so that it changes, or transforms, to the FCC form (**austenite**, or the **gamma phase**). After this change in crystal structure has been achieved, the steel is hot-rolled, meaning that it is rolled while still hot, or in the gamma form.[*]

This hot rolling has an effect on two structure levels, both of which are illustrated on the next page. First, and obvious, the steel bar is made longer and thinner, i.e. the **macrostructure** has changed. Second, and less obvious, the grains have also been flattened, something we sometimes call "pancaking". The original **equiaxed microstructure**, which means that the grains are approximately the same size in all directions, has been changed into a **pancaked microstructure**.

During the pancaking the grains have suffered gross deformation, something which we know is produced by the motion of millions of dislocations. After the rolling the metal crystals are literally full of dislocations and under normal circumstances at these temperatures the atoms are very mobile and would move around to try to restore the original non-dislocated order, forming new crystals in a process we call **recrystallization**. In addition the crystals prefer to be equiaxed rather than pancaked so this makes the boundaries to move.

Here is where our materials science knowledge becomes useful. We know that by adding the alloying element niobium to the steel we can form very small precipitates (50 atoms across) of niobium carbide (NbC) (something which is done when the steel is first formed). These small precipitates stop recrystallization because they form on the grain boundaries and stop their motion. Because of this the pancaked grain structure is retained.

---

[*] NOTE: Steels can also be cold-rolled, which strengthens by work hardening. We mentioned the possible use of this for producing railroad lines (Page 98). In this case the material needs to be annealed between every few passes through the rolling mill to keep it soft enough to continue rolling. The reason for this is identical to that which we mentioned for a silversmith or blacksmith (Page 99).

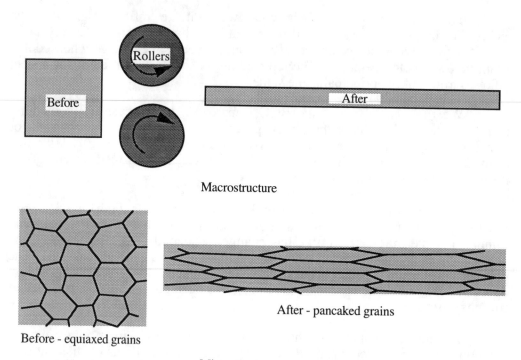

Macrostructure

Before - equiaxed grains

After - pancaked grains

Microstructure

Illustration of the effect of hot rolling on macrostructure (above) and microstructure (below).

The hot-rolled steel sheets are then allowed to cool, and below about 900°C the atoms do everything possible to change back to the BCC arrangement. To change their arrangement the atoms have to have some space to move around and the place where this can occur most easily is at the grain boundaries. If you look at the diagram of the grain boundary on page 119 you will see that there are some large interstices between the two crystallites which give the atoms just enough space to start to rearrange themselves.

In other words the new BCC crystals start to form along the grain boundaries which are pinned in position by the niobium carbide precipitates. These new BCC crystals grow until they bump into each other with the result that new grain boundaries are formed between them.

Illustration of what happens when a hot-rolled HSLA steel cools. The upper diagram shows the pancaked FCC grains. During cooling the atoms rearrange themselves to the BCC crystal structure, and find the space to do this at numerous points along the grain boundaries (center diagram). These nuclei continue to grow until the crystallites meet each other. Because opposing boundaries in the rolled material are very close the crystallites do not grow much before this happens.

Now think what happens. In the direction in which the rolling force was applied, the original grain boundaries in the hot-rolled steel are very close together. As shown in the above diagram, the new crystals grow at many locations along these boundaries and they cannot grow any larger than the small dimension of the original pancaked grains because they meet each other approximately half way across the original grains. The material is now fully BCC and there is no need for further change. The consequence is that a very fine grain size has been produced. It is this fine ferrite grain structure (new microstructure) which produces the high strength in these steels.

Notice that the size of the final BCC grain depends on the height of the pancaked FCC grains as shown in the following graph. The more the rolling, the smaller the grain size and the less dislocation motion which is possible.

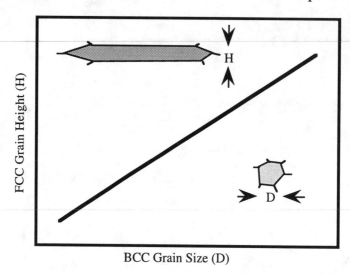

The final BCC grain size depends on the height of the pancaked FCC grains.

In addition, our experiments show that the smaller the grain size, the larger the **yield strength**. You can see from the table of properties on the next page that the change is quite dramatic. Notice that the Young's modulus has not been changed.

Finally, let's consider how this new material has been developed by using some of the principles we have learned earlier. The science behind its manufacture involves two major factors:

- a phase transformation occurs (FCC to BCC) when steel is cooled below around 900°C.

- small precipitates of NbC can be formed at the grain boundaries and they stop the boundaries from moving.

Note that we cannot control the phase transformation. We take advantage of it during the processing. We control the rolling temperature and make sure it is higher than the BCC to FCC transition temperature. We control composition by adding an impurity (Nb) which we have determined will form precipitates along the grain boundaries. We can also control cooling rates to optimize desired properties, but discussion of this aspect is outside the scope of this chapter.

What is the effect on properties?

Notice that in these materials we have not stopped the dislocations from moving completely as we have done in work hardening and precipitation hardening, where the dislocations are pinned and unable to move. In this case we have effectively stopped them from forcing the next grain to deform or yield, hence the change in yield strength. The biggest property change is therefore in the yield strength, as can be seen from the table of properties given below. These new materials are stronger than conventional sheet steels and the table shows some of these differences. You can see that both ultimate tensile strength and yield strength have increased quite remarkably, but that the stiffness, or Young's modulus is unchanged. The fact that the steel can take nearly three times the force without beginning to show a permanent deformation is what allows us to use thinner sheet metal in our autos. Some car manufacturers have reported decreased warranty claims for body dents as a result of using these steels.

Property	Conventional Steel	Comparable HSLA Steel	Change
Young's Modulus (psi)	30×10^6	30×10^6	no change
*Ultimate Tensile Strength (psi)	43×10^3	80×10^3	85% stronger
*Yield Strength (psi)	24×10^3	70×10^3	190% stronger

The thinner HSLA steel used for automobile bodies saves weight and consequently improves fuel economy. We may think today's cars are "tinny" but they do stand up to the rigors of everyday use. Unfortunately our reaction is more psychological than scientific!

---

* **Yield strength** - the stress at which a material begins to deform permanently.
 Ultimate tensile strength - the stress at which a material fails or breaks.

QUESTIONS: Chapters 10-13

1. Adding lithium to magnesium changes the crystal structure from _____.
    (a) BCC to FCC (b) FCC to HCP (c) HCP to FCC (d) HCP to BCC (e) HCP to CCP.

2. Which of the following structures would give the most brittle metal?
    (a) FCC (b) BCC (c) HCP (d) CCP (e) amorphous

3. Aluminum-lithium alloys are very strong because of _____.
    (a) work hardening (b) precipitation hardening (c) grain refining (d) zone refining
    (e) chain stiffening

4. The magnesium-lithium alloys mentioned are _____ than pure magnesium.
    (a) lighter (b) more conductive (c) more ductile (d) both a and c (e) all of these

5. The hot rolling process used in the manufacture of steels changes which structure level(s)?
    (a) microstructure (b) atomic structure (c) macrostructure (d) both a and b
    (e) both a and c

6. When we anneal a work hardened material we reduce the number of _____.
    (a) vacancies (b) dislocations (c) interstitials (d) planes (e) impurity atoms

7. The term grain refining means _____.
    (a) purifying the grains (b) changing crystals into grains (c) changing the macrostructure
    without changing the microstructure (d) decreasing the grain size (e) none of these

8. Which of the following is in order of increasing ductility?
    (a) gold, zinc, amorphous iron (b) amorphous iron, zinc, gold (c) gold, amorphous iron,
    zinc (d) zinc, gold, amorphous iron (e) none of these is in the correct order

9-13.   When we make HSLA steels we hot roll the material. This changes the ___9i___
    structure and the ___9ii___ structure. The grain boundaries are pinned by ___10___ so that
    the grains remain ___11___. When the material cools there is a change in ___12___
    structure from FCC to BCC. The end result is that we have ___13___.

9. (a) crystal, macro (b) atomic, micro (c) crystal, micro (d) micro, macro
    (e) crystal, atomic
10. (a) dislocations (b) nickel carbide precipitates (c) niobium carbide precipitates
    (d) vacancies (e) substitutional impurities.
11. (a) pancaked (b) needle-like (c) amorphous (d) rigid (e) irregular
12. (a) crystal (b) macro (c) atomic (d) electron (e) micro
13. (a) purified the grains (b) enlarged the material (c) produced a denser material
    (d) refined the grains (e) eliminated dislocations

14. Fine grained metals are stronger because there are more _____ to stop dislocation motion.
    (a) slip planes (b) grain boundaries (c) dislocation tangles (d) vacancies (e) point defects

15. Which of the following is not true of HSLA steels compared with regular steels?
    (a) lighter (b) stronger (c) stiffer (d) both a and b (e) both a and c

16 For HSLA steels, the ___ the grain size, the ____ the yield strength.
    (a) larger, larger (b) smaller, smaller (c) smaller, larger (d) there is no connection between the two (e) none of these is correct

17-28.   HSLA steels and Aluminum-Lithium (Al-Li) are both ___17___, which indicates that they both involve ___18___. The alloying element of importance in HSLA steels is ___19___, whereas in Al-Li it is the lithium which is added to the aluminum. In both cases there is only a small amount of the alloying element added, in fact only about ___20___ lithium is added to aluminum to produce a 10% ___21___. In both these materials the alloying element produces ___22___ but their positions in the crystals and their functions are quite different. In HSLA steels the ___22___ are formed ___23___, while in Al-Li they are formed ___24___. The purpose of ___22___ in HSLA steels is to ___25___. In Al-Li their purpose is to ___26___. The strengthening mechanism used in HSLA steels is ___27___, while in Al-Li it is ___28___.

17. (a) cermets (b) alloys (c) semiconductors (d) composites (e) insulators
18. (a) electron/hole pairs (b) a ceramic-metal mix (c) fibers (d) a mixture of metals
    (e) no free electrons
19. (a) europium (b) silicon (c) titanium (d) chromium (e) niobium
20. (a) 1% (b) 3% (c) 5% (d) 7% (e) 10%
21. (a) volume increase (b) volume decrease (c) weight decrease (d) strength increase
    (e) increase in electrical conduction
22. (a) dislocations (b) activators (c) a matrix (d) precipitates (e) cracks
23. (a) at the surface of the material (b) at grain boundaries (c) throughout the material
    (d) on dislocations (e) at no particular location.
24. (a) at the surface of the material (b) at grain boundaries (c) throughout the material
    (d) on dislocations (e) none of these
25. (a) decrease conductivity (b) increase ductility (c) pin dislocations (d) reduce corrosion
    (e) pin grain boundaries
26. (a) decrease conductivity (b) increase ductility (c) pin dislocations (d) reduce corrosion
    (e) pin grain boundaries
27. (a) grain refining (b) work hardening (c) crosslinking (d) precipitation hardening
    (e) crystallization
28. (a) grain refining (b) work hardening (c) crosslinking (d) precipitation hardening
    (e) crystallization

29-38. Aluminum-lithium alloys are the aluminum industry's answer to the threat posed by ___29___ to replace aluminum in aircraft. Each ___30___ (by weight) addition of lithium reduces the density of aluminum by 3.5%. Lithium in aluminum is a(n) ___31___ impurity. Below the ___32___, it is dissolved in the aluminum. Above the ___32___ a two-phase mixture occurs. This two phase mixture takes the form of delta prime precipitates in an aluminum-lithium ___33___. The precipitates form ___34___. In order to effectively ___35___ the material there must be ___36___ precipitates to ___37___. Al_3Li is the formula for the precipitates. This is known as a(n) ___38___.

29. (a) HSLA steel (b) carbon fiber composites (c) titanium (d) polymers (e) ceramics
30. (a) 10% (b) 3.5% (c) 1% (d) 7% (e) 1.75%
31. (a) substitutional (b) intrinsic (c) activator (d) ordered (e) interstitial
32. (a) melting point (b) precipitation hardening point (c) solubility limit (d) refining limit (e) recrystallization point
33. (a) composite (b) melt (c) steel (d) laminate (e) solid solution
34. (a) at grain boundaries (b) near the surfaces of the piece (c) randomly (d) in rows (e) both a and d
35. (a) strengthen (b) stiffen (c) alloy (d) both a and b (e) all of these
36. (a) many small (b) few small (c) many large (d) few large (e) either a or d
37. (a) pin dislocations (b) blunt cracks (c) destroy dislocations (d) absorb defects (e) heal cracks
38. (a) alloy (b) ceramic (c) composite (d) intermetallic compound (e) solid solution

14. POLYMERS ARE NOT JUST PLASTIC

Plastics, or what to a materials scientist are known as polymers, pervade every aspect of our lives. In addition to the natural polymers which account for much of our bodies and most living things around us, there are now thousands of man-made polymers which we use for clothing, household items, automobiles, furniture, appliances, electrical and thermal insulation, etc. Polyethylene, PVC, Teflon®, nylon, polypropylene, polyester, acrylic, and polycarbonate, among many others, are words which appear frequently in advertisements and are used more and more in our everyday language. Many people are unaware that paints and adhesives are also plastics nowadays, and much of the improvement in these materials is the result of plastics technology, or Materials Science.

It may be surprising to many that the first man-made polymers were not discovered until the turn of the last century, and many of those were accidents. While some of these new discoveries were used during the second world war, it was not until after then that some began to be available for public use. Nylon was used for parachutes, polyethylene for electrical insulation in radar installations, and Teflon® in the atomic bomb. The author well remembers the bartering power enjoyed by the GI's in England after that war as a result of their access to 'nylons', which at that time was an accepted synonym for ladies' hose.

There are three main types of polymer. Rubber is an **elastomer**: it can be stretched by large amounts and returns to its original length when the stress is removed. Polyethylene is a **thermoplastic**: it becomes soft when heated so that it can be shaped, and then becomes rigid again when cooled. Epoxy resins are **thermosets**: they become more rigid when heated because the chains become crosslinked with covalent bonds -more about that later.

As we have already seen (Page 41), polymers (many mers - where a mer is the repeating atom group) are based on a chain of carbon atoms which are held together by very strong covalent bonds. If these bonds are so strong, why is it that these materials are often very flexible, sometimes elastic and often plastic? We don't see this behavior in diamond and other covalently bonded solids.

The reason is twofold. The first lies in the fact that in most polymers the atoms are not bonded in a three dimensional network but in a linear chain. We saw that the 'straight' polyethylene chain is kinked (Page 58), zigzagging back and forth along its length. This is a consequence of the directionality of these covalent bonds. The following photographs of a model of a polyethylene chain may help you to visualize this.

'Side' view of polyethylene chain model showing the zigzag nature of a straight chain.

'Top' view of above model.

However, in a linear chain the bond only has a reference to the adjacent bond in the chain, which means that it can rotate around a cone, as illustrated in the following diagram, and still maintain the desired angle with the previous bond. As a consequence the bonds in the chain are able to wiggle around in all directions. In a polymer this can happen because of the rotational ability of the bonds.

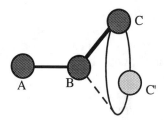

Using atoms A and B as reference atom C can lie anywhere on the rim of the indicated cone, i.e. could be in the C' position. The three atoms will always have the same angle between them.

The second reason for flexibility is that there are only secondary bonds between chains and these are too weak to prevent this bond rotation and the chains from sliding over each other. This is quite different from the rigid 3D network of covalent bonds which exists in diamond or silicon, for example.

The following photograph of a polyethylene chain illustrates how these chains can twist and turn in all directions. Model kits for organic chemistry such as used for these photographs, are available in many academic bookstores, and it may be helpful to obtain one to convince yourself of what we are illustrating. An old Rubik Snake is also a good model for this twisting ability.

Photograph of convoluted polyethylene chain. Note that any three consecutive (black) carbon atoms have the same angle between them.

The weakness in polymers is therefore this weak van der Waals bond between the chains. What we have to do to strengthen the material is to somehow stop these chains from moving easily over each other.

Here again there are several methods we can use but there are three common approaches; crosslinking of chains, chain stiffening, and chain crystallization. In the first the chains are linked together with covalent bonds, in the second some large atom groups are attached to the chains to inhibit their bending and movement, and in the third the chains lie straight and parallel to each other to maximize the van der Waals attraction.

Chain crosslinking

This is perhaps the easiest of the three to understand. The carbon chains are usually separate and can therefore easily move over each other. If we can insert some permanent links between adjacent chains we can restrict their relative movement. To do this we need an atom which can form covalent bonds with two carbon atoms and so start to produce a three dimensional covalently bonded network of atoms. In rubber we add sulfur, a process known as **vulcanization**, to cross-link the rubber chains and thus stiffen the material. Natural rubber flows easily and is of little practical use. The sulfur atom (atomic number 16) needs two electrons to complete its octet, and gets these by sharing electrons (bonding covalently) with two of the carbon atoms in nearby chains. This prevents the chains from unfolding and moving past each other. Eventually, if we add enough sulfur, the rubber becomes a rigid black solid called **ebonite**, which for many years was used for bowling balls and the cover plates of electrical outlets and switches.

A rubber band placed in the window for a few weeks will become brittle because oxygen, with the help of the sunlight, not only produces some cross-linking, but also some chain rupture. Now you can see why carbon black in car tires is necassary to keep light out. It helps stop the rubber from becoming brittle.

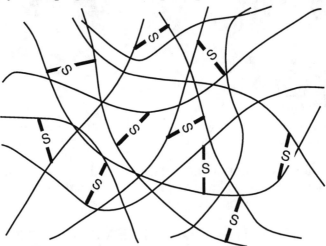

Sulfur atoms form two covalent bonds with polymer chains to produce crosslinking.

Chain stiffening

The second, and perhaps most successful method of making strong polymers is to make it more difficult for the chains to move to new configurations and also to move past each other. The secret to this process is to replace some of the small hydrogen atoms on the polyethylene chain with large groups of atoms such as benzene rings (C_6H_6), which produces polystyrene, but even single large atoms help. Now when the carbon atoms try to rotate their bonds around the cone they cannot do so because the large groups get in each other's way; there is a sort of atom group collision, something known as **steric hindrance**. The large groups therefore stop the chains from being flexible by simply getting in the way of bond rotation.

Polystyrene
(shaded area
is one mer)

In addition, the large groups on the chain produce an effective roughening so that adjacent chains do not slide past each other so easily. It's like putting grains of sand on paper. Two sheets of sand paper do not slide over each other as easily as do two sheets of regular writing paper.

The chain stiffening produced by the benzene rings in polystyrene is enough to make it a hard plastic with a softening temperature of around the boiling point of water. A similar effect is produced in Plexiglas® (polymethyl methacrylate) using (CH_3) and ($COOCH_3$) groups. It is also a hard, stiff plastic.

Plexiglas®

In today's world one of the strongest polymers is polycarbonate. It is used for lenses in protective eyewear, football helmets, car headlamp lenses, and for many household articles such as toilet tanks. It is extremely stiff and strong and gets this property from the large bulky atom groups both in and on the carbon chain, as well as from the presence of oxygen atoms in the chain which do not form the angular bonds we see between carbon atoms. The two bonds from oxygen are directed 180° to each other, i.e. the oxygen produces a straight, rigid segment in the chain. The atomic arrangement in the polymer is shown below.

Polycarbonate

Chain crystallization

The third approach is to crystallize the polymer. This involves packing the chains in a parallel closely packed arrangement as discussed earlier for polyethylene. Indeed polyethylene is the most crystallizable polymer available because the chains can be 'straightened' as shown earlier (Page 58) and there are only small hydrogen atoms on the chains which do not get in each others' way, i.e. they produce no steric hindrance. The van der Waals bonds are quite weak, but as shown in the diagram on page 42, the chains only come close to each other on a few occasions. When the carbon chains are far apart the bonds are very weak. When the chains are crystallized, i.e. arranged in a tight parallel configuration, the bonds are naturally stronger and there are more of them. The chains therefore do not move as easily and the material is stiffer, or stronger. The principle is exactly the same as that used by a carpenter in joining two long pieces of wood. They are first planed to be very straight and smooth so that they make contact over their whole length. The glue then makes a strong bond. If they only made passing contact every few inches the bond between them would be much weaker, and of course the finished article would look peculiar!

In addition to polyethylene we can also produce crystals of polyvinylidene chloride (Saran® wrap) and polypropylene. Another polymer with which you are familiar is Teflon®, simply polyethylene with all the hydrogen atoms replaced with fluorine atoms. In all these the atom groups attached to the main carbon chain are small.

```
 H   H   H   H   H  CH3 H   H   H  CH3 H
 |   |   |   |   |   |   |   |   |   |   |
-C — C — C — C — C — C — C — C — C — C — C —    Polypropylene
 |   |   |   |   |   |   |   |   |   |   |
 H  CH3 H  CH3 H   H   H  CH3 H   H   H
```

```
Cl   H  Cl   H  Cl   H  Cl   H  Cl   H  Cl
 |   |   |   |   |   |   |   |   |   |   |
-C — C — C — C — C — C — C — C — C — C — C —    Polyvinylidene chloride
 |   |   |   |   |   |   |   |   |   |   |
Cl   H  Cl   H  Cl   H  Cl   H  Cl   H  Cl
```

```
 F   F   F   F   F   F   F   F   F   F   F
 |   |   |   |   |   |   |   |   |   |   |
-C — C — C — C — C — C — C — C — C — C — C —    Polytetrafluoroethylene
 |   |   |   |   |   |   |   |   |   |   |     (Teflon )         ®
 F   F   F   F   F   F   F   F   F   F   F
```

To summarize: the weakness in polymers is the weak van der Waals bonds between adjacent polymer chains. We can strengthen by three methods:

Crosslinking: using atoms such as oxygen and sulfur which insert bridges between chains and thus inhibit their sliding over each other.

Crystallization: puts the chains very close together over long distances, thus increasing the bond strength between them and therefore strengthening them.

Stiffening of chains: by adding large side groups, stops bonds from rotating and also roughens the chains to make it more difficult for them to move past each other.

In many polymeric materials two of these three methods are used in combination. One with which you are familiar is Dacron® (polyethylene terephthalate or PET- no need to remember this complex name, unless you want to impress somebody!) which, even though it only has a moderately stiff chain, is strong because it also exhibits some crystallinity.

Polymer chemists have become very clever at producing new polymers with combinations of these strengthening characteristics, and also at inventing some new ones. A way of producing a polymer which is both strong and flexible is considered in our case study on high impact polystyrene (Chapter 16) where we shall be introduced to copolymers, in which two different polymers, one stiff and the other elastic, are arranged in the same chain. The possibilities are infinite and hundreds of new polymers are made each year, many of which are too complex for us to consider. In the next chapter we shall look more closely at polyethylene, which is undoubtedly the most common polymer we encounter every day.

Conclusion

We have seen that polymers like metals and ceramics have weaknesses which can be overcome by altering their structure. This can involve the atomic structure (sulfur added to rubber) or the 'microstructure.'

The term microstructure was placed in quotes because it is somewhat difficult to apply the term to polymers in the sense we have applied it to metals and ceramics, which are mostly crystalline. As we have seen, most polymers do not show much crystallinity, and for those that do, it is perhaps the fraction of the material which is crystalline, rather than the crystal size, which is important. For polymers we shall take 'microstructure' to refer to the arrangements and characteristics of the *chains,* rather than to those of the *crystals.* Polymer scientists often call this the chain 'architecture.' Do the chains have large appendages? How are they arranged? How long are they? Etc. All these are factors unique to polymers, and can often be modified by suitable processing. We shall see some examples of this in the next chapter.

15. CASE STUDY: POLYETHYLENE, THE MOST COMMON POLYMER

We have already noted that the word "polymer" means many parts, or many mers. In polyethylene the mer is ethylene, a gas formed from carbon and hydrogen. You probably won't ever encounter it as a gas, although it is interesting to note that it is used commercially to promote the ripening of tomatoes. We don't find large quantities of ethylene occurring naturally so have to produce it from other raw materials. Before we discuss the ways ethylene, and polyethylene, are produced we shall look at its chemical formula and the formulae of some related compounds called paraffins.

The paraffins

The word paraffin comes from the Latin and means "not very reactive." If somebody mentioned the word "paraffin" to you in a word association game, you would probably say "wax", paraffin wax being a white solid sold in supermarkets as a sealant for jelly. In England "paraffin" denotes what is known in the USA as kerosene, and "liquid paraffin" is a laxative. All uses describe materials which are mostly mixtures of what are known to a chemist as paraffins.

Earlier in the book we saw that a carbon atom has four outer, or valence electrons, which can form four covalent bonds with other carbon atoms to produce diamond. Most of what we call Organic Chemistry is related to the countless number of ways a carbon atom can form four bonds with different surrounding atoms. In this chapter we shall only deal with cases in which all these surrounding atoms are hydrogens, compounds called **hydrocarbons**. A very simple way this occurs is when a carbon atom forms covalent bonds with four hydrogen atoms and acquires an octet of electrons by sharing the one electron of each hydrogen. The resulting compound is called **methane** and has the chemical formula CH_4. The methane molecule consists of a central carbon atom with four surrounding hydrogen atoms situated on the corners of a tetrahedron. Methane is a gas at room temperature and is the major component in natural gas. A model of a methane molecule is shown in the following diagram.

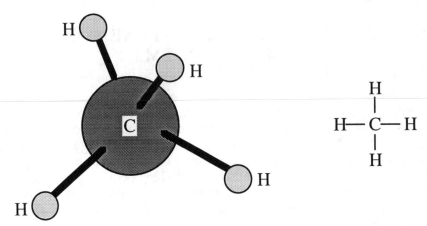

Methane molecule with carbon atoms covalently bonded to four smaller hydrogen atoms on the corners of a tetrahedron. The diagram on the right shows the way the atom arrangement is usually shown for simplicity. When you see such diagrams remember that the atoms are not all in the same plane.

A similar compound called **ethane** is also found in natural gas. Its molecule has two central carbon atoms, each of which shares an electron with the other to form a covalent bond, the remaining three valence electrons on each carbon atom forming covalent bonds with hydrogen atoms to give a molecule with the formula C_2H_6. As suggested earlier, ethane is also a gas.

Propane is a gas which you have probably encountered as the fuel used for barbecues and camping gas stoves. It is the next logical extension to the series of compounds started by methane and ethane. At the center of the molecule are a line of three carbon atoms, the middle one of which forms covalent bonds with the adjacent two. If you think about this a little, or look at the diagrams, you will see that this leaves the central carbon atom with two electrons to form covalent bonds, while the other two carbon atoms are left with three electrons as was the case with the carbon atoms in ethane. These eight electrons form bonds with hydrogen atoms to give a chemical formula C_3H_8.

It should not be difficult to now go to the next possibility. Instead of a line of three carbon atoms we have four. Think of the additional carbon atom being added to the middle of the existing three and forming covalent bonds with the two adjacent atoms. This leaves it with two valence electrons to bond to hydrogen atoms. The resulting compound, a gas called **butane**, has a formula C_4H_{10}. You have probably heard of it as a fuel used in cigarette lighters. The following diagram illustrates molecules of methane, ethane, propane and butane.

Don't forget that the four bonds from the carbon atoms point to the corners of a tetrahedron, so that the line of atoms shown is zigzag rather than straight.

The first four paraffins.

The four compounds, methane, ethane, propane and butane are the first four members of a series of compounds called paraffins. The next member of the series is obtained by simply adding one carbon and two hydrogen atoms. The general chemical formula is therefore obtained by taking a number (n) of CH_2 units and adding the two hydrogen atoms from the ends, giving C_nH_{2n+2}.

In many lighters you can see through the plastic case and you may have noticed that the butane is a liquid. This is because the butane molecules are under pressure. They have been squeezed together until they bond together. The same occurs in the metal cylinders of propane gas used for barbecues. All gases turn into liquids if the molecules or atoms come close enough together and bonds form between them. This can be accomplished by lowering the temperature, by applying a high pressure, or by a combination of both. What type of bond forms in these circumstances? As already mentioned for the inert gases (Page 39) the bond is usually of the van der Waals type.

Van der Waals bonds in paraffins

At this point it may be helpful to remind ourselves how van der Waals bonds form. At any instant in time the atom, or molecule, finds that it has more electrons on one side than another with the result that the atom or molecule becomes polar. One side of the atom or molecule tends to be negatively charged and the opposite side positively charged, and two such units can therefore attract each other, positive attracting negative. A consequence of this is that the van der Waals bond becomes stronger the larger the number of electrons in the atom or molecule. Why?

Imagine two molecules, one with 100 electrons and another with 200 electrons. If at any instant one in a hundred electrons finds itself on the wrong side of the atom, a dipole is formed. In the molecule with 100 electrons there would be 49 on one side and 51 on the other, a difference of two. In the other molecule the corresponding numbers would be 98 and 102, a difference of four. It is this larger difference in charge, or larger polarity, which produces the stronger bond.

This can be clearly seen for the paraffins by looking at the boiling points of the liquids. Remember that materials (liquids) boil when the heat energy is large enough to break the bonds between the atoms or molecules. The stronger the bonds the more energy is needed to break them, thus giving rise to higher boiling points. Here are the boiling points for the paraffins we mentioned above. (Note that since all values are negative, a smaller number is a higher temperature.)

methane	ethane	propane	butane
-161°C	-89°C	-42°C	-1°C

You can see that at room temperature butane doesn't need much encouragement to form a liquid. We don't have to lower its temperature much in order to get it to liquefy, and for the same reasons we also don't have to squeeze it much to accomplish the same thing. As a result it can be kept liquid in a quite thin plastic container. Propane, on the other hand, is more difficult to liquefy, and is usually pressurized inside a metal container.

As you might imagine, as the molecules become larger the boiling points get higher. After butane we have pentane, whose boiling point is 36°C. In other words it is a liquid at normal room temperatures. By the time we get to $C_{20}H_{42}$, a compound called eicosane, the boiling point is over 200°C and the melting point is around 37°C. This means that the bonds are now strong enough to hold the molecules together as a solid even on the hottest day.

At this stage you may be realizing why polymers are usually solid. The compound just mentioned, eicosane, has a 'chain' of 20 carbon atoms. Polymers have chains of thousands of atoms, and we might therefore reasonably expect the bonds between these chains to be quite strong. We shall come back to this later.

Ethylene

By now you must be wondering where ethylene comes into the scheme of things. It too is a compound of carbon and hydrogen, but it is not a paraffin because it has a different bonding arrangement between the carbon atoms.

When we discussed the combination of two carbon atoms to form ethane we joined then with one covalent bond, i.e. they shared one pair of electrons. What if they decide to share two pairs of electrons and form two covalent bonds between themselves? They then each have only two remaining electrons to form covalent bonds with hydrogen atoms, with the result that the molecule consists of two carbon atoms and four hydrogen atoms (C_2H_4). This is ethylene. We say that the molecule consists of two carbon atoms with a **double bond** between them, and two hydrogen atoms bonded to each carbon atom.

Although you may not have encountered ethylene gas, you may have come across **acetylene** gas as used in oxy-acetylene welding. In an acetylene molecule there are also two carbon atoms but they decide to share three pairs of electrons between themselves, forming a **triple bond**, and consequently only have one electron each left to bond to a hydrogen atom. Acetylene therefore has the formula C_2H_2. Molecules of ethylene and acetylene are illustrated below.

$$\begin{array}{cc} H & H \\ | & | \\ C = C \\ | & | \\ H & H \end{array} \qquad\qquad H - C \equiv C - H$$

Ethylene   Acetylene

Polyethylene

In the 1930's scientists were curious about the effects of really high pressures on gases. Among the gases investigated was ethylene. The ethylene was placed in a very strong, rigid container and squeezed using pressures over 1000 times greater than atmospheric pressure. This was the equivalent of about ten tons per square inch, or an elephant on tip-toe! When the container was opened a "white waxy solid" was found to have been formed. We now know that the polyethylene had polymerized into something similar to what we know as paraffin wax. It turned out that there was accidentally a small amount of oxygen in the ethylene, which was crucial to the reaction. This rather crude experiment led to investigations into how the polymerization process could be controlled to make a useful product - the polyethylene we know today.

The large amounts of polyethylene manufactured nowadays obviously require enormous quantities of ethylene, and we should perhaps be wondering where such quantities can be found, especially since we have already mentioned that we are unlikely to encounter ethylene gas in everyday living. The answer is that the ethylene has to be manufactured. It is either produced from ethane, found in natural gas, or from products of the petroleum refining industry. In both cases the ethylene is produced by a process called **cracking**. For ethane the process is quite simply the splitting (hence the term cracking) of the ethane molecule (C_2H_6) into ethylene (C_2H_4) and hydrogen (H_2). Note that the numbers of atoms balance, something a chemist calls 'balancing the equation'.

The formation of polyethylene from ethylene occurs by a process called **addition polymerization** and involves the use of high pressures, high temperatures, and catalysts. Different pressures, temperatures and catalysts (processing) give different types of materials with different structures and properties. Remember, this is what Materials Science is all about.

This is not the place to enter into a long and detailed discussion of the meaning of the term "catalyst". You have probably heard of it in reference to the catalytic converter on your car, perhaps without really knowing what it is, except that it is something to do with cleaning up the emission gases. A catalyst can simply be thought of as a chemical which initiates a chemical reaction, or helps it take place. In the case of polyethylene manufacture the catalyst causes a rupture of one of the two covalent bonds between the two carbon atoms in the ethylene molecule. As a result, each carbon atom in the molecule has an electron which is looking for something with which to form a bond. We call these **unpaired electrons** because they are not satisfied until they have paired up with another electron to form a covalent bond. One of these unpaired electrons becomes satisfied by bonding to the catalyst, while the other one is left hanging, looking for something to react with. What then happens very quickly is that a neighboring ethylene molecule decides to join this reactive unit. One of its double bonds breaks and an unpaired electron on one end pairs up with the unpaired electron on the first molecule to form a covalent bond.

At this point the molecule joining up is itself left with an unpaired electron at the other end and the same thing happens between it and another ethylene molecule. You can see that we have started a process which can just keep going as more and more ethylene molecules join up and a long chain is formed. In fact the addition of extra ethylene mers occurs so quickly that it takes less than a hundredth of a second to produce a chain of 1000 mers. (Note that each mer contains two carbon atoms and four hydrogen atoms.) This addition polymerization process is illustrated on the following page, where the catalyst is simply designated by the symbol X and * represents a reactive bond. We shall later refer to some specific catalysts used, but their composition is not important for this discussion.

$$
\begin{array}{ccccc}
\overset{\displaystyle H}{\underset{\displaystyle H}{|}}\ \overset{\displaystyle H}{\underset{\displaystyle H}{|}} & & & \overset{\displaystyle H}{\underset{\displaystyle H}{|}}\ \overset{\displaystyle H}{\underset{\displaystyle H}{|}} & \\
C=C & + & X \longrightarrow & X-C-C- & *
\end{array}
$$

Ethylene   Catalyst   Reactive unit

X–C–C–* + C=C ⟶ X–C–C–C–C–*

Reactive unit   Ethylene   Larger reactive unit

X–C–C–C–C–* + C=C ⟶ X–C–C–C–C–C–C–*

Ethylene

The addition polymerization mechanism for polyethylene.

Of course, if the ends of two chains, each with an unpaired electron come close together, these two electrons can pair up to form a covalent bond and there are no further additions to the chain. As a result chain growth stops, as shown in the diagram on the next page. Polymer scientists refer to this as termination.

Chain branching

During this rapid polymerization process you can well imagine that there are plenty of opportunities for mistakes. In some cases a mer adds to the side of a chain such that a hydrogen atom is replaced by another ethylene mer, which in

$$X-\overset{\underset{\displaystyle H}{|}}{\underset{H}{C}}-\overset{\underset{\displaystyle H}{|}}{\underset{H}{C}}-\overset{\underset{\displaystyle H}{|}}{\underset{H}{C}}-\overset{\underset{\displaystyle H}{|}}{\underset{H}{C}}-\overset{\underset{\displaystyle H}{|}}{\underset{H}{C}}-\overset{\underset{\displaystyle H}{|}}{\underset{H}{C}}-* \quad + \quad *-\overset{\underset{\displaystyle H}{|}}{\underset{H}{C}}-\overset{\underset{\displaystyle H}{|}}{\underset{H}{C}}-\overset{\underset{\displaystyle H}{|}}{\underset{H}{C}}-\overset{\underset{\displaystyle H}{|}}{\underset{H}{C}}-\overset{\underset{\displaystyle H}{|}}{\underset{H}{C}}-\overset{\underset{\displaystyle H}{|}}{\underset{H}{C}}-X$$

$$\longrightarrow \quad X-C-C-C-C-C-C-C-C-C-C-C-C-X$$

Illustration of how polymerization terminates by the combination of two reactive units.

turn starts the formation of another chain branching off the first. This process of **chain branching** illustrated below, is a very important feature of the resulting polymer's structure and hence affects its properties. Some important parameters are the number of branches which form and their length. These can be controlled by the changing the processing conditions (pressure, temperature, catalyst).

Chain branching in polyethylene. Remember that hydrogen atoms are very small and that the atoms do not all lie in the same plane. They therefore do not interfere with each other as may appear to be the case here.

As an analogy think of a length of wire. A straight length of wire can be wound onto a spool very efficiently. Adjacent turns of wire lie very close to each other, in fact they tend to close pack in the same way that spherical metal atoms can be considered to pack. If we now put a large number of short branches on our wire, in other words make barbed wire, we find that we can no longer wind the wire as efficiently onto the spool. The reason is **steric hindrance**. The short branches get in each other's way. On the other hand if we attach just a few long branches to the wire, these long wire branches can bend over and lie parallel to the wire to which they are attached. The result is that we can again have a fairly efficient packing of wire on the spool. If you think about it, you will readily see that barbed wire would be ineffective if the spurs (branches) were all two feet long. They would simply bend over under their own weight and you could climb over the fence without difficulty.

The same sort of features are apparent in different types of polyethylene. While the best packing occurs with linear chains, a small amount of long-chain branching still allows the chains to pack very efficiently, whereas short-chain branching does not, especially if there is a lot of it. There are several, related results of this:

- short-chain branching produces a lower density material - if the chains of atoms are closer together there is more weight per volume.

- short-chain branching makes for a lower crystalline content in the material - chains have to be straight and parallel to form polymer crystals.

- short-chain branching produces weaker materials - there is more bonding between straight parallel chains.

These effects are similar to those mentioned in the previous chapter in talking about individual chains. However, when a branch folds over to lie parallel and close to the parent chain the effect is almost the same as when the two chains are unconnected.

Different polyethylenes, their manufacture, properties and uses

There are two major polymerization processes used commercially for the production of polyethylene. One occurs at very high pressures (~20,000 psi) and moderate temperatures (200°C) and uses an oxygen-containing catalyst. This process produces considerable short-chain branching and the resulting product is known as low density polyethylene (LDPE). The second process uses titanium and aluminum chlorides as the catalyst with much lower pressures (~200 psi) and a slightly lower temperature (100 to 175°C). Under these processing conditions high density polyethylene (HDPE) with far fewer short-chain branches is formed. The reasons for the differences in these products are well outside the scope of this book.

HDPE is used extensively for garbage cans, dish pans, pipes, etc. A large plastic can of paint or driveway sealer is likely to have HDPE embossed on the bottom indicating the type of material from which it is made. These applications take advantage of the much higher strength and stiffness of HDPE.

On the other hand, plastic wrap and plastic bags are often made of LDPE. This material has a lower strength and is more flexible, although it is still a tough material. Don't forget that along the chains of carbon atoms in these large polymer molecules there are still very strong covalent bonds.

The following table gives some property comparisons for these two different polyethylenes. You will readily see that the density difference is really quite small, whereas the property differences are much larger. Incidentally, the theoretical density of a single polyethylene crystal is almost exactly that of water (1.00 gm/cc).

	HDPE	LDPE
Density (gm/cc)	0.96	0.92
Tensile strength (psi)	5,500	3,000
Young's modulus (psi)	180,000	40,000

These data clearly illustrate how the properties of a material can be changed using different processing techniques. Remember that the two materials contain the same atoms and the same polymer chains. Using our classifications of structure we would say that only the microstructure is different, although in this case we are not just concerned with the size, shape and orientation of the crystals, but also the fraction of the material which is crystalline.

Another difference between these two types of polyethylene, which you have certainly seen, is their different transparencies. A polyethylene film made of LDPE, and used for the bags which find many uses in the kitchen, are translucent. This has the big advantage of allowing you to see what's inside the bag without opening it. On the other hand polyethylene garbage cans are opaque and, if no pigment has been added during manufacture, are white. We shall later come across this same phenomenon in discussing glass ceramics (Page 178), where we shall give it a fuller explanation.

You are probably aware that a large single crystal of sugar is colorless and transparent, while a bowl of the same substance looks white and opaque. The reason for the opacity of the granular sugar is that light is scattered at the boundaries between the crystals. In HDPE the light is scattered whenever it passes from amorphous to crystalline regions, and vice versa, and hence the material looks white. In a LDPE film there is less crystallinity and little light scattering, hence the light passes through and the film appears transparent when very thin. Indeed all amorphous polymers are usually transparent and colorless. Opacity and color are produced by various pigments and fillers which are added to the raw material during manufacture of the article.

Another polyethylene product takes advantage of the strong covalent bonds which exist along the chain. Fibers in which these chains are aligned along the fiber length have a high strength and a high Young's modulus, for similar reasons as mentioned for carbon fibers (Page 193). In the latter it is covalently bonded sheets of carbon atoms lying along the fiber whereas here it is linear chains. These polyethylene fibers are 'gel spun', which means they are pulled from a material which is sort of half way between a solid and a liquid. (You've probably seen the term used for some toothpastes, and you know what Jell-O® is.) In this gel the polymer chains do not get as tangled as in a solid, and it is therefore easier to pull them into straight alignments.

Finally, it is important to mention that polyethylene is a thermoplastic material. As mentioned in the previous chapter, this means that the material softens when heated and hardens when cooled. The process can be repeated over and over again without problems. This is because heat energy is sufficient to break some of the weak van der Waals bonds between chains, which are then able to more easily slide over each other. This property allows the material to be easily pressed and stretched into the many polyethylene articles we encounter everyday and is somewhat responsible for their low manufacturing cost. This property also makes polyethylene an ideal candidate for recycling (Page 157). Just keep a look out for the recycling symbol on articles marked HDPE and LDPE.

Propane gas → baby oil → paraffin wax → polyethylene

We started this chapter by discussing some simple hydrocarbons called paraffins. If you look at the diagrams of the molecules you will see that the progression methane to ethane to propane to butane, etc. is accomplished by adding a unit of CH_2 to the previous molecule. You should have now noticed that CH_2 is simply half an ethylene mer, and that a polyethylene molecule without any branches is therefore simply an enormous paraffin. At room temperature, as the molecules get larger, or chains get longer, the material changes from a gas to a runny liquid to a viscous, oily liquid, to a wax, and eventually to the polymer we know as polyethylene. The composition (atomic structure) has not changed, simply the chain length. This is a structural variable which is not available in ceramics and metals and is a unique feature of polymers.

Indeed, this raises another variable which polymer chemists are able to control: the distribution of chain lengths, or what they usually refer to as the molecular weight distribution. This variable is one which we have not considered in our discussion, but it is also very important in determining the properties. Indeed there is yet a third commercial polyethylene product known as ultrahigh molecular weight polyethylene (UHMWPE), in which the processing is optimized to give really long molecular chains. In this material molecular weights greater than a million are common. This corresponds to over 70,000 carbon atoms, or a chain length of around 0.01 mm. The material is commonly used to line the socket of an artificial hip joint, because of its inertness in the human body, its low friction and excellent wear characteristics.

Conclusion

Although the details of the processing are complex, you have seen enough to appreciate that, starting with the same atoms (carbon and hydrogen) in the same molecule (ethylene) we are able to produce a wide variety of materials, just by changing the processing (temperature, pressure, catalyst. What started as a rather accidental discovery back in the 1930's has led to a host of different polyethylenes which we would now probably find difficult to live without. Such has been their effect on our daily lives.

We have now come to the end of a journey which started with a molecule with one carbon atom (methane) and ended with a molecular chain containing tens of thousands. All are related hydrocarbons. Perhaps the next time you use baby oil you will think of it as low molecular weight polyethylene!

16. CASE STUDY: FROM RUBBER TO HIPS TO ABS

No, ABS has nothing to do with an antilock brake system and HIPS has nothing to do with hip joint replacements, but you will probably have these materials on your car and around your house. These are names given to a family of plastics, based on the three basic chemicals which go into them. Acrylonitrile is the basis of polyacrylonitrile (PA), the acrylic fibers (Dacron®, Orlon®, etc.) you may have in your sweater or blanket. Poly**b**utadiene (PB) is an elastic polymer (**elastomer**) used as a synthetic rubber. And **S**tyrene is the basis of polystyrene (PS), which we have already discussed, used for plastic drinking glasses and quite brittle. ABS is simply a complex polymer based on these three constituents. HIPS stands for high impact polystyrene, a somewhat simpler polymer using only PS and PB but with some of the same properties as ABS. But enough of that for now, we need to go back in history.

History

Natural fibers such as wool and cotton are polymers, often quite complex compared to the ones we make in today's chemical industry or the laboratory. Compared to wool, the use of rubber, a naturally occurring polymer known as an elastomer, is relatively new. It occurs naturally and is collected as the sap, known as latex, from a rubber tree. Over 400 years ago Columbus and other explorers found South American Indians had formed it into a ball which was used much as a rubber ball is used today for various games. The first practical use was probably when it was found that it could be used to 'rub out' pencil marks, and from this we get the name. In the early 1800's it was used for waterproof clothing and boots (Wellington boots) but had many disadvantages. Besides its offensive odor, it would freeze and become brittle in winter, and in a hot summer it would flow like a viscous liquid. The wearer literally found his boots around his ankles!

In the 1840's the technique of stopping the flow of rubber by **vulcanization** was discovered, and Thomas Hancock (UK) and Charles Goodyear (USA) were awarded patents for the invention. By 1860 the rubber industry had already reached an annual $5 million turnover. We have already discussed the process in some detail (Page 132) and there is no need to go into it again now.

To put the matter into perspective we need to go back to the periodic table on page 7 . You will see there that every element has an atomic weight, which is the weight in grams of 6.02×10^{23} atoms. Carbon has an atomic weight of 12, oxygen 16, hydrogen 1, etc. A benzene molecule (C_6H_6) has a **molecular weight** of $(6 \times 12) + (6 \times 1) = 78$. A polymer chain is one large molecule and therefore has a large molecular weight. In any piece of polymer there are millions of chains of different lengths, and hence different molecular weights. Indeed, one way of changing the properties of a polymer is to change the average length of the polymer chains, or in other words, the average molecular weight. Many polymers have average molecular weights of tens of thousands: for natural rubber it is greater than a million. The atomic structure of the rubber chain is shown below. You can see that the repeat unit (mer) consists of five carbon atoms, four of which are in the chain, and eight hydrogen atoms, giving a weight of 68 for this unit. This means that a chain with a molecular weight of one million (10^6) will contain about 15,000 of these units, meaning a chain of 60,000 carbon atoms. On an atomic scale these chains are very, very long.

Natural rubber

The properties of rubber

The long-chain natural rubber molecules are not cross-linked but are considerably entangled, like loose knots in a ball of wool with which a kitten has been playing. In this state the chains can slowly move over each other and, as long as there is enough time, the rubber can flow. That's why the rubber boots ended up around the wearer's ankles.

You may at some time have played with 'Silly Putty' and found the same phenomenon. If you leave a ball of it on the table, it slowly creeps into a flat pancake. If you drop the ball on the floor it bounces. If it's very cold you can pull it quickly and it breaks in an almost brittle manner. If it's warm and you pull it slowly, it will pull out to very long lengths. The reason for these differences is mainly one of time, and also of temperature. Given enough time, the chain tangles will unravel as the chains flow over each other, and the material 'flows'. If deformation is sudden the chains do not have time to disentangle and the material is resilient. Just think how important this property of rubber is when you next drive over a pot-hole!

Rubber is elastic because of the very long chain molecules it contains. We've already seen how some chains, including rubber, can wiggle about all over the place. Because of a basic scientific principle known as **entropy** (which essentially means 'disorder') the chain does not want to be straight. It prefers the greater disorder of a somewhat tangled state. If we pull a piece of rubber so that the chains straighten, they will automatically return to their original convoluted state when the force is removed. Sometimes the rubber chain is known as an **entropic spring** because of this effect.

Diagram of how a rubber chain stretches as an entropic spring between crosslinks.

Vulcanization must be just enough to stop the chains from flowing past each other, as they do in the natural state, but not too much so that they are locked up and the spring is gone. If we lock the chains together completely, we form the hard brittle solid called ebonite.

The synthetic rubbers, including polybutadiene, which has the following very simple formula, have a similar resiliency to natural rubber.

Polybutadiene

Notice that there are no bulky side groups on the chain. The atomic structure is what you get when you replace the CH_3 group on the natural rubber chain with a hydrogen atom.

Polystyrene

We have already seen in the previous chapter how the benzene rings on this polymer chain produce enough steric hindrance to make the chains, and hence the material, very inflexible at room temperature. Not only is it rigid but it is also very brittle.

Just as in metals and ceramics we discussed atoms getting enough energy so that they can move around, in polymers heating often results in the motion of whole chains. The thermal energy overcomes the weak van der Waals bonds between chains so they can slide over each other more easily, in addition it is enough to get the bonds rotating, making the chains more flexible. Because of this, polystyrene becomes softer above 100°C. The temperature at which this change from a brittle solid to a ductile one is called the **glass transition temperature**. Below this temperature large chain motion is frozen and the material is brittle and breaks like a glass. Above this temperature the polymer chains are very flexible and are moving around making the material ductile. All polymers have a glass transition temperature and hence exhibit this behavior. Fortunately for us the glass transition temperature for rubber is rather low. You wouldn't want your tires to be brittle in winter, especially when the pot-holes develop.

Taking advantage of both materials - high impact polystyrene

Polystyrene and rubber are, as we have seen, quite different materials. The former is tough and hard, but brittle. The latter is resilient but not really strong. Is there any way of taking advantage of both properties so that the polystyrene will withstand impacts? The answer is 'yes' and is found in HIPS.

What if we were to make a mixture of the two polymers, such as by placing small particles of the butadiene rubber within the polystyrene glass? We can do this using various mixing techniques to produce what we call a **blend**. Unfortunately this produces very little improvement, and the reason is easy to see from the diagram on the following page. The crack is prevented from going straight through the polystyrene and has to negotiate a path around the butadiene particles. It stays between the polystyrene chains and, because it goes round the rubber particles, it takes a longer path. The longer path means that more bonds have to be broken and more energy is needed to break the material. Unfortunately the difference is not great and there is little improvement.

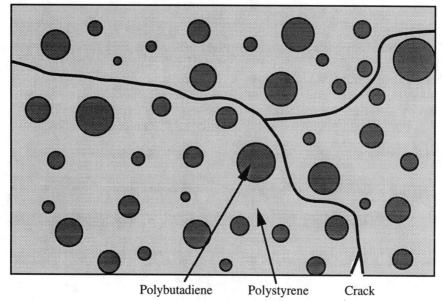

Polybutadiene   Polystyrene   Crack

A crack passing through a polystyrene-polybutadiene blend.

Polymer chemists have developed an answer to this problem by designing two types of **copolymers**: block copolymers and graft copolymers.

A copolymer (co - meaning together) is a combination of two or more different monomers *in one chain*. We have so far talked of polymers with chains made by joining thousands of the same repeat unit (or **mer**), but there is nothing to stop a clever polymer chemist from making a chain with different mers at different places in the chain. Just imagine taking two or three different gold and silver chains, cutting them into different lengths and then joining them randomly to form a new chain. That is what we do with polymers to form a copolymer. In the situation just described we would have effectively produced a **block copolymer**, which has just one chain with segments or blocks of different polymers along its length.

Diagram of a block polymer. The chain consists of A mers and B mers.

A **graft copolymer** takes advantage of the fact that we can, for example, remove a small hydrogen atom attachment from the chain and replace it with another carbon atom which starts a new chain. In other words we have branching, or we have grafted a new, and in this case a different, chain onto the original one. In the case of HIPS we have a chain structure something like that shown below, a main polystyrene chain with polybutadiene branches.

Diagram of a styrene-butadiene graft copolymer. The main polystyrene chain has butadiene branches.

In HIPS we still have polybutadiene (PB) rubber regions in a polystyrene (PS) matrix, but now we have this graft copolymer added to the mix. The graft copolymer acts to join the two components in a much stronger manner because the grafted rubber chain prefers to be in the rubber while the polystyrene chain wants to be in the polystyrene matrix. We can think of the main PS chains of these graft copolymers lying in the matrix, wrapping themselves round the PB particles, with the PB branches sticking like tentacles into these particles. We have essentially joined the two different phases (PB and PS) together with what you can think of as rubbery linkages.

Any crack which now tries to pass round these PB particles, as illustrated on the previous page, has to negotiate the network of rubbery chains connecting the matrix to the polybutadiene. The result is an amazing increase in the toughness of the material. Any crack is sort of trapped around the polybutadiene particles and spreads in all directions producing crazing of the polystyrene in this area. In fact a strong blow to the material can produce an almost foam-like structure around the PB particles. In so doing these must be a tremendous increase in the number of broken bonds, which absorbs the impact energy and hence the material does not break through. The energy is used in producing these crazes.

With HIPS copolymer we have made a material with the rigidity and surface gloss of a glassy polystyrene, but with some of the resiliency of rubber, a material we call a **high impact polymer**. You will probably find it in the dashboard of your car, in the lining of your refrigerator, in computer and telephone housings, etc. In fact any place where we need a really tough material.

ABS plastics

Those clever polymer scientists have not stopped with just combining polystyrene and polybutadiene, they have produced a whole family of high impact polymers based on polystyrene/polybutadiene but with an additional ingredient, polyacrylonitrile. These materials use the same principles discussed above, but the additional ingredient allows a wide range of different materials to be produced.

There may be acrylonitrile mers included in either or both of the rubber and polystyrene chains. Things get very complex and there is no need for us to be concerned with the details. We can simply note that adding acrylonitrile to the rubber chain makes it stiffer, and adding it to the polystyrene chain will change the glass transition temperature. Hence we can design an ABS material with desired properties. Keep your eyes open for mention of ABS in advertisements. You'll truly be surprised at the number of instances in which it is mentioned.

Some final thoughts on polymers - the recycling problem

In 1960 there was hardly any polymer material in a car. Today there is an average of 300 pounds. Even though they are very durable, over 20% of all polymers produced are used for less than a year, and some items are used for only a few hours or even minutes. Just think how long we use the clamshell container for a hamburger before it is thrown away! Here is the problem in a nutshell. The use of polymers has grown tremendously in recent years, but their limited time of use has presented us with a disposal problem. Note that the problem is really just one of disposal, polymers themselves are quite safe because they are so stable and durable. Many people consider recycling to be the answer, but the problems are enormous.

In this chapter we have seen that many plastics are combinations of two or more polymers. In fact many items of everyday use are even more complicated that. Take for example the common two liter soda bottle shown in the following diagram. It contains at least five different polymers, of which one is itself a copolymer.

Diagram showing the common components of a plastic soda bottle.

Simply taking this bottle and trying to melt it and form it into something different just doesn't work. Many polymers just don't mix, and if they do, the product is awful. Just think what you would have if you went into a gourmet restaurant, took a plate of each menu item, mixed them together and then tried to serve the result to the clientele! It just wouldn't work. The analogy holds for mixing polymers. So you have to separate the components of the soda bottle before you can recycle, but how do you do it? At present the answer is that it has to be done by hand at considerable cost. Indeed, it is usually cheaper to make new materials than recycle old ones.

Another problem is that while a thermoplastic polymer such as polyethylene can be heated and softened (melted) so that various items of the same polymer can be mixed together and reformed into a useful product, a thermosetting polymer cannot be reused in this way.

A solution would perhaps be to burn them. One estimate says that if all plastics produced in the USA were to be incinerated there would be sufficient energy produced to light every home and office in the country. However, such action simply turns a solid waste problem into an atmospheric pollution problem. Burning PVC releases poisonous dioxins into the atmosphere.

At present there is no adequate solution to this dilemma. The purpose of this brief discussion is to point out that the problems are much more complex than is usually understood.

Conclusion

This study has introduced you to some of the many ways we can manipulate polymer chains. If you imagine buying a variety of metal chains, different metals, different link sizes, different patterns, you could join them together in a wide variety of ways. The same is true of polymers, which is why there seems to be a never ending discovery of new ones. By suitable processing, which is far too complex to explain here, the polymer chemist can make a most amazing array of materials, most of which will probably never be commercialized. Some, however, will certainly have significant effects on our future way of living.

Much current research is aimed at degradable polymers. But the problems are immense. How long do we want things to survive? If the plastic ring arrangement around your six-pack of soda collapses when you pick it up because it has been sitting in the sun for a couple of weeks, you would not be very happy. This is but one example of the problems current research is trying to solve.

QUESTIONS: Chapters 14 - 16

1. We call a mixture of different polymers a _____.
   (a) homopolymer (b) copolymer (c) branch polymer (d) block polymer (e) blend

2. Which of the following is not true about the great majority of polymers?
   (a) electrical insulators (b) thermal insulators (c) easily bent into shape (d) composed of chains of carbon atoms (e) all of these are true.

3. What important plastic material uses graft copolymers?
   (a) Lexan (b) Plexiglas (c) polycarbonate (d) ABS (e) polystyrene

4. Crystalline polymers are stronger and denser than amorphous ones because _____.
   (a) there is greater van der Waals bonding between their chains (b) their chains are stacked closer together (c) their chains tend to be longer (d) all of these (e) none of these

5. High density polyethylene (HDPE) is less flexible than low density polyethylene (LDPE) because it is
   (a) less crystalline (b) more crystalline (c) crosslinked (d) less defective (e) none of the above

6. Vulcanization uses _____ to make rubber stronger. The element used is _____.
   (a) chain stiffening, Li (b) chain crosslinking, Nb (c) chain crystallization, Li (d) graft copolymerization, S (e) none of these is correct

7. Polymers in the glassy state are
   (a) crystalline (b) ductile (c) brittle (d) linear (e) none of these is correct

8. A polymer made of two mers A and B with the chain below is called a _____.

   A-A-A-B-B-A-A-B-A-A-A-B-B-B-A-A-B-A-A-A-A-A

   (a) chain copolymer (b) block copolymer (c) graft copolymer (d) alternating copolymer

9. Polystyrene is a polymer which has a benzene ring attached to the carbon chain in place of every fourth H atom in polyethylene. The stiffer of these two polymers is ____. The stiffening is caused by _____.
   (a) polystyrene, crosslinking (b) polyethylene, work hardening (c) polystyrene, chain stiffening (d) polyethylene, chain refining (e) polystyrene, crystallization

10. The two types of bonds in polymers are
    (a) covalent, secondary (b) ionic, secondary (c) metallic, secondary
    (d) covalent, ionic (e) ionic, metallic

11-12.   A rubber chain is known as a/an ____11____ because it automatically returns to a/an ____12____ state when the force is removed after being stretched.

11. (a) crosslinked spring (b) graft copolymer (c) branched copolymer (d) copolymer spring (e) entropic spring
12. (a) convoluted (b) amorphous (c) crosslinked (d) crystalline (e) coiled

13-26.   Polymers are based on chains of carbon atoms held together by ____13____ bonds. This gives the chains high strength, but the weakness in polymers which gives them flexibility is ____14____. Below a certain temperature, called the ____15____ temperature, polymers become brittle. For polystyrene, often encountered as styrofoam, it is ____16____. The simplest and most common polymer is polyethylene, in which each carbon atom in the chain is attached to two hydrogen atoms. In polystyrene one of every four hydrogen atoms is replaced with a ____17____ . This makes the chain stiffer because of ____18____. Some important materials are made using a mixture of polymers called a(n) ____19____. HIPS is a more complex polymer which includes chains called a ____20____ which join ____21____ inclusions to a polystyrene matrix. In ____21____ car tires the material is stiffened by ____22____ the chains using ____23____ atoms and also by adding ____24____. Some ____22____ also occurs when ____21____ is exposed to air and ____25____ for long times because ____26____ atoms can do the same thing as does ____23____ . In addition the ____24____ helps by keeping the ____25____ out.

13. (a) hydrogen (b) ionic (c) covalent (d) metallic (e) both b & c
14. (a) dislocations (b) crosslinks (c) bonds missing electrons (d) secondary bonds (e) surface defects
15. (a) critical (b) recrystallization (c) glass transition (d) solidification (e) annealing
16. (a) well above 100°C (b) around room temperature (c) below 0°C (d) over 1000°C (e) about 100°C
17. (a) fluorine atom (b) chlorine atom (c) benzene ring (d) sulfur atom (e) none of these
18. (a) steric hindrance (b) crosslinking (c) grain refining (d) work hardening (e) crystallization
19. (a) alloy (b) copolymer (c) bipolymer (d) amalgam (e) blend
20. (a) blend (b) block copolymer (c) bipolymer (d) graft copolymer (e) bridging polymer
21 (a) rubber (b) acrylic (c) carbide (d) interstitial (e) carbon
22. (a) crystallizing (b) hardening (c) crosslinking (d) lengthening (e) reducing
23. (a) carbon (b) sulfur (c) oxygen (d) lithium (e) phosphorus
24. (a) dislocations (b) precipitates (c) impurities of any sort (d) carbon blacks (e) nothing extra is added
25. (a) acids (b) sunlight (c) pollution (d) heavy use (e) oil
26. (a) carbon (b) sulfur (c) oxygen (d) nitrogen (e) hydrogen

27. One of the reasons polymers are flexible is that _____.
    (a) they have strong C-C bonds (b) H atoms are attached to C atoms
    (c) they have a 3D structure (d) they are crosslinked (e) covalent bonds can rotate

28-34. ABS plastics are based on polybutadiene [PB]/polystyrene [PS] ___28___ copolymers.
The polyacrylonitrile [PA] is simply added to obtain a range of materials with slightly
different properties. PS is a stiff, strong polymer because of ___29___ whereas PB is
___30___ . The material consists of PS which contains some PB. The PB/PS copolymer
serves the purpose of ___31___ . The resultant material is known as a high ___32___
polymer. When used alone, PS is very ___33___ at room temperature because ___34___ .

28. (a) graft (b) alternating (c) block (d) reciprocating (e) condensed
29. (a) high crystallinity (b) bulky side groups (c) crosslinking (d) larger atoms
    (e) stronger bonds between C atoms
30. (a) lighter (b) elastic (c) less stiff (d) biodegradable (e) glassy
31. (a) increasing flexibility (b) joining the PB and PS together (c) pinning dislocations
    (d) thermal conduction (e) making longer chains
32. (a) intensity (b) impact (c) density (d) conductivity (e) rigidity
33. (a) elastic (b) conductive (c) transparent (d) brittle (e) flaky
34. (a) it has flexible chains (b) it has free electrons (c) light energies are greater than
    the band gap energy (d) it is below the glass transition temperature (e) it contains
    weak bonds

35-44.   The simplest and most common polymer has only ___35___ atoms on a carbon
chain, ___36___ ___35___ atoms to each carbon atom, and is called ___37___ . A strong
___37___ fiber can be made by aligning these chains so that they are ___38___ each
other. This can be accomplished by a process called ___39___ . We can also make
strong and more rigid ___37___ by ___40___ the polymer. This increases the ___41___
between chains. Sometimes we add side branches of the same polymer chain to the main
chain. If these side branches are ___42___ and many, their addition has the same effect as
placing large side groups on the chain. This is called ___43___ . This type of ___37___ ,
referred to as ___44___ , is used for garbage bags where flexibility is needed.

35. (a) hydrogen (b) oxygen (c) fluorine (d) nitrogen (e) both a and b
36. (a) one (b) two (c) a varying number of both (d) four
37. (a) polypropylene (b) PVC (c) polystyrene (d) polyethylene (e) polycarbonate
38. (a) parallel to (b) perpendicular to (c) across (d) outside (e) at an angle to
39. (a) pulling (b) extrusion (c) gel spinning (d) weaving (e) stretching
40. (a) annealing (b) crystallizing (c) extruding (d) increasing the number of
    hydrogen atoms on each carbon atom of (e) both a and d
41. (a) attraction (b) repulsion (c) distance (d) both b and c (e) both a and c
42. (a) as long as the original chain (b) long (c) short (d) straight (e) both b and d
43. (a) steric hindrance (b) interference (c) immobilization (d) deactivation
    (e) crosslinking
44. (a) ABS (b) LDPE (c) HDPE (d) SBS (e) PVDC

17. HOW HEAT AFFECTS MATERIALS

In the last few chapters we have examined some of the basic properties of metals and polymers, together with some specific examples of recent developments in these areas. Now we shall turn our attention to ceramics, which we have defined as oxides, carbides, nitrides and borides. To most people ceramics mean the traditional clay based materials such as found in plates, cups and saucers, casseroles, etc. We have also mentioned glass as being a ceramic based on silicon oxide. We usually consider such items as being fragile. Stores remind us of this even before we buy, with their "If you break it, you've bought it" signs. Almost everybody has broken a plate or glass at some time and is well aware that they rarely bounce. Before we approach ways in which we can make strong ceramics there is another subject we need to introduce: the effect of heat on materials. At this stage we shall not confine our attention to ceramics

There are many possible ways in which materials react to heat. We know that if heated enough they glow and become red and then white hot. If they are magnetic they lose that property. Most polymers cannot be heated very much before they begin to decompose. We have also seen that the atoms move around more and that there are more vacancies created, etc. However, for our purposes, there are only two properties to consider. These are known by the scientific terms, thermal conduction and thermal expansion.

Thermal conduction

Just as materials show different efficiencies at conducting electricity they also have different heat conducting properties. Our everyday experience tells us that the best conductors are metals. The reason for this is quite simple. The heat is carried through the metal by the movement of electrons. One electron can carry very little heat but there are so many free electrons in a metal (they are the 'glue' which holds the atoms together) and they travel so quickly that they are very efficient heat carriers. Effectively what happens is that each electron picks up some thermal energy from the heat source, runs down to the cold region, where it leaves the heat, and then runs back for more. Obviously, the electrons cannot just stay in the cold region or else they would all end up there and it would acquire a large negative charge which would push back any other electrons which tried to bring more heat (remember that like charges repel each other). There is therefore a balanced flow with as many coming as going, something we call

dynamic equilibrium in scientific jargon. A metal seat feels cold because the electrons in the metal quickly take on the heat from your body, carry it away and come back for more! Obviously, this does not happen with wood.

Because heat in metals is transported by electrons, we would expect anything which interferes with the electron motion to reduce the heat conduction. Perhaps the most familiar effect is the result of adding impurities to a metal. A cast iron pot, rather old-fashioned nowadays, is a good conductor of heat and is still used for cooking by some people. The modern stainless steel pans are much nicer to look at but do not conduct the heat nearly as well. This is why they usually have a bottom cladding of copper or aluminum to distribute the heat. If you use a cheap, thin stainless pan with no bottom cladding for cooking, the ring marks from the burner are clearly visible inside the bottom afterwards. The stainless steel does not distribute the heat sideways. The reason for this is that the carbon, nickel and chromium impurities which are added to iron to make stainless steel, get in the way of the free flowing electrons and hence reduce the heat flow. When discussing point defects (Pages 74-77), we saw that they cause distortions to the regular arrangements of atoms in the crystal, and these interrupt the clear straight paths the electrons would otherwise have through the material.

Other materials also conduct heat, although not nearly as well. This is because they have no free electrons. The heat causes the atoms to vibrate, as we have already seen. In ceramics, which have strong ionic and covalent bonds, the movement of one atom causes the adjacent atoms to move as well. Just think of beads threaded on a string. When we make one move up and down (oscillate) the adjacent ones also move and a wave is set up in the string. Such a wave motion of atoms in a crystal is called a **phonon**. You may have a coiled cord on your telephone and sometimes, when talking, you pinch a few coils together then let go. A wave travels down the cord and sometimes is reflected back from the other end. You may have seen the same effect when playing with a Slinky. This is very much like the way a phonon travels through a material. The term phonon arises because the wave travels at the speed of sound (nothing to do with the telephone, really!). The heat energy transported by such waves, or phonons, travels much more slowly through the material than do electrons, hence the conduction is not as efficient.

In materials such as polymers, where atoms are linked by very weak bonds, the movement of one atom may produce motion of adjacent atoms in the same chain, but produces little or no motion of atoms in adjacent chains. Heat conduction is therefore even more difficult than in ceramics and only occurs moderately efficiently when an atom is forced to vibrate so much by the heat that it bumps into an adjacent atom and thus transfers some of its heat energy to that atom. The process obviously proceeds very slowly and inefficiently.

To summarize, metallic bonds produce the best heat conductors because of rapid electron motion. Covalent and ionic bonds produce worse conduction by atom waves (phonons) being set up in the material. Weak secondary bonds (van der Waals and hydrogen) produce the worst thermal conductors because they cannot conduct heat until the atoms knock into each other. The three following diagrams illustrate these methods of heat transfer.

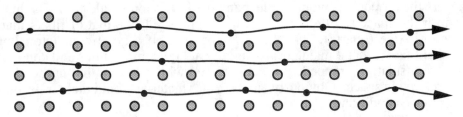

Free electrons move between atoms (metals)

Atom waves or phonons (ceramics)

Atom vibrations and knock-on (polymers)

Illustrations of the three ways heat can be carried through a solid material.

The absolute worst conductor of heat (best insulator) is a vacuum, or failing that, still air. We use the former in vacuum flasks to keep things hot or cold and the latter when we insulate houses or design winter clothing. Both fiberglass house insulation and down filled jackets use trapped air to insulate against heat loss.

A modern application of this principle is the tiles used as the insulating skin of the space shuttle. Of course one requirement of such a material is that it does not melt at the temperatures we need to insulate against. If this were to happen, the air pockets would be lost and the insulation would fail. The material used for the space shuttle tiles is composed of a felt-like mat of fibers made of silicon dioxide (quartz). The silica is not of itself a good conductor, but the important fact is that it maintains its rigidity at high temperatures and continues to hold the insulating, trapped, still atmosphere, which is very thin at the altitudes encountered in space. Obviously any polymer material would melt or decompose under those conditions.

25 microns

Photograph of a space shuttle tile.

Thermal expansion

The expansion of materials when they are heated is something we are all probably familiar with. We put expansion joints in railroad lines, bridges, etc., to allow them to expand without buckling in hot weather. You have probably noticed the gaps which are left to allow for this.

The fact that materials expand tells us that when they are heated not only do the atoms vibrate, but they also move further apart. The amount they move depends to a large extent on the strength of the bonds. We might naturally expect weak bonds to allow atoms to move further apart for a given heat input than do strong bonds, and to a good approximation this is the case.

Polymers usually expand more than metals, which expand more than ceramics. A graphite crystal expands a lot perpendicular to the planes (van der Waals bonds) but very little parallel to the planes (covalent bonds).

A simple thermostat can be made using two metals with different thermal expansions, joined in what we call a bimetallic strip. When heated, the one with the larger expansion forces the other to bend over as shown. Remember that the inside of a curve is always shorter than the outer, so the strip bends over in the direction of the metal with the smaller expansion. If this strip is part of an electrical circuit and the room temperature is high enough, the strip bends away from an electrical contact, breaking the circuit and turning the heat off. As the room cools, the strip straightens up and makes contact, turning the heat on again.

In today's world we can make thermostats by taking advantage of other properties of materials, but the bimetallic strip remains a cheap means of temperature regulation for household use.

A simple thermostat using thermal expansion of a bimetallic strip.

A similar device is used in garage door openers. When you activate the opener, not only does electricity flow to the motor, but also through a small heating coil around a bimetallic strip. This causes it to bend and make a contact which connects the electric power to the light bulb, thus turning it on. When the door has been raised, the power is disconnected and the bimetallic strip begins to cool. After a couple of minutes it has cooled sufficiently to return to its original position, breaking the contact and the light goes out.

The two thermal phenomena we have discussed are very important as we talk about ceramics. These are strongly bonded solids and as a consequence they have low thermal expansions and very poor thermal conductivity. This means that a ceramic plate heated on one side will expand a little while the other side is still cold and, for the moment, does not expand. This is analogous to our thermostat in that we have something which start out the same length on both sides but now has one side longer than the other. As a result, the expanded side pulls the cold side and the material wants to bend. We know what happens to a ceramic if you try to bend it. It breaks!

18. CERAMICS: DO THEY HAVE TO BE BRITTLE?

Why are ceramics usually brittle?

We have now seen why metals are usually ductile, how we can make them stronger and stiffer, and why a few metals such as zinc are quite brittle; now we turn our attention to ceramics. If we drop a china mug and a pewter tankard we know that we can expect the tankard to survive with maybe a dent, but we also expect the mug to break into a hundred pieces. Not only will it break, but it will break catastrophically.

The reason for the big difference lies in the types of bonds which are involved. In metals, we have nondirectional, rather fluid, metallic bonds, while in ceramics we either have strong, directed covalent bonds, or ionic bonds between positive and negative charges which are quite closely packed, and hence are quite immobile and have fixed positions.

Because of the existence of directed, rigid, covalent bonds, it is very difficult to move dislocations in these materials. Also, the ions make movement of planes very difficult, even using dislocations, because in the process of moving planes of ions over each other, it is usually necessary to move positive ions over positive ions and negative ions over other negative ions. As you know, like charges repel each other, so that there is a great resistance to this movement.

The bonds are quite strong and there is not really an easy way to deform the material. When a ceramic or a glass breaks it usually does so catastrophically. The reason for this is easy to see once we realize what the basic weaknesses are in ceramics or glasses. The answer to the problem is not dislocations, but surface imperfections or flaws in the form of small cracks or scratches.

When a person wants to cut a piece of glass, a diamond point is first used to put a surface flaw (scratch) on the material, and the glass is then broken. The break, or fracture, follows the scratch. The glass has not really been 'cut', but has been broken in a controlled manner by taking advantage of the fact that glasses and ceramics break at surface flaws. While you can see the scribe mark a glass cutter puts onto a piece of glass, the surface cracks and scratches in ceramics do not have to be visible to be important, and often aren't.

Take the simple model shown below. The material is carrying a load which is shared by, let's say, a thousand atoms. Each atom takes one thousandth of the load and transfers it to the next atom through the bonds which connect them, shown as vertical dashed lines. So long as the bonds are strong enough the material does not break because when the material breaks, the bonds between the atoms are what give way. The load is transferred up the material until we reach the crack, which is shown as being four atoms deep. Now it becomes necessary for the load to be redistributed so that it can be carried by four fewer atoms, but it is not shared equally by the remaining 996 bonds. The remaining bonds don't just all carry 1000/996 of what they were previously carrying. The ones at the crack tip end up carrying proportionately more than their fair share.

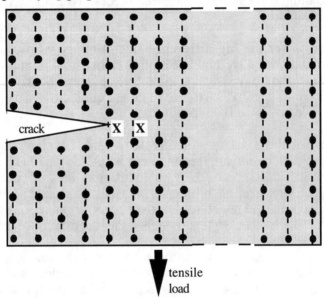

Illustration of what happens at the tip of a crack. The sample is being stretched by a tensile load, but four bonds are broken and cannot carry any load. The two bonds marked X are longer than the others (more strain) because they are carrying more load. They will therefore be the first to break.

In some cases this extra load becomes more than the bonds between the atoms at the crack tip can bear and therefore the bond between them breaks. This places more load on the adjacent atom, which is already somewhat overloaded, and its bond breaks also. The crack grows very rapidly and in a very short time the whole material has broken. You can perhaps see how this can happen when there is a sudden increase in the force on a material, such as when it is dropped.

Your experience has shown you that ceramics and glasses break suddenly, what we call **catastrophic failure**, while metals usually stretch before they break. The reason for this sudden failure is what is described above. We say that the surface cracks and scratches are **stress concentrators**; they concentrate the load on the atoms, or rather the bonds, at the crack or scratch tip.

Before we move on we should ask why cracks are not so important in metals. We have mentioned several times that for most metals there are many different atom planes which are close packed and can slide over each other. Because of this, a surface crack or scratch in a metal is usually very quickly blunted as shown in the following diagram. Slip of planes in ceramics is very difficult, so cracks grow rather than get blunted. Another way of looking at the situation is to say that crystalline boundaries stop crack propagation in ceramics whereas in metals any slip plane can do the same.

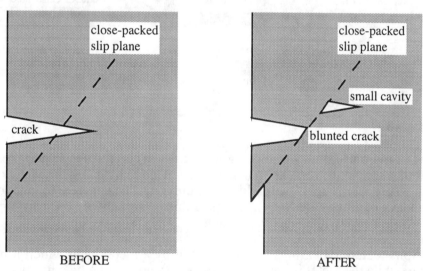

BEFORE   AFTER

Illustration of how a surface flaw in a metal becomes blunted by movement of atoms on a slip plane. Blunt cracks are not as important as are sharp cracks.

How then can we strengthen ceramic materials? As with dislocations there are two possibilities: we either eliminate the cracks or stop them from propagating (growing). There are several ways of tackling the problem but we shall mention only a few.

Flame polishing

A simple approach can be used with a glass. Remember that glasses are formed from a molten viscous liquid state. Small cracks form in the surface when the glass cools in the same way that a dried rain puddle leaves a cracked, or crazed, surface. One way of getting rid of them is to remelt the surface layer. We call this **flame polishing**. A flame is passed over the cracked surface and remelts just the few layers of surface atoms. These then solidify with many fewer cracks than they had before.

Diagram of the flame polishing process.

Compression

The more usual way of closing the cracks in ceramics is to compress the material thus forcing the cracks shut. This can be done by using the material in a situation where it only sees loads which compress it. The concrete foundations of tall and heavy buildings are fine examples of this. Alternatively one can surround the ceramic material with something which is always pressing on it.

Some ceramic bearings are surrounded by a metal band which it placed over them while the metal is very hot. The band starts out being smaller than the ceramic part but expands on heating so that it can be slipped over the part in the same way that metal rims used to be fitted to wagon wheels. When the band cools it shrinks and compresses the ceramic which can then survive knocks much better. The metal band hugs the ceramic very tightly and the compression forces the cracks to close. This is the reason why ceramics are usually stronger when compressed than when pulled: compression closes cracks.

In glasses we can adopt a rather unusual approach. We use a type of atom gun to fire large atoms (ions) into the surface. These atoms need a lot of space and therefore elbow their way in, pushing surrounding atoms away. Of

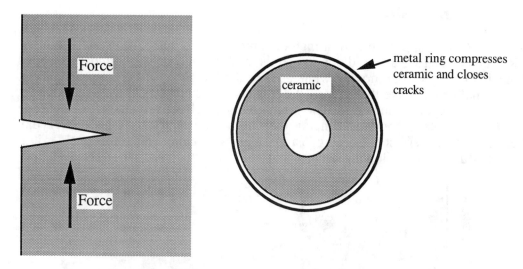

Use of compressive force to close surface cracks in a ceramic.

course one of the ways they can get this space is to force any surface cracks and scratches to close. What this does is to effectively make the surface atoms see some compressive force. In this case the compression is exerted within the surface of the material by the large atoms rather than by an external load.

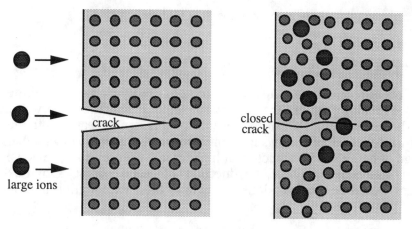

Ion implantation of large ions (left) closes crack (right).

Smaller grain size

A third approach to limiting crack motion is to make the crystals smaller. Remember that we also did this in metals, but in that case the boundary stopped the dislocations from moving whereas here it stops the *crack* from propagating. The smaller we make the crystals the less chance there is of the crack growing, and the stronger the material. The grain boundary effectively does for a ceramic what a slip plane does for a metal, they both blunt cracks. A good everyday example of this effect is Corning Ware®, a glass ceramic. We shall consider it in a case study in the following chapter.

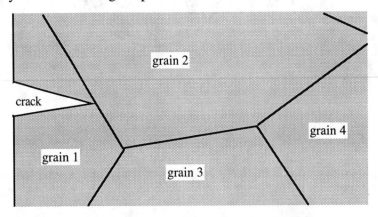

Grain boundary stops crack from propagating.

Nanophase ceramics

Recent research has shown that the possibility exists for making ductile ceramics by making the grain size very, very small. Smaller than we have ever previously considered. Part of the reason for this new research is the relatively recent discovery of ceramic superconductors (Chapter 27), which have the advantage of being superconductors at higher temperatures than previously found for other materials, but lack the ductility of metal wires. Obviously their brittleness would be a tremendous obstacle to their exploitation in commercial devices.

The technique used is to heat the ceramic in a vacuum furnace to a temperature at which it vaporizes. A cold rod is placed inside the furnace so that the ceramic condenses on it. By carefully controlling the conditions, particles can be produced which are only a few atoms in diameter. These are then squeezed together at very high pressures so that the particles join or **sinter**. These new materials have quite different properties from the traditional coarser-grained ceramics with the same chemical composition. Because of the ultrafine grain structure they are known as **nanophase materials**. We shall probably hear a lot more about them in the years ahead.

Conclusion

To summarize: the weaknesses in ceramics and glasses are surface defects, cracks and scratches. To strengthen the material we have several options:

eliminate surface defects: flame polish a glass to remelt the surface to heal cracks, etc.

close surface defects: apply external compressive load; implant large atoms in surface.

limit surface defect motion: make crystals smaller; cracks stopped by boundaries.

To close on a practical note, we can often prolong the useful life of glass objects by stopping them from getting scratched. Reusable beverage bottles are often sprayed with a very thin plastic layer when they come off the production line. This stops the hard glass surfaces from rubbing against each other which would cause surface scratches and make them more liable to break.

Nowadays we use windshields in our autos made of laminated glass. This is made using two layers of ordinary glass bonded together with a sheet of transparent plastic. This flexible plastic layer holds the glass together so tightly that it will crack but not shatter. The side and rear windows of the automobile are usually made of toughened glass in which the surface layers are put into compression by special cooling techniques. We shall briefly consider the process in the next chapter.

19. CASE STUDY: GLASS CERAMICS FOR COOKWARE

Background

In our discussion of ceramics and glass we have seen that their major weakness is due to surface cracks or flaws which concentrate stress. These defects are usually too small to be noticed but are there nonetheless.

You have perhaps broken a drinking glass by pouring boiling water into it. Why does it break? The answer lies in the presence of these surface flaws. The glass starts out being all at the same temperature, but pouring boiling water into it immediately increases the temperature *inside* the glass. Unfortunately ceramics, of which glass is an example, do not conduct heat very well. Thus for the moment the inside of the glass is hot and expanding while the outside surface is still cold. The situation which exists for this very short time is exactly that which we discussed in the case of the bimetallic strip. One side has expanded more than the other. In this case it is because of different temperatures rather than different materials, but the effect is the same. One side expands and pulls the other with it. As a result there is a tensile stress on the outside of the glass and the cracks are pulled open. There is now increased stress on the bonds between atoms at the crack tip and eventually the glass breaks. We have given a sort-of slow motion description of the process, it all happens so suddenly, but what we have described can be captured with high speed cameras. It is, in fact, what happens.

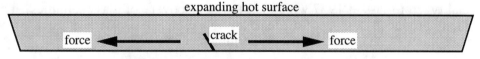

Illustration of how a surface crack is opened by an expanding opposing surface.

Something similar will happen if you take a ceramic pot from the freezer and place it on a hot burner on the stove. Whenever we have a hot expanding surface close to a cold one, the hot surface pulls on the colder surface and possibly opens surface cracks so that the material breaks.

Corning Ware ® is a relatively new material which can withstand such rapid temperature changes without breaking. It is what is known as a glass ceramic, a material which has undergone special processing which turns glass into extremely small crystals. In our discussion of the mechanical strength of ceramics and glass we saw that there are several ways of strengthening the material: flame polishing, compressing the surface, surface ion implantation and making the grains or crystallites smaller. It is this last approach which is used in glass ceramics. We shall now see how it can be done.

How to make a glass with small crystals

We know that surface cracks in glasses and ceramics are stress concentrators. The atoms near the crack tip have extra forces on their bonds which can therefore be broken if the force exceeds their strength. The force they were carrying is then transferred to the bonds between the adjacent atoms, etc. The result is a catastrophic failure. In ceramics we can toughen the material by making the crystallites or grains smaller; the grain boundaries blunt the crack tip and hinder its propagation. But glasses are amorphous, there are no crystallites, no grain boundaries, and the crack cannot be stopped. Glass therefore breaks in the way we are all accustomed to.

What if we could somehow cause small crystallites to form in a glass? There would then be a mechanism for the inhibition of crack propagation. This is what happened accidentally in the discovery of what we now know as glass ceramics.

It was the overheating of a furnace during the manufacture of another special type of glass in 1957 which led to the discovery of glass ceramics. This accident produced a scientific breakthrough which has affected us all. We perhaps know these materials best as Corning Ware®.

The secret of the manufacture of glass ceramics is getting the crystals to form, or **nucleate**. In normal circumstances there are no crystals formed when glass is cooled, however this can be changed by seeding the glass with tiny crystals of an impurity which provide surfaces on which the SiO_2 tetrahedra in the glass can crystallize. We may have done something similar in home or high school chemistry experiments. By suspending a crystal of sugar on a thin cotton thread in a concentrated sugar solution we can get the crystal to grow over a period of time because it acts as a nucleus on which the sugar molecules can arrange themselves. We sometimes call this process **seeding**, in the same sense that we refer to cloud-seeding to try to get raindrops to form in a cloud. The nucleating agent used in glass is titanium oxide. It is added as very, very fine particles. You can appreciate how small they must be when you know that in the glass there can be as many as a trillion (10^{12}) nuclei in a cubic millimeter (a cube with an edge length of 1 mm). This may seem like lot of nuclei, but it works out at about one nucleus for every hundred million atoms!

The container or pan is first made as a regular glass object. Because of this it can either be blown or formed in a mold, and then ground and polished to produce, for example, a flat bottom. At this point it appears to be a clear glass-like object. The advantage of this is that the required shape and size can be precisely produced at a low cost. There then follows a special, carefully controlled heat treatment to produce the required **devitrification** (removal of the glassy state: vitreous = glassy). The details of this process are beyond the scope of this discussion The important thing to understand is that the very small TiO_2 crystals are just what is required to nucleate small crystals of SiO_2.

These small SiO_2 crystals are less than one micrometer (one thousandth of a millimeter) across and are quite free of any porosity. Careful seeding and control of the heat treatment can result in as much as 99% of the glass being converted to small crystals. The remaining glass occupies the spaces between the crystals, cementing them together and producing a solid, non-porous material.

The following photograph shows two halves of a Corning Ware® casserole dish. On half is before devitrification and the other after. You should be able to see two differences after the devitrifying heat treatment: (a) the container is now white and opaque, and (b) is slightly smaller than the original. The reasons for these differences are very interesting:

(a) A crystal is an ordered arrangement of atoms, and when things are put in order they take up less room. A neatly stacked pile of bricks takes up less space than when just tipped onto the floor from a wheelbarrow, for example. This accounts for the shrinkage during the devitrifying heat treatment - ordered crystals are formed from disordered (amorphous) glass.

(b) As a result of the numerous small crystals and their associated boundaries, light is no longer able to pass straight through the material, but is scattered at the boundaries so that the material appears white and opaque, the same way that salt and sugar appear white.

The crystals in glass-ceramics are so small and are so strongly cemented together that no surface flaw or crack can easily pass through the many boundaries which confront it. In addition these materials have a very low thermal

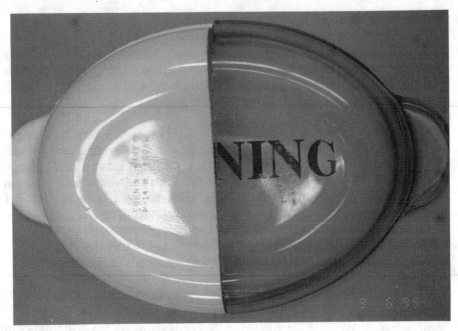

Photograph of Corning Ware® after (left) and before (right) devitrification. Note that the while the edges at the bottom are aligned, the edges at the top are not. The devitrified half is smaller than the original.

expansion so that the hot side of a piece of material does not try to extend the cold side by very much, i.e. it exerts a smaller stress than would be the case if the thermal expansion were large. As a result of this combination of high strength and low thermal expansion, glass ceramics have what we call a high **thermal shock resistance**. We can take the cookware straight from the refrigerator to a red hot burner, and vice versa, without crack or fracture. Remember that these two factors, a small thermal expansion producing less pull, and a high strength, both help to give us the properties of Corning Ware® with which we are familiar.

Glass ceramics and light

Another glass ceramic which you may own is called Visions Ware®. This material looks like a glass in that it is transparent, with a reddish tint, although there is a version called 'cranberry' which is much redder. It is also a crystalline material with a very fine microstructure, so why is it not also white and opaque? You may remember that we earlier discussed polyethylene (PE) and said that low density PE was usually clear, but crystalline high density PE was white and opaque (Page 146). We left an explanation until this point because it relates to the nature of light.

Light is what we know as an electromagnetic wave. We shall briefly describe what is meant by 'electromagnetic' later, but for now we shall focus on its wave nature. Most people think of waves as related to water. If you drop a pebble into a pond, a wave radiates from the point where it is dropped. The following diagram illustrates a simple wave. The distance between the crests or troughs of the wave is called the wavelength, usually denoted λ.

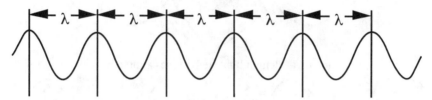

Diagram of a wave, illustrating what is meant by wavelength, λ.

When a light wave strikes a crystal it is scattered. Just think of it as reflection from the surface of the crystal. When the crystals are larger than the light wavelength, the light has no chance of avoiding this scattering, but when the crystals are smaller than the wavelength, there is a chance that the light can simply go around the crystals, as illustrated on the next page.

In Visions Ware® the crystals are even smaller than those in Corning Ware® and the light is able to go round them without being scattered. In other words, the light can pass straight through the material. Another thing about white light which you probably know is that it consists of a range of colors. This is commonly seen in the colors of the rainbow (red, orange, yellow, green, blue, indigo, violet). Each color has its own characteristic wavelength, with red having the longest and violet the shortest.

The following diagrams illustrate the possibility that a red wave could go round a crystal while a blue one could not. In other words the blue is scattered while the red is not. This is what happens to make the sunset look red. When the sun is setting, the light has to come further to reach us. Over this distance the blue light is scattered, or reflected sideways, by atmospheric dust, while the red light comes directly to our eyes with little interruption. Our eyes therefore see more red light than blue, and the sunset is red. In Visions Ware® the same thing happens. Red light passes through the material with little or no interruption, while blue is scattered. Our Visions Ware® pan therefore has a reddish tinge because more of the red portion of the visible light spectrum reaches our eyes uninterrupted than does the blue, some of which is lost due to scattering. Cranberry Visions® has its much redder color because of intentionally added impurities. We shall discuss how impurities produce color in Chapter 23.

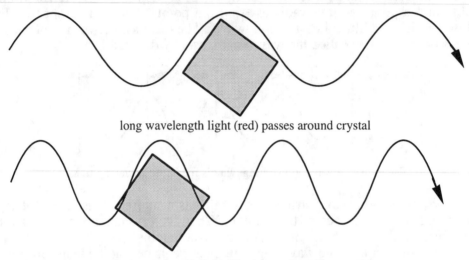

long wavelength light (red) passes around crystal

short wavelength light (blue) is scattered by crystal

Illustration of how red light can pass through a material without being scattered while blue light is scattered. Some red light passes through uninterrupted and the material appears reddish.

Corelle® and toughened glass

Another really strong material is the glassy material called Corelle® which is a sort of opalescent glass. In discussing the bimetallic strip and the breaking of a drinking glass when filled with boiling water, we had two layers of material with one pulling on the other. What if we could arrange for this pulling to be compressive rather than tensile? Any surface flaws would then be closed, and the material made stronger.

The way this is accomplished is quite simple although the processing required to accomplish it required considerable research. We make a three layer sandwich of two different glasses such that, on cooling, the one in the middle shrinks much more than the one forming the outer layers. In addition to having these quite different thermal expansions, or in this case contractions, the two glasses must adhere very strongly together.

When the three layers are shaped in the viscous molten state they have essentially the same dimensions. When they cool the inner layer contracts more than the outer layers and tries to pull them with it. The result is an internal compressive force as illustrated in the following diagram. Any surface flaws which develop during the processing are therefore pulled together and closed.

high thermal expansion glass

low thermal expansion glass

Three layer glass with inner layer contracting more and pulling surface layers into contraction.

The following photograph of a broken piece of the material allow you to see the sandwich structure. Also if you look at the surface of a piece of Corelle® at the correct angle you can often see a fine 'orange peel' structure resulting from the contraction of the outer layers when pulled by the inner layer.

Photograph of the broken surface of Corelle® showing the sandwich structure.

This same principle is used to make toughened or tempered glass. The glass used in windshields nowadays is always laminated with a central layer of tough plastic. However, the side windows are made of **tempered glass**. This material is all made of the same glass but a simple trick is used to produce the layering effect we have just discussed.

The sheet of glass is heated so that it is soft all the way through and the top and bottom surfaces are then cooled very quickly with a blast of cold air.

These outer surfaces therefore contract and become hard. When they do this, the inside is still quite soft because heat does not travel quickly in these materials, i.e. the inside has not had time to solidify. It therefore flows and adjusts to the smaller dimensions of the outside.

The production of tempered glass produces compressive forces on the surface by the delayed contraction of the inside.

The soft inside glass then cools and also contracts, and in so doing pulls on the outer layers which cooled first. As a result these outer layers are pulled into compression, which as we have already seen, toughens the material because it closes any cracks or scratches on the surface.

This type of glass is sometimes called **safety glass** and is also often used in household sliding glass doors.

Conclusion

We have seen in this chapter how the careful choice of materials and the ways they are processed can allow us to overcome the limitations imposed by surface flaws on ceramics. These are materials which many of us use regularly. They are not expensive, but are very high-tech, allowing us to enjoy some of the advances made in materials in recent years. A final word of caution. These materials are not like Pyrex®, which is a glass and quite different.

QUESTIONS: Chapters 17-19

1. The high strength of Corning-Ware® is due to _____.
   (a) a flame polished surface (b) precipitation hardening (c) vitrification (d) cross-linking
   (e) none of these

2. Choose the false option or choose (e). For ceramics _____.
   (a) the bonds can carry load (b) cracks act as stress-concentrators (c) compressive forces
   can close cracks (d) cracks cannot be blunted by grain boundaries (e) all these are true

3. Windshields of cars are made of _____.
   a) polycarbonate b) compressed glass c) tempered glass d) laminated glass
   e) none of these

4. In metals, heat is conducted by _____ while in ceramics it is conducted by _____.
   (a) protons, electrons (b) electrons, phonons (c) phonons, atom knock-on (d) phonons,
   electrons (e) none of these

5. _____ usually expand less than _____ when heated.
   (a) ceramics, polymers (b) metals, ceramics (c) polymers, ceramics (d) polymers,
   metals (e) none of these options is correct

6. Impurities _____ the conductivity of metals.
   (a) reduce (b) increase (c) do not alter (d) have nothing to do with

7. In general, for a covalently bonded material, the thermal expansion would be _____ and the
   thermal conductivity would be _____ than for a metallic material.
   (a) higher, lower (b) higher, higher (c) lower, lower (d) higher, lower (e) none of these

8. In the making of a glass ceramic all the following are involved except _____.
   (a) devitrification (b) nucleation (c) seeding (d) crystallization (e) all these are correct

9. When a metal gets a crack in it the crack usually _____.
   (a) causes the metal to fail catastrophically (b) gets blunted through the slip of planes
   (c) is filled by mobile atoms near the crack tip (d) stops on its own (e) none of these

10. Which of the following is a reason why dislocations don't move through ceramics?
    (a) directed covalent bonds (b) small grains (c) movement of like charges over one
    another (d) both a and b (e) both a and c

11. What is the average grain size in glass?
    a) 0.01 microns b) 0.5 microns c) 5 microns d) 10 microns e) none of these

12. Sintering is a process by which _____.
    (a) atoms are moved toward the middle of a grain (b) surface cracks are removed
    (c) the surface of a material is placed under compression (d) impurities are removed from a
    material (e) ceramic particles are joined at temperatures lower then their melting points

13. Which type of bonds in a material would most likely yield the largest thermal expansion?
    (a) covalent (b) metallic (c) van der Waals (d) ionic (e) bond type does not affect
    thermal expansion

14. Sodium ions in glass are bonded to oxygen atoms by _____ bonds.
    (a) covalent (b) hydrogen (c) van der Waals (d) ionic (e) metallic

15. All of the following are true of glass ceramics except _____.
    (a) very small grains (b) low porosity (c) high strength (d) high thermal expansion
    (e) high thermal shock resistance

16-25. At absolute zero temperature, the atoms in a material are stationary and in fixed
    positions. When the material is heated from this temperature, the atoms move ___16___.
    As a consequence the material ___17___. If only one end of a rod of material is heated,
    some of the heat energy travels to the other end. The way the energy travels depends on the
    material, in particular on ___18___. In metals the energy is carried by ___19___; in
    ceramics by ___20___; and in polymers by ___21___. The best insulating materials
    are the ___22___, but they are not useful at high temperatures such as you would find in
    your furnace because they ___23___. We can greatly improve the insulating properties by
    incorporating some ___24___ into the material. Space shuttle tiles are good insulators
    which use this principle. The material they are made from is ___25___.

    16. (a) further apart (b) more rapidly (c) to form vacancies (d) from a fixed position
        (e) all of these
    17. (a) becomes amorphous (b) expands (c) bends (d) shrinks (e) decomposes
    18. (a) its crystal structure (b) the types of atoms (c) the bonding (d) its microstructure
        (e) its dimensions
    19. (a) phonons (b) photons (c) free electrons (d) atom collisions (e) protons
    20. (a) phonons (b) photons (c) electrons (d) atom collisions (e) electron holes
    21. (a) phonons (b) electron holes (c) electrons (d) atom collisions (e) protons
    22. (a) ceramics (b) semiconductors (c) polymers (d) glasses (e) metals
    23. (a) become brittle (b) decompose (c) are flammable (d) become conductive
        (e) all four are true
    24. (a) precipitates (b) air pockets (c) point defects (d) larger atoms (e) fibers
    25. (a) silicon (b) silica (c) titanium (d) a silicate (e) silicone

26. Which of the following is the worst conductor of heat?
    a) air b) fiberglass insulation c) an iron pot d) a stainless steel pot e) a vacuum

27-36. Ceramics are usually materials in which a metal has combined with ____27____ using ____28____ bonds. Unlike metals they cannot permanently deform, something we know as ____29____ deformation, because ____30____ find it very difficult to move as a result of the ____31____. While metals are usually formed by starting from a molten material, ceramics are formed by ____32____ powders. In metals it is sometimes possible to process a material to produce smaller crystals, such as in ____33____, but in ceramics smaller crystals are usually obtained by starting with a(n) ____34____ powder. Smaller crystals help make both ceramics and metals stronger. In metals they ____35____ , while in ceramics they ____36____ .

27. (a) boron (b) carbon (c) nitrogen (d) oxygen (e) any of these
28. (a) metallic (b) ionic (c) covalent (d) both a and b (e) both b and c
29. (a) plastic (b) polymeric (c) relaxed (d) elastic (e) cooperative
30. (a) vacancies (b) ions (c) dislocations (d) cracks (e) electrons
31. (a) bonding (b) precipitates (c) grain boundaries (d) bulky side groups
    (e) both a and b
32. (a) sintering (b) annealing (c) combining (d) recrystallizing (e) quenching
33. (a) stainless steel (b) HSLA steels (c) aluminum-lithium alloys (d) cast iron
    (e) superalloys
34. (a) purer (b) equiaxed (c) finer (d) coarser (e) acicular
35. (a) induce precipitate formation (b) inhibit dislocation motion
    (c) hinder crack propagation (d) cause dislocation tangles (e) a combination of a and b
36. (a) induce precipitate formation (b) inhibit dislocation motion (c) hinder crack
    propagation (d) cause dislocation tangles (e) a combination of a and b

(37-44) Ceramics are usually brittle because of the presence of ____37____ . When a stress is applied to a ceramic, it tends to ____38____ at the tips of these defects, which means that the bonds at these points are closer to ____39____ . The less deep these defects, the less the stress is ____38____d, because there are fewer broken bonds in the defect which are not carrying their share of the load. When you 'cut' glass you don't really cut it, but place a sharp scratch on the surface where it will ____39____ when you try to bend it. The glass on the outside of the bend gets longer, or in other words has a larger ____40____ , and sees a ____41____ stress, while that on the inside sees a ____42____ stress. The thicker the glass, the ____43____ the increase in length of the outer surface, and the ____43____ the ____40____ and stress. Fracture always starts on the ____44____ of the curve.

37. (a) surface cracks and scratches (b) dislocations (c) point defects (d) precipitates
    (e) forces
38. (a) infiltrate (b) initiate (c) propagate (d) concentrate (e) saturate
39. (a) multiplying (b) fracture (c) becoming covalent (d) releasing their electrons
    (e) slipping
40. (a) modulus (b) strain (c) reactivity (d) stress (e) both a and d
41. (a) compressive (b) shear (c) tensile (d) bend (e) isotropic
42. (a) compressive (b) shear (c) tensile (d) bend (e) isotropic
43. (a) less (b) smaller (c) greater (d) faster (e) slower
44. (a) bottom (b) center (c) end (d) inside (e) outside

20. COMPOSITE MATERIALS - GETTING THE BEST OF TWO (OR MORE) WORLDS

Background

Most materials scientists would admit that composite materials, or 'composites' as we usually call them, are one of today's really important materials developments. Not that such materials are novel. The Biblical account of the captivity of the Israelites in Egypt (Exodus 5) refers to their having to gather their own straw to make bricks. Obviously the purpose of the straw was to increase strength. Nowadays we do not use straw in bricks because we have a better knowledge than they did of how to process the coarse alumina (Al_2O_3) powder to cement it together more strongly. The use of straw to strengthen bricks was a solution to a problem which we have rediscovered in recent years in the form of composite materials. In fact there is now some interesting research being performed on using straw and other natural filamentous material for strengthening rather than some of the more recently discovered man-made polymer fibers.

What do we mean by a composite material? Some fifty years ago we might have answered this question by saying that it was a material made by mixing two other materials which did not chemically react to form a new compound. These two materials simply coexisted in the same solid, which probably exhibited some properties of both of them. Some of the materials we have discussed already fall into this category because they contain mixtures of two or more different materials. Aluminum-lithium alloys have a solid solution matrix surrounding Al_3Li precipitates. HIPS and ABS plastics have polystyrene and polybutadiene regions. Glass ceramics consist of small crystals embedded in a glassy matrix. Corelle® consists of layers of two different glasses.

Today when we talk about composites we usually mean materials in which very strong **fibers** of one material are embedded in another material, called the **matrix**, which completely surrounds them and holds them together. Sometimes the fibers and the matrix are made of different materials, while in others, as is the case with carbon-carbon composites, the two components are made of the same material. Most of these composite materials are very lightweight and have a high strength and a high stiffness. It is these three characteristics which make them very attractive for aerospace applications.

We have already mentioned carbon reinforced composites (Page 105) which are used for aircraft manufacture. These are often made of carbon fibers in an epoxy matrix (something like you can buy at the hardware store in two tubes, which, when mixed and allowed to cure, form a strong bond for cementing articles together). You may have a tennis or squash racket with a frame made from the same material. For years we have made some household articles, liquid storage tanks, car bodies, etc., from fiberglass, a composite consisting of glass fibers in a polymer (probably polyester) matrix. Today we have special polymer fibers (even polyethylene fibers as mentioned on page 147), ceramic fibers, boron fibers, etc., all of which are being used to make composites.

Wood is an excellent example of a natural composite, containing cellulose fibers in a lignin matrix. It illustrates one of the basic problems with fiber reinforced materials, that of anisotropy. A piece of wood has the cellulose fibers going along what we call the grain. We can break a piece of wood much easier along the grain than across the grain. You don't find a karate expert breaking a plank of wood across the grain with a chop of his hand! When broken along the grain the fracture surface is quite smooth because we are producing a fracture between fibers, few, if any, of which are broken in the process. When broken across the grain the fracture surface is very rough because the break has to occur across the fibers themselves.

weak - breaks easily along grain   strong across grain

A piece of wood is easier to break along the grain than across the grain.

We shall now look at some of these new strong fibers before coming back to the composites they are used to manufacture. We shall pay particular attention to carbon (graphite) fibers because they are relatively easy to understand, and are those which you are perhaps most likely to encounter. In the following chapter we shall consider the details of carbon/carbon composites and their manufacture for aerospace applications. Some of these materials can be very expensive, but we have already seen that the economics of air travel can justify using some very expensive materials.

Strong fibers

Modern composites are usually considered to be strong but lightweight. In fact this combination is so important that we often classify materials using a quantity called **specific strength**, which is the strength divided by the density. We shall not be concerned with the units of this quantity because we are really only interested in the relative values, e.g. material A has a value 70% greater than material B. You will see that in the table given later we divide psi by gm/cc, which is mixing systems of units in a way that scientists abhor, but it does give us correct *relative* values. In other words we want to know the percent difference in weight which can be carried by the same weights of different materials, because in many instances (e.g. aircraft) we want to keep the weight as low as possible. We saw when discussing strength (Page 88) that a material can always carry twice the load if we make it twice as thick. Of course this also makes it twice as heavy. If we can replace the material with another which has half the density, but two thirds of the strength, we could achieve a 25% weight saving. The following example will help to explain this.

Example.

A rod of material A, 2" x 1" rectangular cross section, weighs 10 pounds and can carry 300 pounds (150 psi). If we want it to carry 600 pounds we have to double the area of the rod to 2" x 2", and it now weighs 20 pounds.

The same sized rod of material B weighs 5 pounds (half the density of A) and can carry 200 pounds (100 psi or two thirds the strength of A). If we want it to carry 600 pounds, which is three times its current capacity, we must triple the area of the rod to 2" x 3", and it now weighs 15 pounds (three times its original weight).

By replacing material A with material B we have reduced the weight from 20 pounds to 15 pounds, a weight saving of 25%.

If we look at the relative specific strengths (strength divided by weight) we obtain the following values:

$$A : 150 \text{ psi}/10 \text{ pounds} = 15$$
$$B : 100 \text{ psi}/5 \text{ pounds} = 20$$

The specific strength for A is 25% less than for B and indicates the possible weight saving in going from A to B.

When we look at materials from the standpoint of specific strength we find that the ceramics, silicon nitride, silicon carbide, aluminum oxide, boron, graphite, and some of the strong polymers do considerably better than the strongest steel. A table in the following chapter which compares carbon composites with steel will give you an idea of how important this can be.

We have already seen (Chapter 18) that the limiting factor in the strength of ceramic materials is the presence of small surface cracks or scratches. Our experiments show us that the smaller the piece of material we use, the less the chance of having one of these surface flaws large enough to cause the material to break. This is why we use very fine fibers. In fact it appears that fibers may always be the strongest form of any material.

Another aspect of very thin fibers which is worth mentioning is that they can be more easily bent without breaking than can thick fibers of the same material. If you bend a piece of material you always end up with a longer outside edge and a shorter inside edge. The thicker the piece, the longer this outer edge. As we now know, this stretch, or strain, is produced by a stress. The greater the strain, the greater the stress. It follows that there is more stress in a bent thick fiber than in a thin one bent the same amount, and therefore the thinner the fiber, the more it can be bent without breaking.

We earlier mentioned metal whiskers (Page 97) as having strengths close to the theoretically predicted values because they contain no dislocations. By dividing the material up into such small pieces we reduce the effects of cracks, and other defects, and where there happens to be a crack in a fiber in a composite, it cannot find a continuous path through the material to cause fracture because it very soon encounters the less brittle matrix and other unbroken fibers.

Manufacturing fibers and composites

We can manufacture glass and alumina fibers by melting the material and drawing out a fiber - just like pulling taffy. We have already mentioned (Page 147) strong and stiff polyethylene fibers produced by gel spinning. Silicon carbide fibers are made from a polymer in which some carbon atoms are replaced by silicon atoms (remember that they both have the similar electron structures with four electrons in their outer shells, so they can often substitute for each other easily) or they can be made by the deposition of silicon carbide on a carbon fiber using chemical vapor deposition (CVD). Carbon fibers are made either from a polyacrylonitrile (PAN) fiber, the acrylic fibers used in clothing, or from pitch. We shall discuss this in the next chapter.

In manufacturing composites from strong fibers there are many criteria which must be met by the matrix material. First, the fiber and the matrix must not react. You cannot just pour a molten metal around carbon fibers because you often end up with a carbide and the fibers have disappeared. This is because there has been a chemical reaction between the metal and the polymer or carbon fibers. Second, the matrix must be somewhat soft so that it does not damage the fiber. If it scratches the fiber we have lost the main advantage of using fibers. Third, it must adhere well to the fiber so that the fiber does not get pulled out of the matrix when a force is placed on it. In some respects the matrix must hug the fiber just as wet ground holds a wooden stake. You may be able to move the stake, but it is very difficult to pull it out of the ground.

Sometimes the matrix can be melted and poured around the fibers without damage. In some cases the matrix is deposited between the fibers using a CVD process. In others a powder of the matrix can be mixed with the fibers and then sintered together. There are obviously many different processing techniques which can be tried, each with its own limitations. We shall discuss the use of liquid pitch for producing the matrix in carbon/carbon composites in the case study in the next chapter.

Some current application of composite materials

The use of straw to make bricks which we mentioned earlier is an illustration of the use of fibers to reinforce ceramics, which break easily because of cracks. The fibers bridge the cracks and carry the load so that the crack does not propagate. This is similar to the effect of the graft copolymer chains in HIPS and ABS plastics. We have used this principle to reinforce cement using asbestos and both glass and carbon fibers, and on a much larger scale with steel reinforcing rods.

An automobile tire is a composite material consisting of an elastomer (itself reinforced with carbon black) as the matrix, which is reinforced with thin steel wires (steel belted radials) or strong polymer fibers, especially the aramid fibers such as Kevlar®.

Commercial application of composite materials with metal and ceramic matrices is becoming more common. The Toyota automobile company has used ceramic fibers to reinforce parts of aluminum alloy pistons in diesel engines, and aluminum alloy struts reinforced with boron fibers are used in the midsection framework of the US space shuttle. In the future we shall probably see ceramic materials such as silicon nitride or silicon carbide used to reinforce a matrix of the same material, just as we use carbon fibers to reinforce carbon in carbon-carbon composites. These materials would be strong and crack resistant, able to withstand high temperatures, and as such, ideal for aircraft engine manufacture.

As is the case for polymers, there are always new composite materials being produced, and research in this particular area of Materials Science is currently very active.

21. CASE STUDY: CARBON/CARBON COMPOSITES

Making the fibers

If you place a piece of fabric, whether of natural or man-made fibers, onto a hot coal or a hot burner on your stove, you will see it shrink, shrivel and turn black. What you are witnessing is the **carbonization** of the material. Any other atoms on the polymer chain such as hydrogen, oxygen and nitrogen are driven off by the heat, and a mass of carbon is left behind. Of course, if there is a supply of air to the material the carbon will eventually burn and form carbon dioxide gas, but it is the carbonization which we are interested in.

In most cases the carbon left behind when the other elements have been driven off is amorphous. There are no graphite crystals produced. However, we discovered some twenty five years ago that if we use a single acrylic fiber and heat it while pulling on it to stop it shrinking and shriveling, we can produce a carbon fiber which contains regions of the planes which make up the graphite crystal (Page 13). What's even more important is that these planes lie parallel to the fiber length. The importance of this fact is that this places the strong covalent bonds between the carbon atoms along the fiber length. When we try to stretch this fiber we are pulling on these strong bonds. Further heating at temperatures above 2000°C, in an inert atmosphere to prevent oxidation, causes these little pieces of plane to join up so that we have quite large graphite planes along the fiber length. It is this which makes these fibers both strong and stiff.

More recently we have discovered ways of doing the same thing starting from the black viscous liquid left after gasoline has been removed from crude oil, something we call petroleum pitch. The pitch is what we call a **thermoplastic** material, which means that heat makes it plastic. At room temperature it is a hard brittle solid, but at higher temperatures it becomes a viscous liquid which can be pulled out into a fiber in the same way that we can pull taffy. Remember that we saw something similar when we talked about the glass transition temperature for polymers (Page 152). This pitch contains many large molecules consisting of several benzene rings (Page 132) linked together, and if you think about it you will see that after removing the hydrogen atoms these hexagonal molecules can easily link together to form small graphite planes of carbon atoms.

The hot liquid pitch is placed in a container with a small hole in the bottom through which it is pulled to form a thin fiber, a process known as **spinning**, the term used for the production of wool and cotton fiber from the raw material. When this is done the large molecules slip through the hole in the edge-on orientation (sideways), as shown in the following diagram, simply because this is the easiest way through. We then heat the fibers to drive off the other atoms (hydrogen, nitrogen, oxygen, etc.) and are left with hexagons of carbon atoms lying parallel to the fiber length, just as we had in the method starting with acrylic fibers. Further heating at high temperatures (above 2000°C) then causes these little planes to join up and produce a strong, stiff fiber.

Illustration of how hydrocarbon molecules become oriented
during the spinning of a pitch-based carbon fiber.

Carbon fibers are strong and stiff because they contain the 'chicken-wire' layers of carbon atoms which are held together by very strong covalent bonds, and these planes lie parallel to the fiber length. When you pull on a fiber you are trying to stretch and break these bonds, which are the strongest bonds known.

Using different manufacturing techniques (processing) we can make a large variety of fibers with different properties and microstructures. Depending on the type of pitch used and the dimension of the hole through which the fiber is spun, we can produce fibers with the graphite layers wrapped around the fiber in concentric rings, while in others the layers can radiate from the center of the fiber like spokes on a wheel. In all cases the important point is that the layers lie parallel to the fiber length. The following diagrams show the types of graphite plane orientations you would see when looking at the ends of the fiber, which is about a hundredth of a millimeter in diameter. We can also produce fibers with different strengths by changing the temperature to which they are eventually heated, and the time we keep them at that temperature.

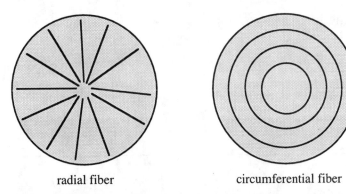

radial fiber   circumferential fiber

Two different types of carbon fiber showing how the layers are arranged along the fiber

Carbon fibers are also very stiff (high Young's modulus), another consequence of the strong, stiff covalent bonds in the graphite layers. As we mentioned earlier (Page 91), stiffness is often the property which is of paramount importance. Many lightweight new materials may be very strong but they cannot be used for such things as aircraft structures because they are not stiff enough. Here again we are interested in how much stiffness we can get for a certain weight of material, so we also define a **specific modulus** which is the Young's modulus divided by the density. Carbon fibers are used in many sporting goods on account of their stiffness rather than their strength.

The following table gives the strengths (UTS) and Young's moduli (stiffnesses) of medium strength carbon fibers and compares them with the values given for the high strength low alloy (HSLA) steels on page 125, and with those of typical carbon/carbon composites made with all the fibers parallel in one dimension (1D) and with fibers lying in three dimensions (3D). The table also shows the densities and the relative specific strengths and specific moduli of the

Material	Carbon Fibers	3D C/C Composite	1D C/C Composite	HSLA Steel
Density (A) (gm/cc)	1.8	1.8	1.8	7.8
Tensile strength (B) (10^3 psi)	300	25	95	80
Specific strength* (B/A) x 10^{-4}	16.6	1.4	5.2	1.0
Young's modulus (C) (10^6 psi)	35	10	18	30
Specific modulus* (C/A) x 10^{-6}	19.4	5.6	10.0	3.8

We are only concerned with the relative values of these quantities and no units are given. For example, a 1D carbon/carbon composite has 5.2 times the strength of the HSLA steel and over two and a half times (10/3.8) the stiffness.

materials. The advantage of carbon fibers and their composites are obvious. They give us higher strength and greater stiffness for less weight.

You will notice from the above table that 1D composites seem better than 3D. This is because in 1D material all the fibers are in the same direction, as they are in wood. Because the force is pulling in that direction, all the fibers are sharing the load and are being stretched, and the strength and modulus shown are measured along this direction. These materials show a large anisotropy. In the 3D material only a third of the fibers are parallel to the direction of the force and so bearing the load. Each fiber therefore sees three times the stress and stretches more. The 3D composite is therefore not as stiff as is the 1D composite but is more isotropic. In 1D all the fibers are bearing the load, whereas in 3D only a third do so.

When carbon fibers first became available commercially in the 1970's they cost up to $500 a pound. Today reasonable quality fibers can be obtained for $20 a pound, although they can cost several times this amount for special grades. Don't forget that you get a lot of fibers in a pound because of their low density. The following photograph shows carbon fibers alongside a human hair and a fiber of alumina (Al_2O_3) to give you an idea of the size. Typical carbon fibers have a diameter of 10 microns (one hundredth of a millimeter).

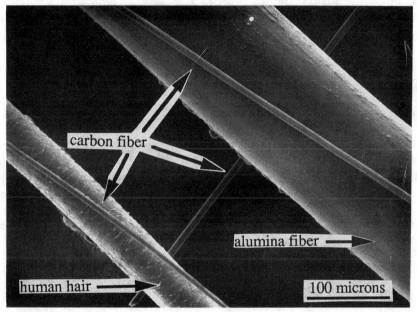

Photograph of three carbon fibers together with a human hair and an alumina (Al_2O_3) fiber.

The matrix

While fibers of any material may be strong and stiff, their uses in this form are rather limited. They can obviously be braided and twisted into a string or rope, but in order to obtain a rigid material which we can use for structural applications, aircraft wing struts, tennis racquet frames, golf club shafts, etc., we have to place the fibers in a matrix.

As mentioned in the previous chapter, the matrix we use has to satisfy the following criteria. It must be somewhat soft so that it does not scratch the fibers, which usually means that it will either be a metal or a polymer. It must also adhere well to the fiber surface so that the fiber is not easily pulled out of the matrix, and it must blunt any cracks which pass through a fiber and then try to cross the matrix. It is this last criterion which gives rise to one of the really valuable properties of fiber composites: they do not fail just on account of one fiber breaking.

For our carbon fibers we use a matrix of either polymer or carbon. It is very difficult to reinforce metals with carbon fibers because if we try to pour molten metal around the fibers there will be a chemical reaction to produce a metal carbide, and the thin carbon fibers are soon lost.

For the matrix we often use an epoxy resin, which sets hard when cured. We can easily coat the fibers with this material and fill the spaces between them, a process called impregnation. This sticks them together to form a solid body. This material is called a **carbon fiber reinforced plastic** (CFRP) and is the type of carbon fiber composite you will find in sporting goods. Carbon fiber manufacturers produce a tape of fibers which are already coated and held together with the uncured epoxy, something called prepreg tape. It is then common to have a form or model of the required finished article made and then wind this tape around it to obtain the required shape. After curing, we now have a solid body of the desired CFRP part. For sporting goods the carbon fibers used do not need to be the strongest available and the product can often be produced without much of a price increase over those made from more conventional materials. Such was not the case fifteen years ago.

Such CFRP composites are not of use at high temperatures because the polymer matrix decomposes and the material ceases to be what it was designed to be. At this point we can probably see how we can form a carbon matrix, because when the polymer matrix decomposes into its constituent elements (hydrogen, oxygen, and possibly nitrogen) it leaves behind the carbon, just as we saw when talking about carbon fiber manufacture. In fact by heating a carbon fiber reinforced plastic we produce a crude **carbon/carbon composite** (carbon fibers in a carbon matrix).

Carbon/carbon composites have the great advantage of not only being able to withstand very high temperatures, they also retain almost all their strength up to temperatures as high as 2500°C. Their one major drawback is that they burn if allowed to come into contact with any oxidizing atmosphere at temperatures above around 500°C.

We mentioned that heating a carbon/epoxy composite would produce a *crude* carbon/carbon composite. This is because the epoxy does not leave behind much carbon, or to use the technical jargon, it does not have a 'high carbon yield'. When we make carbon/carbon composites for practical use we need to find something we can use to fill the space between (impregnate) the fibers which gives a high carbon yield. Sometimes we use a polymeric resin, but the more likely candidate for this purpose is the same type of pitch from which we also make the fibers. This pitch impregnant can give carbon yields greater than 60%.

The principles of manufacture are quite simple, but the process is very time consuming and expensive. The fibers are first arranged in the manner required and hot pitch is forced between them by high pressures. The resulting material is then placed in a furnace and heated very slowly (baked) to release the other elements (oxygen, hydrogen, etc.) in the pitch in their gaseous form. This must be done very slowly so that the escaping gases do not all come out in one big blast and blow the part to pieces.

After baking, the part is placed in a higher temperature furnace (as hot as 3000°C) and heated so that the small graphite layers in the carbon produced by the pitch join up in the same way we mentioned in making the fibers themselves. We now have a strong carbon matrix holding the carbon fibers together.

Unfortunately, the carbon matrix produced contains many pores through which the gases escaped. Only a fraction of the pitch is left behind, and therefore only maybe a half (depending on the carbon yield) of the original space between the fibers has been filled. We now get rid of some of this remaining space, or porosity, by repeating the whole cycle of impregnation, baking, and heating at high temperature. Each time we repeat the cycle we further reduce the porosity of the article we are making by a half, so that after four impregnations we have a sixteenth of the porosity remaining. For some special aerospace applications the cycle is repeated around ten times, each cycle giving diminishing returns.

The whole process of as many as ten impregnations can take a few months and consumes a tremendous amount of energy. It is not cheap to heat materials to 3000°C, let alone do it ten times. The energy costs are tremendous. You can now perhaps see why some of these special carbon/carbon composite materials cost thousands of dollars per pound.

An alternative, and also expensive, way of creating the matrix is to flow a gas such as methane, through the woven fibers at a high temperature. The heat cracks the methane into hydrogen, which escapes, and carbon which is deposited (chemical vapor deposition again) between the fibers.

The photograph below shows a typical carbon/carbon composite. You can see the individual fibers and distinguish them from the carbon matrix. In some cases the matrix has not adhered well to the fibers, while in others there is apparently a good bond between them. This illustrates some of the problems we encounter in making this advanced material.

The composite

While we have now seen something of the processing which goes into the manufacture of one fiber reinforced composite material, we have to still consider the arrangement of the fibers within the article we are making. As mentioned earlier with reference to wood (Page 188), the fibers only give strength in a direction along their length. Engineers perform very complex calculations to see where and in what direction the stresses in a part will be, and then attempt to manufacture the composite part with the fibers arranged in the directions where strength is needed.

Note that this implies that we cannot just make a block of composite and cut off a piece from which to make our part. We can do this with a billet of steel because the material has isotropic properties. The presence of fibers in a composite automatically makes the material anisotropic.

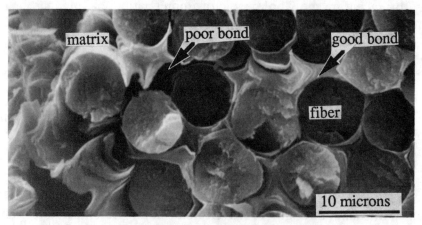

Photograph of a carbon/carbon composite showing fibers and matrix.

If all the fibers are arranged parallel to each other, we only have strength in one direction, just like a piece of wood. To obtain strength in two dimensions we can place layers of fibers in different directions, as we do in a piece of plywood. With fibers there is also the possibility of weaving them into two-dimensional mats for incorporation into the composite. For three dimensional strength there are special machines which weave or braid the fibers into a three dimensional form for impregnation. You can see that there are numerous ways in which the fibers can be arranged, and for some special applications the only way these arrangements can be achieved is by having skilled personnel weave and lay the fibers into the required arrangement by hand. Here again there are tremendous costs involved.

The following diagrams illustrate some of the weave patterns which have been used for fiber composite manufacture. We should note that there is no reason why we cannot use short lengths of chopped fiber to make the composite, but these do not allow us to weave and arrange the fibers in the ways that are possible using continuous lengths.

2D WEAVE   3D WEAVE

Weave patterns for fibers used in carbon/carbon composites.

We have mentioned several times the great cost of some of these materials and you may be wondering how these can be justified. An illustration will help you see why we are sometimes willing to pay thousands of dollars for a pound of lightweight, strong composite. A telecommunications satellite contains electronics for several message-carrying channels. For each channel the weight involved is around 2 - 3 pounds and the channel can be rented for several millions of dollars a year. If you could provide the manufacturer with a new material which would save enough weight in the casing and rocket construction to allow the installation of an extra communication channel, just imagine how much you could charge for this material! Carbon/carbon composites are also used as heat shields for space vehicles on reentry to the earth's atmosphere, being the only material which can really stand up to the extreme conditions encountered during this event. This shield protects hundreds of millions of dollars worth of equipment, so what value can we place on it? The fact is that there are some applications for materials in today's world for we which we are quite willing to pay very large sums of money. Some carbon/carbon composites may cost several thousands of dollars for one pound, but in some applications they are worth it.

Currently carbon/carbon composites are being used for aircraft brakes (originally used in the supersonic Concorde where it is claimed they produce a weight saving of over half a ton), as heat shields for space vehicles, and for rocket nozzles. Some progress has also been made in taking advantage of carbon's biocompatibility (it shows almost no adverse interactions with body tissue) in developing carbon/carbon plates for joining broken bones, and carbon/carbon prostheses for hip joints, etc. We can tailor our composite so that it has almost the same stiffness and density as bone, which is an added advantage over the traditional metal prostheses.

CFRP materials are currently being used in aircraft frames and even for the frames of the seats, where they not only have a weight advantage but can also be made thinner, enabling operators to pack in more passengers. (Not an advantage for us consumers!) It is reported that the A320 Airbus will use CFRP in the fin and tailplane with a weight saving of almost one ton. This translates into a fuel saving of over a quarter of a million gallons per year, assuming the same passenger load.

Why does a composite work?

To understand how composites gives us the advantages that they do we will consider a very simple situation; one where the fibers are all aligned in the same direction as shown in the next figure. If we pull on this material both the fibers and the matrix will stretch by the same amount so long as there is good adhesion between them. Otherwise the fibers will pull out of the matrix. We can therefore say that the strains in the fibers and the matrix are the same.

Now remember that the fiber is normally much stronger and stiffer than the matrix, and stiffness is given by stress/strain (Page 91). If the fiber has a higher stiffness but the same strain as the matrix, this means that it has the higher stress, i.e. the fibers are carrying almost all the load. Because of this high load

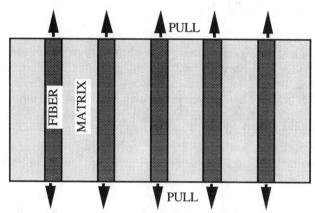

When a composite is stressed the matrix and fibers have equal strains.

on the fibers, some of the cracked fibers will break, but for the whole piece to break the crack has to pass through the matrix, which is usually plastic and almost rubbery compared to the fiber. The matrix therefore does not break, and as a consequence the load which was carried by the broken fiber has to be borne by another part of the composite.

Once a fiber in the matrix is broken any force will now try to pull the fiber from the matrix, and the result is what we call a shearing force (Pages 46 & 86) along the boundary between the broken fiber and the matrix. You can think of it as a type of friction between the fiber and the matrix. As long as the fiber stays in the matrix the load is carried by this frictional force through the matrix and returns to the fiber on the other side of the break. In other words the broken fiber ends are prevented from separating by the adhering matrix; shear forces occur in the matrix and the force gradually returns to be carried by the fiber. At a short distance from the break the fiber is carrying as much load as it did previously.

A good analogy to this shearing force holding the broken fiber in the matrix, is found in trying to remove the stake we put in the ground to support a tree or plant. Moist earth is somewhat plastic like the matrix in a composite. The rigid stake, wood or metal, is like the broken fiber. Trying to pull the stake out of the ground is like trying to pull the fiber from the matrix; it is held tight by the frictional shear forces between it and the soil. You can try a simple experiment to demonstrate this by holding a finger of one hand tightly in the other hand. There is a certain amount of 'give', but you cannot easily pull the finger out unless you relax your grip.

Another contribution to the strength of a composite is the fact that there are individual fibers in the material, and even though they may all break at some point along their length, as discussed above, these breaks will all be at different points along the material's length. If the fiber fractures were all lined up, it would, of course, make it very easy for a crack to pass right through the material and failure would occur, but this is not going to happen where hundreds of thousands of fibers are concerned. This is why fibrous materials, such as wood, are so difficult to break across the grain. Not only do we have to break the fibers, we also have to pull them out of the matrix, which is why we need good adhesion between them and the matrix. In the following photograph of a broken carbon/carbon composite you can see some fibers pulled out of the matrix as well as some broken ends.

Fractured carbon/carbon composite. The black holes are where fibers have been pulled out. The visible fibers have been pulled out of the matrix of the other half, and in some cases you can see small pieces of matrix adhering to them.

Conclusion

Carbon/carbon composite materials have become very important lightweight materials used in aerospace. Unfortunately they are very expensive and burn in air when hot. There is much current research being performed aimed at preventing this oxidation but at present there is no perfect solution. For our everyday purposes the use of carbon fibers in a polymer matrix produces adequate materials, and there are now many examples of their use in sporting goods, racing automobiles and aircraft.

QUESTIONS: Chapters 20-21

1-5.   For some applications such as an internal strut of an airplane wing we are more concerned with the strength and stiffness we get for a pound of material rather than the strength and stiffness themselves. We call the ratio of the strength to the weight, or rather the density, the ___1___. A 10" long rod of material A with a square cross section of 2" x 2" breaks under a tensile load of 8,000 pounds. Its ultimate tensile strength is therefore ___2___. This material has a density of 20 pounds per cubic foot. Material B has an ultimate tensile strength of 5,000 psi and a density of 50 pounds per cubic foot. The material with the higher ___1___ is therefore ___3___. If the rod of material A was 10.5" long when it broke its strain at that time was ___4___. Materials with the highest ___1___ values are usually ___5___.

   1. (a) absolute strength (b) tensile strength (c) specific strength (d) shear strength
      (e) bend strength
   2. (a) 2000 pounds (b) 2,000 psi (c) 800 psi (d) 4000 psi (e) 4000 pounds
   3. (a) A (b) B (c) they are both the same (d) there is not enough information to say
   4. (a) 0.05 (b) 5 (c) 5% (d) both a & c are correct (e) both b & c are correct
   5. (a) elastomers (b) metals (c) composites (d) minerals (e) plastics

6-12.   Composites have always occurred in nature. Wood consists of ___6___ fibers in a lignin ___7___. It breaks easily along the grain (along the direction of the fibers) because the break occurs only in the ___7___. In this case the break is smooth. When broken across the grain, the break is rough. This is because ___8___.

      Composites are very strong because, not only are the fibers strong and difficult to break, they also ___9___. Unfortunately wood has a large UTS (ultimate tensile strength) in only one direction, the grain direction. In order to make a material which is strong in two directions we make plywood. But now the UTS measured along the sheet decreases because ___10___. Man-made composites using carbon fibers are used in sporting goods where they have a polymer ___7___, but for the high temperatures in rocket nozzles a ___11___ ___7___ must be used. In many cases, conventional materials such as steel are stronger but ___12___.

   6. (a) polyethylene (b) carbon (c) lignin (d) cellulose (e) polyester
   7. (a) solution (b) mixture (c) concentration (d) matrix (e) gel
   8. (a) fibers are broken (b) fibers do not all break in the same plane (c) some fibers do
      not break (d) both a and b (e) both b and c
   9. (a) have a high Young's modulus (b) are very elastic (c) have to be pulled out of the
      surrounding material (d) are usually polymers (e) both a and d
  10. (a) the glue between the plies makes it weak (b) only half the fibers give the strength
      (c) fibers are weakened by processing (d) both b & c (e) strength does not decrease
  11. (a) titanium (b) aluminum (c) boron (d) carbon (e) none of these
  12. (a) are less flexible (b) are stiffer (c) are much heavier (d) have no durability

13-22.   The carbon and polymer fibers used in the commonly available composite materials today have a high strength because they have _____13_____. These fibers are held in a matrix which serves to support them. The matrix must _____14_____ and in addition must _____15_____. Carbon/carbon composites are made from carbon fibers which are strong because _____16_____. The fibers are made from pitch by using a _____17_____ process. At room temperature pitch is a brittle solid because it _____18_____, but at higher temperatures it becomes a viscous liquid. The fibers are arranged in the required manner and then the softened pitch is allowed to flow around them to form the matrix. It is also easy to surround the carbon fibers with a(n) _____19_____ matrix. We might like to make this composite using a metal matrix such as by allowing molten aluminum to flow round the fibers, but we cannot because _____20_____. An aluminum matrix would allow us to overcome a major problem with carbon/carbon and carbon/_____19_____ composites, that is that they _____21_____. The major reason why carbon/carbon composites can cost thousands of dollars per pound is the vast amount of _____22_____ used in their manufacture.

13. (a) covalent bonds parallel to the fiber length (b) light atoms
    (c) an ion-implanted surface (d) very small crystals (e) a small cross sectional area
14. (a) not react with the fibers (b) not damage the fibers (c) not be brittle (d) a & b
    (e) all three, a, b & c, are correct.
15. (a) allow the fibers to slide easily in the matrix (b) form a strong bond with the fibers
    (c) keep the atmosphere away from the fibers (d) both a and b (e) both b and c
16. (a) they contain carbon atoms (b) they contain few impurities (c) the graphite planes are aligned perpendicular to the fiber length (d) the graphite planes are aligned parallel to the fiber length (e) carbon is inherently strong.
17. (a) CVD (b) refining (c) quenching (d) spinning (e) rolling
18. (a) has surface cracks (b) is below its glass transition temperature
    (c) contains impurity atoms (d) has large grains (e) is strongly crosslinked
19. (a) ceramic (b) polymer (c) silica (d) nanophase (e) amorphous
20. (a) the aluminum is not strong enough (b) aluminum is difficult to melt
    (c) aluminum has too many dislocations to be very strong (d) molten aluminum reacts with carbon (e) aluminum is expensive
21. (a) are too soft (b) are too expensive (c) are brittle (d) burn or decompose at high temperatures
22. (a) man hours (labor) (b) energy (c) time (d) pitch (e) machining

22. ELECTRONS IN MATERIALS

We have already seen (Page 29) that the electrons in an atom are arranged in shells which fill from the inside out. Before we develop a model for electrons in solid materials we must remind ourselves of the following:

(1) There are $2n^2$ electrons in each shell, where n is the number of the shell. There are therefore 2 electrons in the first shell, 8 in the second shell, 18 in the third, etc.

(2) Atoms link up with bonds to get 8 electrons in the outer shell, (like the inert gases).

The reason the electrons arrange themselves in this way is simply a matter of energy. Whatever electrons and atoms do in a material is often in an attempt to lower their energy as much as they can.

If you take a weight tied to a piece if twine and twirl it around in a circle the weight has energy. If you lengthen the twine and want the weight to make a circuit in the same time you have to give it more energy because it has to move faster. The bigger the radius of the orbit, the more energy the weight will have. The same is true of electrons orbiting a nucleus except that only certain orbits, and hence certain energies are allowed. This is a result of the quantum theory, and is something which is outside our normal experience. Our cars have a certain number of gears, and when we shift from one gear to another we make a different range of speeds available. We can accelerate and decelerate without difficulty within any range. The electron in an orbit around the nucleus of the atom has a fixed speed (energy), and when it shifts to a larger orbit (outer shell) it has a higher speed, but there are no speeds in between. There is a quantum leap from one orbit to the other. We cannot imagine driving a car under such conditions. You would make, for example, a quantum leap from 10 m.p.h. to 25 m.p.h. when changing from first to second gear.

This idea of fixed energies gives rise to the idea of an energy ladder for the electrons moving around the nucleus of an atom. If an electron is to move to an outer shell it needs an increase in energy, just as you need energy to climb one rung on a ladder, or one step on a staircase. In an atom, the difference between the energies of adjacent steps becomes lower the higher up the ladder you go. Eventually the electron gets to the top of the ladder and is now no longer in a fixed orbit around the atom but is free to leave the atom, i.e. the atom is now a cation.

The shell structure we have already mentioned (Page 30) tells us that there are more electrons in a shell as we go away from the nucleus of the atom. We incorporate this into our ladder model by saying that there is more space for electrons on our energy ladder the higher up the ladder we go. The lowest step can accommodate only two electrons, the next one eight electrons, etc. In fact things are a little more complicated than this because each step or level has some little steps within it which we can call sub-steps or sub-levels. A truer picture is therefore the step diagram shown below. The second step has two sub-levels, holding 2 and 6 electrons, the third step has three sub-levels which can hold 2, 6, 10.... electrons, etc. We usually refer to the main levels by the number of the shell, and, for historical reasons, we give the sub-levels the letters s, p, d, and f. This gives rise to the model shown.

The energy 'ladder' for electrons moving around the nucleus of an atom.

There are three important points we must make about this diagram before we continue. First, the height of the step between 1s and 2s is perhaps a thousand times greater than the step between 2s and 2p. In other words the vertical scale is very distorted. We have to do this in order to get the diagram on the page. Second, it is impossible for an electron to have any energy other than those corresponding to the position of a step. Movements between steps are possible, but they involve quantum leaps as far as energy changes are concerned. The electrons do not accelerate or decelerate: their energy changes abruptly. Third, the positions of the steps are different for each atom, with step heights getting larger the higher the atomic number. An electron dropping from 2s to 1s in copper (atomic # 29) will therefore lose more energy than an electron doing the same thing in aluminum (atomic # 13).

You may be wondering how we know about this energy ladder and such things as sub-levels, and the answer is not difficult to understand. We simply look at the energies electrons lose when they fall to a lower level. Before we can discuss this we need some background concerning the units used to measure the energy of an electron.

The electron volt

Perhaps the energy unit you are most familiar with is the **calorie** (the amount of energy needed to increase the temperature of a gram (1 cm^3) of water by 1°C). There are 1,000 of these calories in a food calorie (it should really be called a kilocalorie), which is the calorie unit used on cereal boxes, etc. These units are much too big to be a convenient measure of the energy of an electron. You are well aware than the more massive a moving article, the more energy it has. Better to be hit by a fast tennis ball than by a truck with the same velocity! Because the electron has such a small mass we need a new unit, and the one we chose is called the **electron volt,** denoted by the symbol, **eV.** It is the energy an electron picks up when it moves between a potential (voltage) difference of 1 volt. For example, a regular C cell battery for a flashlight produces a voltage of 1.5 volts. An electron moving from the negative pole to the positive pole of the battery would pick up an energy of 1.5 eV. There are 2.6 x 10^{19} eV in one **calorie,** so one of these food calories is equal to 2.6 x 10^{22} eV.

From this it should be clear that the electron volt is an exceptionally small amount of energy, but that should not surprise us, after all the electron is a very small particle. Even when traveling through a copper wire (electric current) at a fast speed one electron has little energy.

The atomic energy ladder

As already stated, the energy ladder is an illustration of a scientific principle known as the quantization of energy. The electrons can only have certain energies, corresponding to the steps on the ladder. There is no possible energy between the steps. Another consequence of the quantum theory is that if an electron needs 2 eV to reach the next step and we provide it with energy in packets, or quanta, of only 1.5 eV, the electron is never able to make the jump to the next step.

If you throw a ball up a staircase it can land on the stair immediately below its highest point but it cannot reach the next stair until you increase its energy to get it that much higher. There is no intermediate energy level on which it can rest. Then the ball will reduce its energy by falling down the stairs and it will lose energy in discrete amounts. It may drop down two stairs, then three, then one, etc.

If we wish to move an electron to a higher step on its energy ladder, we have to provide it with energy. We can do this using heat, an electrical voltage, light, x-rays, etc. Sometimes we can even do it by hitting a piece of material very hard. The electron will only stay there if there is no lower level to which it can fall. If there is room on a lower level the electron will lower its energy by tumbling down to this level, sometimes stopping briefly at an intermediate level or even by starting a cascade in which several electrons each move down one level rather than one electron moving down two or three levels. The electron usually stays on the higher step for a very short period of time, often too short to be noticed, before falling to its original level.

When it falls back to a lower level the electron loses energy, and the question we have to answer is: how does this energy appear? What state is it in? How do we recognize it? If we drop a clay pot on the floor it loses energy. Where does the energy go? Some will undoubtedly go into breaking bonds in the material (it shatters). Some will be noticed as sound. Another part of the energy causes the floor to vibrate, although probably not enough for us to notice. In other words, the energy is given off in at least three different forms. When an electron falls from one level to another it loses its energy in only one way, the emission of **radiation**, which may be in the form of visible light rays, x-rays, ultraviolet rays, etc. The energies of these radiations correspond to the differences between the energies of the different steps. It is from this emission of radiation that we gather much of our knowledge about the electron energy ladder in atoms. We shall confine our immediate discussion to the emission of visible light, but you should remember that the same principles apply to the production of x-rays, ultraviolet and infrared rays. Indeed these are essentially the same things, the only difference being in their energy. While visible light rays do not harm our eyes, we know that one reason for wearing sunglasses is to protect from ultraviolet light (higher energy), and eyesight can be lost by staring into a beam of x-rays (even higher energy). The three radiations differ only in their energy, higher energies doing more damage.

Light emission from atoms

If you dip a piece of fabric or paper into a salt (NaCl) solution and then place it in the hot flame of a bunsen burner, you will see the flame produce a bright yellow light. The heat of the flame causes the sodium chloride to vaporize to sodium and chlorine atoms, and also has enough energy to cause the outer electrons in the sodium atoms (atomic number 11, 2 + 8 + 1), which sit on the 3s step, to jump to higher steps on their energy ladder. These electrons immediately come tumbling back down to their original step. It turns out that when they pass from the 3p step to the 3s step they lose 2.1 eV in energy, and this is the energy of yellow light. The step model for this process is shown below. Note that light is **emitted** from the sodium **atoms** in the vapor.

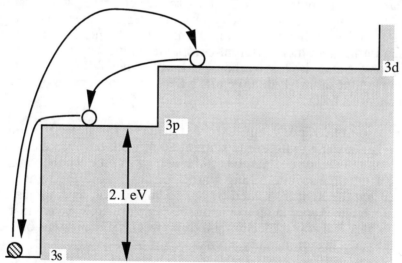

Energy ladder for a sodium atom's outer 3s electron. If it is given an energy quantum large enough to raise it to a higher level it will return to its original level, possibly as shown. The drop from the 3p to the 3s results in an energy loss of 2.1 eV, which is the energy of yellow light.

Before we leave this diagram notice that we have provided the electron on the 3s level with enough energy to go above the 3d level but there is no step there, so it settles on the 3d level and then jumps back to the 3s, usually via the 3p. In other words it behaves like we do, sometimes going up and down stairs two at a time and sometimes one. Notice also that it is the jump between the 3p and 3s levels which produces the yellow light. The jump from the 3d to the 3p level involves a smaller amount of energy and does not produce visible light.

As you know, white light consists of a number of colors, each of which has a different wavelength and a different energy. We call this the visible spectrum. You may have already learned to remember the colors of the rainbow by the abbreviation ROYGBIV (red, orange, yellow, green, blue, indigo, violet). These different colors of the visible light spectrum have different energies:

red..violet

1.7 eV................................3.1 eV

where yellow is around 2.1 eV.

A simple way of testing a substance to find out the different metals it contains is to take a platinum wire, dip it into hydrochloric acid, then into a powder of the material, and then place it in the hot flame of a bunsen burner. The metals react with the hydrochloric acid to produce chlorides which vaporize and emit light in a similar way to that which we have already mentioned for sodium. The outer electrons in the metal atoms are moved to higher levels by the heat of the bunsen burner and then different colors are emitted by the different atoms depending on the energies lost by their electrons as they fall back to their original energy level in the atom. Lithium emits a deep red, calcium an orange-red, and potassium a violet color.

In a sodium vapor lamp, used extensively for street lighting, a high voltage does the same thing to the sodium atoms, but because the sodium is a solid at room temperature it first has to be heated to produce the vapor. That's why these lamps have quite a long warm up time before the light is emitted. Remember that the light is emitted by the sodium vapor, as is indicated by the name. The mercury vapor lamp works on the same principle except that the color is bluish because it involves electron jumps between different steps on a different energy ladder, i.e. that of mercury atoms.

You can now see how we can obtain information about the energy ladder for electrons in atoms. We simply look at the energies of the radiation they emit when their electrons jump down from one step to another.

Unfortunately the model we have developed so far only applies to single atoms. When we put many atoms together to make a solid the electrons interact to form bonds and the situation becomes more complicated, but in some respects it becomes more simple. We must therefore now turn our attention to electrons in solids.

The band energy diagram

If we put N atoms together we obviously need space on the energy ladder for N times the number of electrons. The material does this by creating N times the number of levels on the energy ladder. The complexity involved is obvious when we note that in any piece of solid material we can handle there are at least 10^{22} atoms! How can we manage a model which now needs ten billion trillion times the number of energy levels?

The result is that we now have a model for which we cannot draw the individual steps because there are so many of them. In fact it is like having a ramp of energies. However we must remember that this ramp consists of small discrete steps with only a certain number of electrons allowed on each step. The energy difference between adjacent steps on this ramp is very, very small, being only around 10^{-23} eV (about 10^{-45} food calories). Very small indeed! The model we draw is therefore as shown below.

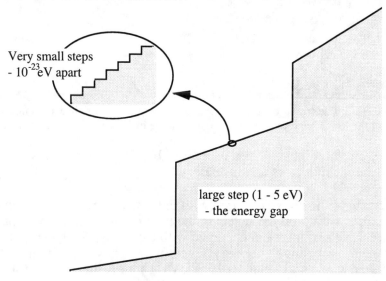

Energy ladder (ramps) for electrons in a solid.

We call these energy ramps **bands** of energy because there exits a range (band) of energies within which the electrons can essentially have any value - differences of 10^{-23} eV are so small as to be negligible. Remember, however, that these bands contain millions of millions of discrete energies which we call energy levels. The large jumps between bands we call **band gaps.**

The diagram we usually draw to represent this model is the view you would have of the above ladder if you looked at it from the front rather than from the side and is called a **band energy diagram**. We draw only the upper two bands: the last one to have any electrons on its levels and the next empty band.

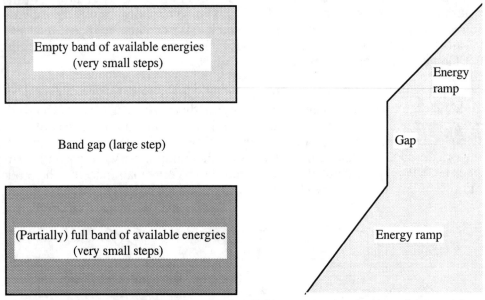

Front (left) and side (right) diagrams of available energies (bands) in a solid material. Note that the lower band may have all or only some of its steps full of electrons.

There are three basic types of energy band diagrams: those for metals (conductors), semiconductors and insulators.

Referring to the above diagram with only two energy bands, **conductors** have no electrons sitting on the levels in the upper band, and a lower band with only the lower levels of the band occupied with electrons. This means that these electrons can move to higher energy levels when they are given very small amounts of energy, even as small as 10^{-23} eV. There is then a gap, followed by another band of available energies.

Semiconductors have a lower band of energies with electrons filling all the steps within the band. There is then a gap (usually less than 2 eV) before the next band. The electrons in semiconductors therefore need at least 1 - 2 eV in order to move to the next available energy step.

Insulators have essentially the same band arrangement as semiconductors but the band gap is much larger. Large energy quanta (usually over 5 eV) are needed to lift an electron to a higher energy level in these materials. We shall soon see that this is very unlikely using electrical voltage, although we can calculate the voltage necessary to do so.

Remember that the electrons in these materials need energy quanta equal to, or greater than, the energies mentioned in order to change what they are doing. This includes moving to produce an electrical current. The three different possibilities are illustrated in the following diagrams.

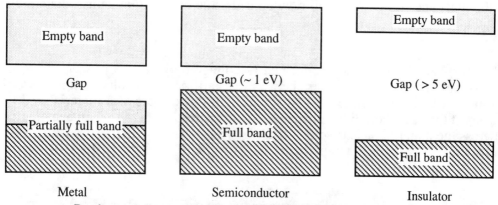

Band energy diagrams for three major classes of electrical materials.

Notice that materials do not oblige us by having gaps which are either small (~ 1 eV) or large (> 5 eV). There is a wide range of all possible band gap energies in all the materials at our disposal. Our division at 2 eV is purely arbitrary.

In silicon, the most common semiconductor, the band gap energy is 1.1 eV, in germanium 0.7 eV, and in diamond it is nearly 6 eV. These all have the same atom arrangement (crystal structure). Diamond is an insulator; silicon and germanium are semiconductors.

What energy quanta are we concerned with?

We must now consider what these different band energy diagrams mean in terms of what we can and cannot do with electrons in solids. Once again we go to that branch of physics called quantum theory. It is somewhat frightening to undergraduate physics majors because of its mathematical complexity. However the results we need are really simple and quite understandable. As mentioned earlier, energy comes in packets called quanta. For example, red light comes in quanta of 1.7 eV. If a material has all the levels in the lower energy band filled and there is a band gap of 2 eV, we can shine red light on the material all day and an electron will never be able to jump the gap up to the next step on the energy ladder. The electron cannot increase its energy at all and no electricity can flow. The energy packets are discrete and are absorbed singly. They do not add together.

The major types of energy we shall be concerned with are electrical, heat (thermal) and light. We shall now consider the energy quanta associated with them.

Electrical Energy. Here the quantity which determines the energy is the **"voltage gradient"** which is defined as voltage divided by distance. In terms of energy quanta, a voltage gradient of one million (10^6) volts per cm is worth about 2 eV. For example, if we have a 5 cm thick sheet of a material and we connect the household line voltage (120 volts) across it, there is a voltage gradient across the material of 120 volts/5 cm = 24 volts per cm. In this case the energy quantum is (by taking a simple ratio) around $(24/10^6) \times 2$ eV $= 4.8 \times 10^{-5}$ eV.

Illustration of a voltage gradient of 24 volts per cm across a material.

If the band gap energy of a material is 2.5 eV, and a voltage of a million volts were placed across an 8 mm thick piece of this material, the voltage gradient would be 1.25 million volts per cm. Since we get around 2 eV per million volts per cm, a voltage gradient of 1.25 million volts per cm would give an energy quantum of 2 x 1.25 = 2.5 eV, just enough to shift electrons across the gap. The material will therefore now conduct electricity. This phenomenon is known as **breakdown**. All insulators will breakdown, i.e. lose their insulating property, if enough voltage is placed across them.

Thermal Energy. This form of energy is unusual in that at any temperature (except absolute zero) there is a range of energy quanta available so that we cannot give an exact value. At a temperature T in Kelvin (°Celsius + 273) the **average** energy quantum is T x 0.86 x 10^{-4} eV. Therefore, at room temperature (~300K) the average thermal energy quantum is 300 x 0.86 x 10^{-4} = 0.026 eV. At 2000°C the mean thermal energy quantum is about 0.2 eV. However, one must remember that there are some quanta which are much larger than this. This is quite different from light quanta where each color has a fixed energy.

Light Energy. We have already seen that visible light has energy quanta (called **photons**) with energies from 1.7 to 3.1 eV. Ultraviolet light has energy packets of higher energy and infrared light has lower energy. X-rays are physically identical to light waves but they have much higher energies and are not seen by the human eye.

It is worthwhile considering the above statements in light of our everyday experience. We have already seen that very large voltage gradients are needed to increase the energy of (move) electrons in a material with a band gap of 2.5 eV. To accomplish this with heat we have seen that at 2000°C the *average* quantum is 0.2 eV, but there will be a few quanta as large as 2.5 eV, meaning that there will be a few electrons which can increase their energy. However, by just shining blue light (2.7 eV) on the material there will be plenty of energy quanta large enough to enable many electrons to increase their energy. If we were asked to rank the energies of these three phenomena we would almost certainly place them in reverse order. We are more afraid of electricity than heat and light. The reason for this is that we are large bodies and the quantum theory does not apply to us as it does to small electrons. We respond to the total energy rather than to the size of the individual energy quanta.

Electrical conduction

We can now better understand the band energy diagrams for the three different materials. Electrical conduction is the movement of electrons under the influence of a voltage. In a metal the electrons are free and are moving about all over the place, with just as many going in any direction as in the opposite direction, so that there is no net electron flow. In order to produce a net flow, which we call current, we have to increase the speed, and hence the energy, of some of the electrons. If we apply a voltage of 120 volts across a 25 meter (2500 cm) length of copper wire, a situation which may be typical of an average house, the voltage gradient is

$$\frac{120 \text{ volts}}{2500 \text{ cm}} = 0.048 \text{ volts/cm}$$

which gives an energy quantum of around 10^{-7} eV. However, this is more than enough to lift the electron to higher levels within the band of energies, (remember the levels in the band are about 10^{-23} eV apart) and hence the electrons can accept the energy, increase their velocity and thus produce an electric current, i.e. the material conducts. Remember that it is only the electrons in unfilled bands which can accept such small energy quanta and hence produce an electric current.

In a regular flashlight we may only use a 1.5 volt cell and the wire may be around 10 cm long. This gives a voltage gradient of 0.15 volts/cm which is even larger than we calculated for household wiring.

For both insulators and semiconductors there are no energy levels for the electrons to go to except for those across the gap. Normal voltage gradients are not enough to provide this energy (1 - 2 eV) so the electrons cannot go to higher energy levels, cannot increase their velocity, and therefore no current is produced. The materials are therefore not good conductors. In order to conduct electricity the electrons have to first be moved to a higher band which contains no electrons. Once they are in this now partially filled band they can accept the small energy quanta provided by the voltage and produce the net electron flow which we call an electric current. Shining visible light (1.7 - 3.1 eV) on silicon (gap energy 1.1 eV) moves many electrons over the gap. These can now further increase their energy using the small quanta provided by a battery and an electric current will be produced.

Another way of looking at the energy gap is to think of it as the energy required to make an electron free. In metals they are already free; in other materials they need a certain amount of energy (an energy quantum) to strip them from the covalent or ionic bonding state in which they exist. For example, electrons in diamond are held very tightly in strong covalent bonds. Silicon has the same crystal structure and is also covalently bonded but the bonds are not as strong. It is therefore easier to strip electrons from the bonds in silicon than it is in diamond. This corresponds to a smaller energy gap in silicon (1.1 eV) than in diamond (~6 eV). Once the electrons have crossed the energy gap in a semiconductor or insulator, they are free to conduct electricity. Any small electrical voltage is enough to increase their energy by the 10^{-23} eV necessary to go to the next level.

We now have a simple picture of the electrons and their energies in solid materials. This will enable us to understand a wide variety of phenomena. In closing this section we may note that any solid can be made to conduct electricity if the electrons are given enough energy to cross the energy gap. This energy can come from any of the sources we have mentioned. In fact any material will conduct electricity if heated to a high enough temperature (assuming it doesn't melt or decompose first), or is exposed to high energy x-rays, or even has light shined on it, so long as the light quanta have an energy greater than the band gap energy. These external influences lift the electrons over the gap and then the voltage can give them energy to go to higher levels in their new band. They are therefore able to take on the electrical energy, i.e. conduct the electricity.

23. ELECTRON INTERACTIONS WITH LIGHT
or
SOME CAUSES OF COLOR

In our discussion of the energy band diagrams we mentioned that the energy gaps between bands are usually a few electron volts. We also know that visible light quanta have energies of a few electron volts, in the range 1.7 to 3.1 eV. Ultraviolet light has larger energies and infrared light has smaller energies. The fact that these energies are about the same as the band gap energies gives rise to some very interesting phenomena which are of great importance to us in our everyday lives. Without them we would not have fluorescent lights, television tubes, and some of the valuable colored gems we use in jewelry.

Before we start to explore some of these phenomena we should mention that there are many different reasons for the coloration of materials. We shall only explore one or two of these. Most materials are colored by very complex mechanisms which are difficult to understand at this level. For example most dyes used in clothing are organic with very complicated molecules giving rise to the color. We shall only consider the color of opaque metals and some transparent gemstones and shall conclude by considering colors emitted from fluorescent lamps and TV screens.

What produces the color? The natural sunlight is what we often call 'white' light. It contains all the colors of the rainbow (ROYGBIV); indeed the rainbow is simply caused by raindrops splitting the sunlight into its component colors. When this light hits a material it is either transmitted (passes through) or is reflected. During these two processes some of the spectral colors may be selectively absorbed or scattered by the material, so that the light which is either transmitted or reflected to our eyes is missing these colors. Instead of being white, it has a color which depends on the colors lost. We have already mentioned an example of this in discussing Visions Ware® (Page 180). Because we shall be talking about energy band diagrams we shall usually refer to the energies of the light quanta. Remember that each color has its own energy.

In the following discussion we must be careful to distinguish light which we see after it has passed through a material (**transmitted** light), as is the case with many gemstones, and light which is **emitted** by the material. Reflection is, as we shall see, really a part of this latter category. We shall be careful to point out which of these two is happening to produce the color.

One problem which arises in discussing color is that of understanding how colors mix, and what happens if some colors are missing. Many people think of mixing paint. You go to the store, select your color from a chart of a thousand shades, and watch the assistant mix the color. Unfortunately thinking in terms of paint can lead us to some wrong conclusions. You can probably well appreciate that if you were to mix cans of red, orange, yellow, green, blue, indigo and violet paint, you would not end up with white. The result would be something awful. Yet this mixture of light produces white light.

A good way to look at the problem is to realize that this mixture of light colors does produce white. Let's take a specific example, using the letters ROYGBIV to denote the colors of the rainbow. If something happens to block out every color reaching our eyes except the red, we see only red. It's simple. Now imagine that your eyes see ROY, the result will be an orange color. Up to this point it seems that the mixing of paint would give a similar answer. Now add green. How does the color change? Our paint mix would start to become rather muddy, whereas our light must be getting closer to white. The progression as we add the remaining spectral colors to our light beam will be R → RO → ROY → ROYG → ROYGB → ROYGBI → ROYGBIV, which means going from red → reddish orange → orange → yellowish orange → yellow → pale yellow → white. Starting at the other end of the spectrum with only violet and then adding indigo and blue, etc. the colors must progressively change from violet to white. A consequence of this is that if just the yellow is missing we see a pale blue, whereas if just the violet is missing we see a pale yellow. The following discussion will be much simpler if you can appreciate what we have just said.

The color of metals

We have already seen that light quanta have energies of 1.7 eV (red) to 3.1 eV (violet). In metals there are electrons in an unfilled band which can often take on all these energies by jumping to higher levels in the band, and they do so. The light is therefore unable to get through without being absorbed by the electrons and the metal is opaque. The electrons go to steps higher in the band but stay there for a very short time. They tumble back down the steps giving out, or emitting, light and this is what gives metals their characteristic luster. We talk of the light being **reflected** but what is happening is that the light energy is being absorbed and then re-emitted. The light does not really reflect as a ball bounces off a wall. A better analog is a baseball being caught by a fielder who immediately throws it to second base in an attempt to get the double-play. The ball is released almost as soon as it is caught. The same is true of electrons in metals and light. The electrons absorb (catch) the light and almost immediately (so quickly that we don't even notice the delay) re-emit it. What is absorbed is emitted, as the electrons are for ever increasing and decreasing their energy.

In all the following diagrams we shall denote quantum jumps which occur with arrows, while those which cannot occur do not have arrows.

In a large number of metals there is at least a 3.1 eV space at the top of the band of electron energies. As a result all the light energy quanta (all colors) are absorbed by the electrons and re-emitted equally, with the consequence that the **'reflected'** light is white. The metals therefore appear silvery. Aluminum, titanium, chromium, iron, silver and nickel are all like this. In other metals there is not as much space at the top of the energy band for the electrons to move to, so that while the red light may be easily absorbed, the blue light passes further into the material and gets lost by other processes outside the scope of this discussion. As a consequence the absorbed light which is **re-emitted** is mostly in the red, orange and yellow part of the spectrum. This is true of copper and gold.

This process of absorption and remission takes place in a very thin layer at the surface of the metal. It is very difficult to make metal foils thin enough to see

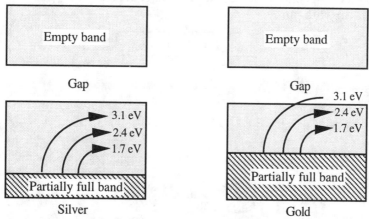

Absorption and re-emission of light in silver and gold. In silver there is enough space in the band of energies for all light energies to be absorbed. When the electrons fall back they therefore emit all colors and the metal is white (silvery). In gold the higher light energies cannot be absorbed. Only the red and yellow end of the spectrum is absorbed and re-emitted and the metal is yellow (gold) colored.

through because the light absorption by the electrons in the material is very, very efficient. One metal which can be made this thin is gold. When beaten to form the gold leaf used for decoration it is very, very thin (1000Å, or one ten thousandth of a millimeter) and you can see through it if you hold it against a strong light. If you ever have a chance to do the experiment you will see that the light coming through is bluish green. Why this color change? The answer is simple. The yellow light you usually see from gold is 'reflected'. The other colors of the spectrum pass deeper into the metal and, if it is thin enough, they can escape from the other side. We therefore have the two complementary colors, yellow and bluish green; together they would approximately make white light. (Complementary colors are those which together would make white light.) What comes through (bluish green) is what is not absorbed, and what is absorbed (yellow) is re-emitted.

The color of pure insulators

A good insulator has a band gap energy of at least 5 eV which is greater than the energies of all visible light quanta. The electrons fill the energy band in the material and cannot take on any energy unless it is enough to cause the electrons to cross the gap. They therefore cannot absorb any of the light quanta so they pass through without any interruption. Because of this, the material is colorless and transparent. The light simply passes through without any absorption because the electrons cannot accept any of its energies. Most good insulators are transparent if they are pure.

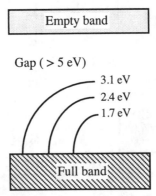

Visible light is unable to move electrons in a good insulator and is transmitted with no absorption. The material is colorless and transparent.

We must emphasize this matter of purity because, as we have seen, impurities are common in most materials, and it is these impurity atoms which are usually responsible for the color and opacity of the material.

The color of semiconductors

You should now be able to see that a piece of silicon, which has a band gap energy of only 1.1 eV, will behave like most metals. All visible light energies (1.7 - 3.1 eV) can be used to make electrons jump across the energy gap. When they tumble back down the energy ladder they emit light of all energies and as a consequence a bare piece of silicon has a metallic luster and looks very much like a metal. The color is **re-emitted** (reflected).

There are also some materials which have band gap energies between 1.7 and 3.1 eV. Let us consider the case of a cadmium sulfide, a material with a band gap of 2.6 eV. Light with energies less than this (red, orange, yellow, green and some blue) will pass straight through because they can do nothing to the electrons in the material. Light with energies greater than 2.6 eV (mostly violet) will be absorbed, or used by the electrons to reach levels in the next band. We therefore see the materials as an orange-yellow because this is the combined color of the light which passes through. In this case the color is **transmitted**.

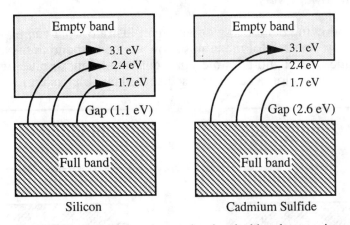

In silicon (left) all light energies can be absorbed by electrons just as they are in a silvery metal. Silicon therefore has a silvery luster and is opaque. In cadmium sulfide (right) only the blue/violet can be absorbed by the electrons and the red/yellow part of the spectrum is transmitted. The material is therefore a yellow-orange color.

This mechanism of producing color is very limited. If you think about it, it must always be the low energies which are passed through uninterrupted (not enough energy to push the electrons across the gap) while it is the high energies which are absorbed. With this process there is no way to produce a blue material because it is always the high energy light (blue) which is absorbed and the low energy light (red and yellow) which is allowed through to produce the color. Remember that the color we see in such cases is **transmitted**. We shall see that to make things blue we need impurities.

Insulators colored by impurities - gemstones

When we add impurities (point defects) to a material they add some steps of their own to the energy ladder, and these steps lie inside the gap. This has the effect of making it easier for electrons to cross the gap. For our purposes, we can divide impurities into two types, those that have more electrons than the atom they replace and those that have fewer. Those that have more are called **donor** impurities because they donate an extra electron or two to the system. Those that have fewer electrons are called **acceptor** impurities because they have room to accept electrons from neighboring atoms. Both types of impurity create extra steps in the gap in the energy ladder. With donor impurities the extra electrons sit on these steps; with acceptor impurities these new levels are empty and can accept electrons from lower levels.

The following band energy diagrams illustrate what can happen in these solids. It is now possible for the jumps shown to correspond to the absorption of red light, while there is no possible jump corresponding to blue light. We can therefore get a blue color because red is absorbed and blue is **transmitted**.

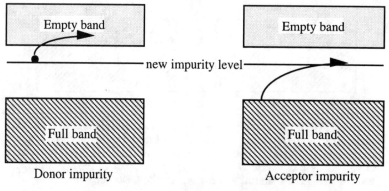

Illustration of new possible absorptions as a result of impurities.

These two types of impurity allow some different jumps to occur, such as those shown in the previous diagram. Some energies can therefore be absorbed which could not be absorbed previously. If these new absorptions are in the range of visible light energies, some color of the light spectrum which was previously transmitted is now lost to absorption in the material. Thus a previously transparent colorless material becomes a transparent colored material.

There are two examples of this with which you are probably familiar. In powder form pure aluminum oxide is white and is used as a fine, abrasive polishing material because of its hardness. A single crystal is colorless and transparent with no particular interest. If we add small amounts of titanium the material becomes a blue sapphire, while small amounts of chromium turn it into a red ruby. In both cases some light is absorbed by electrons using the new levels as steps in the energy ladder. With titanium, red is absorbed and the blue passes through while with chromium the reverse is true.

We already mentioned (Page 15) that adding boron (an acceptor impurity because it has one fewer electron than carbon) to diamond turns the diamond blue, while adding nitrogen (a donor impurity because it has one more electron than carbon) turns it yellow. These colors are also produced by the above mechanism. The following diagrams illustrate what happens.

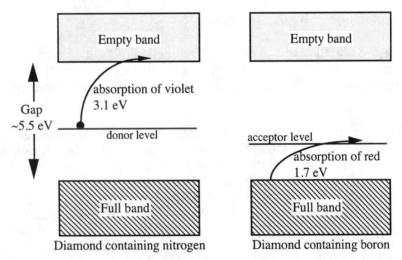

Nitrogen with one more electron than carbon is a donor impurity in diamond. Its extra electron can be freed with blue light, so some blue is absorbed and the diamond transmits a yellow color. Boron has one fewer electron than carbon. A carbon electron can be moved to the impurity level using red light so some blue is absorbed and the diamond transmits a blue color.

The presence of a little nitrogen turns the diamond yellow. A nitrogen atom has one more electron than a carbon atom and this electron sits on the impurity level. An energy quantum of around 3.1 eV is needed to move this electron so some of the blue end of the spectrum is absorbed. The light passing through the diamond is therefore missing some of the blue end of the spectrum and appears yellow. A little boron, which has one fewer electron than carbon, provides an energy step to which one of the carbon's electrons can jump using a quantum of only 1.7 eV (red). Some red light is therefore absorbed and the transmitted light is bluish. In both cases the color is due to **transmitted** light.

The amount of impurity needed to produce these colors is quite small. Replacing one carbon atom in 100,000 with a nitrogen atom produces a yellow diamond, while replacing one in 1,000,000 (a million) with a boron atom produces an attractive blue color. Natural blue diamonds are rare and therefore quite expensive. The Hope diamond at the Smithsonian Institution in Washington D.C. is perhaps the best known example.

Diamond can also be found with different colors. In some cases we have no idea what causes this coloration. For example, there are some very pretty, and valuable, pink diamonds whose color is not understood.

Fluorescence and phosphorescence

There is one further aspect of this interaction of light with materials which we use on a daily basis. It is concerned with the phenomena of **fluorescence** and **phosphorescence**, which together are known as **luminescence**. In both these light is **emitted** from a material.

We have already seen how impurities in insulators introduce extra energy levels in the gap. There is another way we can use these levels. Ultraviolet (UV) light has greater energies than those of visible light (i.e. greater than 3.1 eV) and these energies can be greater than the band gap energy. If we shine UV light on an insulator containing impurities, the UV can lift electrons over the gap to the next band. Once again the electrons don't stay there but tumble back down to the band where they came from. But just as a ball thrown up a staircase will bounce down from step to step, the electron returns to its original level via the impurity level(s). In this way the large quantum of UV light is released in smaller quanta, and one or more of these could be visible light in the range 1.7 - 3.1 eV. The material can therefore **emit** visible light. Because the impurities activate this phenomenon of luminescence, they are called **activators**.

The following diagram illustrates how this happens. The material shown has a band gap of around 4.5 eV so an ultraviolet photon of greater energy can move an electron and is absorbed. The electron returns to its original energy by jumping from one impurity step to another. The diagram shows two impurity levels with an energy difference of 2.1 eV between them. When an electron moves between these two levels a photon of 2.1 eV (yellow light) is **emitted**.

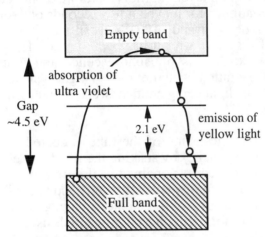

Band energy diagram for an insulator showing how UV light can be absorbed and yellow light emitted.

You can see an excellent display of this phenomenon (luminescence) in most mineral museums. The dull gray rocks are transformed into a wide variety of brilliant colors when illuminated with ultraviolet light.

With **fluorescence** the emitted light only occurs while the UV light is being shined on the material. This is because the electrons are moving up and down the energy ladder so rapidly that we cannot notice any time delay.

You have all heard of, and used, fluorescent lights. They are a relatively new invention, having been invented in the 1930's and brought into more general use in the 1940's. These are tubes which contain mercury and are coated inside with some materials which fluoresce, such as cadmium phosphates, zinc silicate, and magnesium tungstate, the color depending on the impurity used as the activator. The electricity acts on the mercury vapor in the tube, just as in a mercury vapor lamp, causing it to emit the yellow/green light we usually associate with mercury vapor lamps, but it also emits quite a lot of ultraviolet light. This UV light is absorbed by the coating inside the tube which in turn then emits light.

We can have white tubes, pink tubes, special grow-light tubes for plants etc., the colors emitted depending on the impurities in the fluorescent materials coating the inside of the tube.

Phosphorescence occurs when these extra impurity levels are what we can describe as 'sticky'. The electrons stay on an impurity level and take their time returning to the original level. Light is therefore emitted over a much longer period of time and continues for maybe a few seconds or even minutes after the UV light source has been turned off. You can sometimes notice this as an afterglow on your TV screen after it has been turned off, if the room is dark. This phenomenon is known as phosphorescence and is characterized by a noticeable decay of the emitted light after the UV light is switched off. With some minerals you can still see light being emitted twenty minutes after the UV light has been turned off.

In color TV sets the inside of the tube is coated with phosphorescent materials which are given energy by striking them with an electron beam. They then emit light of the colors corresponding to a differences in the energy levels in their energy ladder. Look carefully at a TV picture and you will see that it is made up of small dots or short stripes, of three colors, blue, green and red. Each color corresponds to the dots of different phosphor materials used to coat the screen.

Color TV pictures are better today than they were 30 years ago because of new phosphorescent materials we have discovered. For example, element number 63 in the period table is europium (Eu) which is used as the activator (impurity) in yttrium vanadate (YVO_3) to give brilliant reds. Perhaps this is the only place you will ever come across Europium in your life. It is a rare element, but it has a place in our everyday lives. For the blue we often use zinc sulfide with a silver activator, and for the green, zinc silicate with a manganese activator.

The choice of a phosphorescent material for a color TV tube is quite complicated because, not only does the correct color have to be emitted, it also has to be emitted for the proper length of time. In the USA the TV picture is produced by an electron beam which scans 525 horizontal lines on a screen at a rate of sixty times per second. A new picture is therefore formed every 0.017 seconds. We want the emission to last long enough to bridge the time gap between successive pictures, while not lasting so long that we can faintly see the previous picture when a new one has formed. Getting a phosphor with the correct color and the correct decay time has been the subject of extensive research which has produced better color TV sets.

QUESTIONS: Chapters 22-23

1. Which of the following forms of energy cause fluoresence?
   (a) red light (b) blue light (c) violet light (d) infrared radiation (e) ultraviolet radiation

2. Fluorescence can occur in which of the following materials?
   (a) semiconductors (b) conductors (c) pure insulators (d) insulators with impurities
   (e) fluorescence can occur in all of these materials

3. A yellow diamond gets its color because _____.
   (a) blue light is absorbed (b) yellow light is absorbed (c) yellow light is reflected
   (d) yellow light is emitted (e) none of these

4. The phenomenon when light emission occurs after UV light is removed from a material is called _____.
   (a) phosphorescence (b) fluorescence (c) activation (d) luminescence (e) none of these

5. A very thin sheet of gold transmits _____ light.
   (a) red (b) yellow (c) white (d) orange (e) blue-green

6. The acronym used for remembering the colors in white light is _____.
   (a) ROYBGIV (b) VIBYGOR (c) VIGBYOR (d) BIVGYOR (e) none of these

7. Pure materials with a band gap greater than 5 eV are _____.
   (a) black (b) white (c) violet (d) colorless (e) pink

8. An acceptor level in a diamond exists such that yellow light is absorbed. What color is the diamond ?
   (a) blue (b) black (c) colorless (d) red (e) yellow

9. The energy quanta for visible light are called _____.
   (a) phonons (b) radiation (c) rads (d) electron volts (e) photons

10. The energy of yellow light is _____ eV.
    (a) 1.7 (b) 3.1 (c) 2.4 (d) 2.1 (e) 2.7

11. The highest average energy quantum is found in _____.
    (a) visible light (b) heat at room temperature (c) electrical energy (d) infrared light
    (e) ultraviolet light

12. Materials with a band gap energy less than 1.5 eV are _____.
    (a) red (b) lustrous (c) opaque (d) both a and c (e) both b and c

13-21.   When sodium chloride is heated in a flame it vaporizes and the electrons in the sodium atom are given energy. The outermost electron is lifted up from the 3s step and on its return from the 3p step it loses 2.1eV. As a result ___13___ light is ___14___. A diamond can also be given a slight ___13___ color by adding nitrogen. The nitrogen is a/an ___15___ impurity, and its extra electron can be freed by a quantum of ___16___ light. As a result the ___16___ light is ___17___ and the diamond is ___13___.
A material which gives out light for a few minutes after being exposed to ___18___ is called a/an ___19___ material. This phenomenon is caused by impurities in the material which are called ___20___, and is used in TV picture tubes. The color which is ___14___ depends on ___21___.

13. (a) red (b) yellow (c) fluorescent (d) blue (e) orange
14. (a) transmitted (b) absorbed (c) emitted (d) reflected (e) removed
15. (a) acceptor (b) donor (c) activator (d) substitutional (e) both b and d
16. (a) red (b) yellow (c) green (d) violet (e) orange
17. (a) transmitted (b) absorbed (c) emitted (d) reflected (e) amplified
18. (a) red light (b) ultraviolet light (c) infrared light (d) heat
19. (a) fluorescent (b) incandescent (c) evanescent (d) phosphorescent (e) photonescent
20. (a) activators (b) relaxors (c) modifiers (d) intensifiers (e) acceptors
21. (a) the type of impurity (b) the energy band gap of the material
    (c) the maker of the TV (d) both a and b (e) both a and c

22-32.   A diamond is solid ___22___. Because it is a solid there are now bands of possible energy for the electrons. Between the top two bands there is a large energy step of around ___23___, which is greater than the energy of any color of visible light. As a result no electrons can use visible ___24___ to jump to the next band and the diamond is ___25___, there is no ___26___ of light. In some diamonds boron atoms are present as ___27___ impurities. These boron atoms have one less electron than the ___22___ atom and are therefore ___28___ atoms which produce an extra energy level called a ___28___ level. An electron from the full band can jump to this level using the energy of ___29___ light which is around ___30___ eV . As a result the ___29___ light is absorbed and the diamond appears ___31___ . This ___31___ color is the color of the ___32___ light.

22. (a) boron (b) silicon (c) silicon oxide (d) carbon (e) silicon carbide
23. (a) 6 eV (b) 1000 eV (c) 100 eV (d) 0.02 eV (e) 10 eV
24. (a) photons (b) phonons (c) protons (d) positrons (e) photorons
25. (a) transparent (b) lustrous (c) colorless (d) both a and b (e) a and c
26. (a) absorption (b) transmission (c) reflection (d) refraction (e) emission
27. (a) extrinsic (b) interstitial (c) substitutional (d) both a and d (e) both a and c
28. (a) colorator (b) acceptor (c) receptor (d) activator (e) donor
29. (a) red (b) yellow (c) blue (d) green (e) orange
30. (a) 3 (b) 1.7 (c) 2.1 (d) 2.7 (e) 5.4
31. (a) yellow (b) orange (c) blue (d) pink (e) colorless
32. (a) absorbed (b) transmitted (c) reflected (d) refracted (e) emitted

24. ELECTRONS IN SEMICONDUCTORS

Background

The ability of a material to conduct electricity, which is measured by the quantity known as the electrical conductivity, is perhaps the most variable property that materials have. On the low end we have materials which can insulate from very high voltage gradients, letting no electrons through, and at the high end we have superconductors, materials in which electrons will keep on traveling for ever. We have already briefly discussed (Page 216) the reasons why materials exhibit quite different electrical conductivities. In this section we shall discuss some of the unique properties of silicon and see how it can be used to make some very simple electronic components.

As we saw earlier, metals are conductors because their electrons can take on the energies offered by even as small a voltage source as a 1.5 volt battery. There are energies on the energy ladder to which they can go when they absorb this energy. As a result of this increased energy they can set up a net flow of electrons in the material so that an electrical current flows. We usually refer to them as free electrons. In semiconductors there are no such available energies and something else is needed to lift the electrons up the large step we know as the energy gap between bands.

In the previous chapter we saw that light energies are large enough to do this in many materials, especially in semiconductors, where such events cause the material to have a luster and look somewhat metallic (Page 227). Because of this you never see a bare piece of silicon in your calculator or radio if you open it up. It is encapsulated in something which not only protects it, but also keeps the light out. The silicon 'chips' in the electronics have had their conductivity tailored for the purpose they are to be used for, and letting light in will simply turn all these components into good conductors. We would then have short circuits all over the place!

We also know that heat produces an average energy quantum of 0.026 eV (in future we shall round it up to 0.03 eV) at room temperature (Page 219). There are some quanta which are larger than this value, and at any temperature there may be some of these thermal energy quanta which are also large enough to lift electrons across the energy gap. This will be especially true if we increase the temperature to several hundred degrees Celsius.

In a good insulator light does not have enough energy to lift the electrons over the energy gap, and it therefore remains an insulator when exposed to light and is colorless and transparent. However there are other sources of energy quanta which are certainly large enough to make electrons jump across the gap. Ultra violet light may have enough energy, and x-rays will certainly produce the required jump. As mentioned earlier (Page 221), we can make any material conduct electricity if we expose it to x-rays, or heat it to a high enough temperature.

Tailoring the properties of silicon

The silicon we use in our semiconductors is usually not pure, but it contains specific impurities in well determined quantities. First of all we make ultrapure silicon (Page 78) after which we add impurities in carefully measured and controlled amounts. We have seen in our discussion of color (Page 228) that impurities add new energy steps in the gap between the energy bands, and therefore, in order to be able to control things, we want to start with a pure material which will have none of these extra energy steps, and then add a chosen dopant (impurity) to produce a step where we want it.

Let's start by assuming that we are going to add an impurity which has one more electron than silicon. This impurity is what we call a **donor** impurity. It replaces (substitutional impurity) a silicon atom in the crystal structure and has one more electron than is necessary to form covalent bonds with the surrounding four silicon atoms. If we can find such an impurity which gives a new donor energy level close to the empty energy band, a thermal energy quantum may be able to give the extra electron sufficient energy to jump into the empty band. We now have a conducting free electron.

Every impurity atom we add contributes only one free electron, so the larger the amount of impurity the greater the number of free electrons and the greater the conductivity. In this way we can control the conductivity of the material. At room temperature we would need a donor level about 0.03 eV below the empty band, as shown in the following energy band diagram.

Similarly, we may add an atom (**acceptor** impurity) which has one fewer electron than the silicon and provides an acceptor level about 0.03 eV above the full energy band, as shown in the following diagram. An electron from the full band can then jump to this new level using the thermal energy quantum, leaving a space in the previously full band. Electrons in this band can now move around using this space, much in the same way that atoms can move around in crystals using atom vacancies. We call this space an **electron hole**. We shall discuss the electron hole in more detail later.

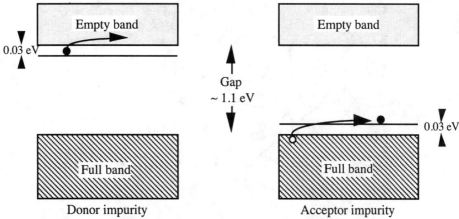

Diagrams showing the impurity energy levels needed in silicon in order that average thermal energy quanta at room temperature can move electrons.

The impurities which produce the energy levels we desire must have electrons whose energies are very similar to those of the electrons in silicon. It makes good sense that these should be the elements which are adjacent to silicon in the periodic table (Page 7). Let's look at it. Here is the section of the table of the elements which is relevant.

B	C	N
Al	Si	P
Ga	Ge	As
3 outer electrons	4 outer electrons	5 outer electrons

It turns out that boron, aluminum and gallium all give acceptor impurity levels about 0.05 eV above the full energy band, and nitrogen, phosphorus and arsenic all give donor impurity levels about 0.04 eV below the empty energy band. In other words just about what we were looking for.

n- and p-type silicon

If we add phosphorus to silicon, we are adding an element which is almost the same size and just has one extra electron. It sits in the silicon lattice as shown in the following diagram.

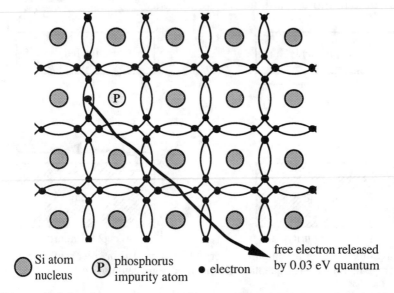

Si atom nucleus   phosphorus impurity atom   • electron   free electron released by 0.03 eV quantum

Diagram of the electron structure of n-type silicon. It takes only 0.03 eV to release the extra electron from the phosphorus atom. It is then a free electron.

Note that this is a simple two-dimensional representation of the three-dimensional crystal structure of silicon. In the diagram, the four surrounding silicon atoms are shown in a plane whereas in reality they are situated on the corners of a tetrahedron. Four of the five outer electrons of the phosphorus are used to form covalent bonds just as the silicon atom would. The extra (fifth) electron hangs around the phosphorus atom because this atom has a larger positive charge on its nucleus than does a silicon atom and therefore has a slightly larger attraction for this extra electron. (Remember that the individual atom is neutral because the number of positive charges on the nucleus is equal to the number of negatively charged electrons which orbit around it.) However a thermal energy quantum gives this electron enough energy to pull itself away from the attraction of the phosphorus and become a free electron. This is the true physical picture of what is happening inside the material. From the energy ladder, or band energy diagram we have used, which is simply a model for the possible energies of the electrons in the material, the thermal energy quantum is enough to lift the electron up to the empty energy band. The impurity atom has **donated** this extra electron to the crystal.

If we put an aluminum atom in place of a silicon atom we have one electron too few to complete the covalent bonds with the surrounding four silicon atoms and the situation results which is illustrated below.

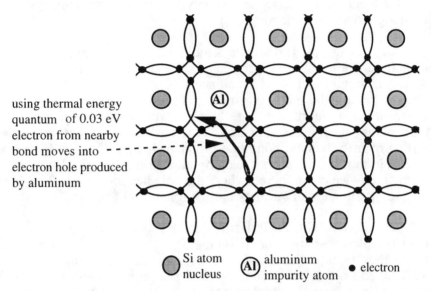

using thermal energy quantum of 0.03 eV electron from nearby bond moves into electron hole produced by aluminum

| Si atom nucleus | (Al) aluminum impurity atom | • electron |

Diagram of the electron structure of p-type silicon. Using a thermal energy quantum of 0.03 eV, an electron from one of a nearby silicon's covalent bonds can move into the electron hole provided by the aluminum impurity atom.

One of the bonds of the silicon atoms to the aluminum is now missing an electron so that there is something which is a kind of electron vacancy. It is just like a missing atom in a crystal in some respects, but it is a missing electron in a bond. Similarly, just as a missing atom (vacancy) allows atoms to move around by jumping into the vacancy, the missing electron allows electrons to move around by moving into this electron vacancy. Naturally we have a term for this electron vacancy. We call it an **electron hole,** or often just a 'hole'. Be careful to note the scientific jargon. A hole is a missing electron in a bond; a vacancy is a missing atom in a crystal.

The energy provided by a thermal energy quantum gives a nearby electron enough energy to jump into this hole, leaving another hole where it came from. An electron from the next atom can then move into this new hole, etc. In other words the aluminum atom in the above diagram **accepts** an electron from an adjacent silicon atom and the chain of electron motion is started. Here again we have just described what is really going on in the material. In terms of our energy ladder model an electron moves from the full band into the acceptor level leaving a **hole** in the band. An electron on a lower step in that band can then use electrical energy to move into the hole. Remember that for electrons to move they must be in an unfilled band. In this case there is only one electron missing from the band but it is enough to allow some movement.

Before going any further we should repeat something we mentioned earlier. A **hole** is a missing electron in a bond. It allows electrons to move by going from one bond to a hole in an adjacent bond. In the same way a **vacancy** allows atoms to move by moving from one atom position in the crystal structure to an adjacent vacant atom position. In other words, it is not just one electron which is moving, but it is the cooperative motion of a large number of electrons all shuffling over to the next bond that produces the net electron flow. We talk about the hole moving because if we compare initial and final pictures of the electron positions we can only tell where the hole has moved to. This is exactly analogous to the situation of vacancy motion for atoms (Page 75).

Silicon doped with an impurity which has an extra electron (i.e. five electrons) is called an **n**-type semiconductor. The impurity donates an extra electron to the crystal. Silicon doped with an impurity which has one less electron is called a **p**-type semiconductor. The impurity accepts an electron from an adjacent silicon atom. [Note that P (phosphorus) creates an n-type material; things can get very confusing!]

We should note in conclusion that at high temperatures, thermal energy quanta are large enough to give the electrons sufficient energy to jump across the whole gap. Also at very low temperatures the thermal energy quanta will not be sufficient even to move electrons as we have just described. This sets limits on the temperatures at which we can use these silicon semiconductor devices. Remember that at high enough temperatures all materials become conductors.

A simple silicon rectifier

Modern electronics depends very much on these two types of semiconductor. In fact we can take one small piece of silicon (a chip) and, for example, place Al impurity atoms in one part adjacent to P atoms in another part. This placing of n-type and p-type semiconductors next to each other is, perhaps, the simplest example of a modern solid state electronics component. We call it a **p-n junction**. We shall now see what happens when we place a voltage across this piece of silicon in an attempt to drive electrons (pass a current) through it.

Notice first that in both the n- and p-type regions of the material the electrons move in the same direction. However in the p-type material the motion of holes is in the opposite direction to the motion of electrons, as illustrated simply in the following diagram.

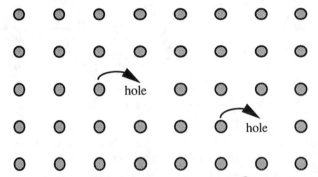

Simple illustration of how when electrons (⊙)move in one direction into holes, the holes move in the opposite direction

Thus in the piece of silicon shown below, if electrons flow from left to right, the extra (free) electrons in the n-type material move to the boundary, as do the holes in the p-type material. The two meet at the boundary where the free donor electrons in the n-type material hop into the holes in the bonds of the p-type material, and continue their motion by moving from hole to hole. In this way the electrons pass across the boundary with no difficulty.

Electron and hole motions from n to p in a p-n junction of silicon. Free electrons in n-type meet holes at the boundary and 'fall into' these holes, thus crossing the boundary.

If we reverse the electron flow, the electrons in the p-type material make their way to the boundary but find no holes to drop into. They therefore are stopped in their motion. Notice they are not free electrons, they move from bond to bond via the holes and there are now no holes for them to move into. The electrons cannot therefore move through the material because they are stopped at the boundary. The only way they can continue to move through the n-type material is to become free electrons, needing 1.1 eV, but there is no way of them getting this energy. As a result electrons do not flow through the material and there is no conduction.

Electron and hole motions from p to n in a p-n junction of silicon. Electrons in p-type move from hole to hole but can only continue to move across the boundary if given enough energy to become free electrons.

We call this device a **rectifier**. It only allows current to pass in one direction, i.e. it is a "one-way only" conductor, and the current is rectified. (In this sense the verb 'to rectify' means to convert AC current into DC.)

Our alternating household electric supply comes at approximately 120 volts, 60 cycles (alternating current - AC). This means that the current changes direction 60 times in a second. The device we have just discussed changes this current into a crude direct current (DC) supply such as is supplied by a regular battery. The following diagram illustrates what happens.

The upper diagram shows a normal AC current which cycles its flow from one direction to another. The rectifier only allows current to flow in one direction.

Of course the previous diagram does not show that the rectifier produces a steady DC current as provided by a battery. There is need for the periods of no current to be filled in and for some smoothing, but how this is done is outside the scope of this text. The little devices provided with some portable electronic items to enable you to power them from the mains electricity perform all these functions as well as reducing the voltage from 120 volts to whatever is needed. Thirty years ago we needed bulky vacuum tubes to perform these same jobs, but now they can all be done can now in one solid piece of material. For this reason we sometimes refer to the technology as **solid state electronics**.

The rectifier is one example of an electronic component. We can also make resistors, capacitors, etc. on a piece of silicon, and one of today's modern silicon chips may contain thousands of such devices on one piece of silicon, something we call an integrated circuit. The different n-type and p-type regions are exceptionally small and the impurity atoms can be fired into the silicon using a special atom gun.

NOTE: When we add impurity dopant atoms to silicon we change the properties by changing the **atomic structure** and hence the **electron structure**.

25. CASE STUDY: SILICON SOLAR CELLS

It seems that in recent years there has been an energy crisis every few years. Not that there is any shortage of energy around; we just don't know how to harness what is available. Every year the sun provides over 1000 times more energy to the earth than we can extract in the form of coal and oil (fossil fuels) during that year. We just have no real way of effectively using it. Some household solar heating devices use the sun to heat water, and others to warm large masses of rock, etc., which then release that heat over an extended period of time. Solar water heaters were used extensively in the Miami, Florida area as long ago as the early 1940's. In today's world there has been, and continues to be, much research on the direct production of electricity from the sun using solar cells. You may have such a power source in your calculator, and some battery powered tools are now being made available with solar charging units. What materials are used in these solar cells and how do they work?

How a solar cell works

There are a few different designs of solar cell so we shall discuss the simplest, which it turns out is very similar to the p-n junction rectifier we discussed in the previous chapter. It consists of a thick layer of p-type silicon with a very thin n-type layer on the surface. Remember that the n-type material contains some free electrons because thermal energy quanta give electrons on the donor impurity level enough energy to jump up to the empty band. Similarly the p-type material contains some electron holes, or some covalent bonds which are missing an electron.

At the boundary where the two types of semiconductor meet, some of the free electrons cross over and fill the holes, i.e. they move from the n-type material to the p-type material where they provide the missing electron to complete the needed two electrons per covalent bond. As a result there is a thin volume at the boundary where there are no electron holes in the p-type and no free electrons in the n-type.

Now we need to remember that both pieces of material (n- and p-type) are electrically neutral before being placed in contact. In the n-type material the extra electrons balance the *higher* positive charge on the nucleus of the dopant atoms (e.g. phosphorus), and in the p-type material the electron holes balance the *lower* positive charge on the nucleus of the dopant atoms (e.g. aluminum). As a result of the extra electrons in the n-type material crossing over into the p-type material the region near the boundary is left with a net positive charge. Similarly the p-type material near the boundary becomes negatively charged. This causes what we call an **electrostatic field** across this boundary, or **junction**. There is a positively charged region on one side and a negatively charged region on the other.

In silicon we have seen that the band gap energy is around 1.1 eV (Page 227). If an energy quantum greater than this enters the silicon it can give an electron the energy needed to tear itself away from the covalent bond (on the energy band model we say that the electron jumps across the energy gap) producing a free electron and an electron hole. Both of these defects provide a means for electron motion. The free electron roams through the crystal just as electrons do in metal conductors. The electron hole allows electrons to move from bond to bond in a cooperative motion. All visible light has energy quanta greater than 1.1 eV so that each quantum is capable of producing an electron and an electron hole, something we call an **electron-hole pair**.

The very thin n-type layer is on the side which faces the sun and the light that hits it penetrates far enough so that some electron-hole pairs are produced in the charged layers between the n- and p-type semiconductors. Now you can see why this n-type layer is very thin; we need the light to be able to produce some of these electron-hole pair defects in the region of the boundary between the two types of semiconductor. Because unlike charges attract, the free electrons go towards the positively charged n-type material. The electrons hopping between bonds also go to the n-type material, meaning that the holes go to the p-type material.

This electron motion towards the n-type material is an electric current. If we can only collect it, we have generated electricity from light. The mechanism is illustrated in the diagrams on the next page.

While we have now basically described the working of the cell, we also have to consider the need to get the maximum amount of light into the cell, and how we are going to get the electric current out. Older solar cells were very inefficient because much of the incident light was reflected from the top surface and did not penetrate to produce the required electrons and holes. In order to solve this problem we place a very thin anti-reflection coating on this top surface. This coating is transparent and very thin so there is no loss of light as it passes through. You may have encountered anti-reflection coatings on your eye glass lenses.

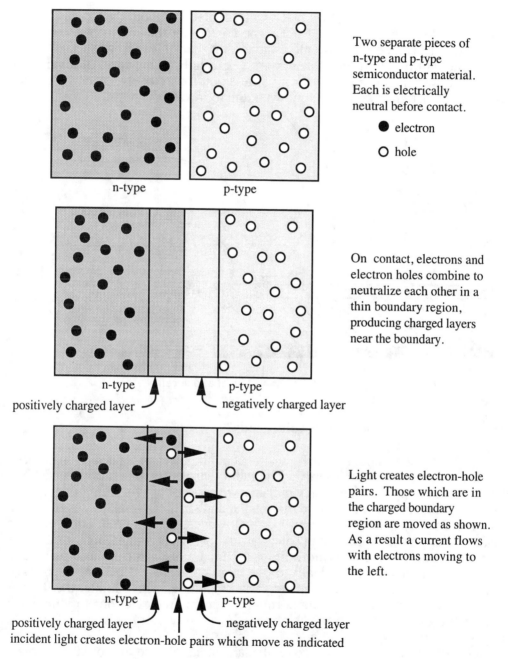

Two separate pieces of n-type and p-type semiconductor material. Each is electrically neutral before contact.

● electron

○ hole

n-type   p-type

On contact, electrons and electron holes combine to neutralize each other in a thin boundary region, producing charged layers near the boundary.

n-type   p-type

positively charged layer ⌐   ⌐ negatively charged layer

Light creates electron-hole pairs. Those which are in the charged boundary region are moved as shown. As a result a current flows with electrons moving to the left.

n-type   p-type

positively charged layer ⌐   ⌐ negatively charged layer

incident light creates electron-hole pairs which move as indicated

Diagrams illustrating the working of a silicon solar cell.

To collect the current we place metal contacts on both the top and bottom surfaces of the semiconductor sheet. The contact on the side of the cell away from the light can be a simple metal layer, but that on the front surface has to allow the light through. For this reason it is usually in the form of a very thin metal grid, which you may not notice unless you look closely. A complete cell may look something like what is shown in the following diagram.

Diagram of cross-section of a solar cell.

What are the prospects for solar cells?

Today only about a tenth of a percent of all power generated by man-made devices comes from solar energy. The main reasons for this are high cost and low efficiency. In the electronics industry we are looking for miniaturization to make our silicon semiconductor parts smaller and smaller. Small pieces of silicon are all we really need for this purpose. However, for the production of large quantities of power using silicon solar cells we want bigger and bigger pieces of silicon in order to intercept more light, produce more electron-hole pairs, and produce a larger current. Ideally these large cells should be single crystals. Polycrystalline silicon contains many grain boundaries which hinder the flow of electrons and also make many opportunities for the free electrons to jump back into the holes they came from. Naturally, large single crystals are difficult to make and are very expensive. There is no practical way of economically manufacturing single crystals to cover the large areas needed to provide the power for even a few houses, let alone industry.

The other possibilities are to use polycrystalline silicon or amorphous silicon. Research is progressing on both fronts and efficiencies are improving. One recent development is the use of amorphous silicon in which the material is deposited from hot gases (CVD) onto a continuous ribbon of stainless steel, 14 inches wide and half a mile long. The efficiency produced, just over 10%, is a record for amorphous silicon cells, and the steel backing provides flexibility which makes its use easier in many circumstances. Even this development holds no great promise since it is estimated that a year's production from a proposed factory would be only about 180 miles of ribbon, representing a 10,000 kilowatt generating capacity. Perhaps it is easier to appreciate these figures if we say that it would need around 200 feet of this ribbon to power a 2 kilowatt electric heater!

Another interesting development uses a polycrystalline film but with the contacts for collecting the electrons buried in the film so that the electrons released by the sunlight have a very short distance to travel before being collected. This means that there is less likelihood of their being scattered by grain boundaries or recombining with the holes. Such a material has been produced with an efficiency of around 15%, still not as good as single crystal silicon (around 25% efficient), but much cheaper to make.

To make large amounts of electric power we must certainly try to improve the efficiency of a cell (today's record is over 30%), but even then it will require enormous areas to produce the millions of watts needed to provide all the power for a medium sized city. A solar power plant generating a thousand million watts, typical of a medium sized conventional power plant, would today need to have about 10 square miles of solar cells (a rectangular area 5 miles by 2 miles, for example). This seems a large area, but just imagine how much of the earth's surface we disturb to mine coal and dispose of the waste! The solar power station would be clean and quiet with no moving parts requiring service and no need for fuel delivery, etc.

There are some other major problems which we should mention. One is the lack of sunshine in some parts of the world and its unpredictability in others. Where there is little sunshine the economics of using these solar cells are extremely unattractive. Even in those areas of the world where sunshine is almost guaranteed, solar power is expensive, costing up to 7 or 8 times that from fossil fuels (oil and coal), even though costs have fallen by 70% in the last decade. Another problem is that solar cells produce direct current (DC) and this would need to be converted to alternating current (AC) before being supplied to our homes to operate the appliances we now own. This again costs money and results in loss of power.

A recent report from South Africa indicates plans to electrify rural health clinics using solar power systems. Lighting and refrigeration, which consume relatively small amounts of power compared to heating and industrial machinery, are natural candidates for the use of solar power. This is particularly true for remote areas where the cost of extending power lines is in itself enormous. Emergency telephones recently installed on the campus of The Pennsylvania State University are also solar powered for these same reasons. Like many recent applications, the solar cells provide power to charge batteries, which in turn power the apparatus. Otherwise the telephone would only work during daylight hours when the sun is shining! For the immediate future you are still only likely to see solar cells being used to directly power electronic equipment using small currents, such as a watch or calculator.

There have been reports that a relatively new semiconductor, gallium arsenide, will give rise to greater efficiencies for solar cells. However its much greater cost may prevent any real developments in applying it for this purpose.

Camera photocells

While discussing solar cells we should note that the light meters built into all cameras nowadays also use a silicon cell, but their structure and mode of operation are quite different from the solar cells we have just discussed. They work because silicon becomes a conductor in the presence of light. A battery tries to pass a current through the silicon but is unable to do so in the dark. The light produces electron-hole pairs and the material can now conduct. The stronger the light source, the greater the number of electron-hole pairs produced, and the greater the current flow. The photocell's electrical conduction is therefore a measure of the light intensity.

Night vision goggles

While solar cells convert light into electricity, night vision goggles, of which many people were first made aware by the movie "Silence of the Lambs", convert electricity into light. Their operation is also something we can understand with the background knowledge we now have. There is always some light out there in the darkness; our eyes just don't see it because of their low sensitivity.

The following diagram should help you understand the description which follows. Bear in mind the sizes mentioned are much smaller that the sizes shown and the diagram is not to scale.

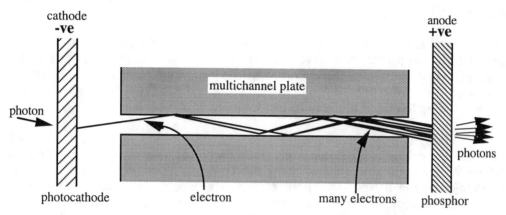

Diagram of the essential working of night vision goggles.

The unit has a conventional front lens through which light photons pass and an image is produced on a thin plate called a photocathode, which is attached to the negative terminal of a battery. At this stage the number of photons is so small that the image is invisible to the human eye. We have seen, for example, that a photon of visible light (energy 1.7 - 3.1 eV) can produce a free electron in silicon. The thin photocathode is also made of a special material in which free electrons are produced by photons, and because it is has a negative voltage applied to it, the electron produced by the photon is ejected from the rear of the plate and pulled towards an anode, attached to the positive battery terminal. On the way to the anode the ejected electron has to pass through something called a multichannel plate.

Note: the cathode is the negative electrode; a cation (positive ion) is so called because it is attracted to the cathode. Similarly for the anode and the anion. This is often confusing.

The multichannel plate is about an inch in diameter and fifteen thousandths of an inch thick, and consists of thousands of very thin glass tubes (channels), each much thinner than a human hair. The electron enters one of these fine tubes and immediately strikes its wall, which is coated with a specially developed material which also emits electrons when given energy. These electrons are also pulled by the anode to the far end of the tube and in so doing ricochet along the tube, producing more and more electrons each time they hit the wall. These electrons are also being accelerated by the battery so their energy, and hence their ability to produce more electrons, increases the further they go. As a result, a stream of electrons is produced at the back of the multichannel plate from one of these tubes when only one entered it.

Now the stream of high energy electrons hits a phosphor screen where bright light is produced, as discussed in the previous chapter. The resulting image is viewed through the eyepiece of the goggles. What is really seen is a series of dots from the original image produced on the photocathode, each corresponding to one of the very fine tubes in the multichannel plate.

You may be wondering how so many collisions can occur in such a short tube (0.015 inches long), but you must remember that we are dealing with light whose wavelength is much shorter than this. Where does the light energy come from? From the battery which accelerates the electron so that it has enough energy to produce the emission of more electrons, which in turn are accelerated to produce even more, etc. Electrical energy has been converted into light energy.

Night vision goggles were originally developed for military purposes and were bulky and quite expensive. Nowadays they have been made much smaller and quite cheap Russian made versions have recently appeared in mail-order electronics catalogs. They are now therefore readily available to everybody.

Conclusion

This chapter has shown how electrical and light energies can each be converted into the other. All types of energy can be converted into other types. We see this most obviously in electrical energy in our homes which can be converted into heat, light, sound and mechanical (kinetic) energies. The conversion of one form of energy into another is something we depend on tremendously in our everyday lives. In the cases considered here it is the development of special electron and light emitting materials which makes it possible.

26. CHANGING THE CONDUCTIVITY OF MATERIALS

We have so far talked about the conduction of electricity in materials as being caused by the motion of electrons. These electrons can be thought of as things which carry charge. In scientific jargon we call them **charge carriers**. The more carriers there are, the better the material conducts electricity. In some respects this is a matter of common sense. The more trucks we have, the faster we can shift a large load. There is, of course, another factor involved in our analogy, and that is the speed at which the trucks move. Continuing the analogy, it is not only the speed shown on the speedometer which is important, but how direct is the route taken. Driving from Pittsburgh to Philadelphia at 55 m.p.h. will get us there in under six hours, but not if we have to go via Buffalo! If we were to take the latter route, our effective speed would be halved.

What we are concerned with in the movement of electrons in a material is this effective speed, something we call the **electron mobility**. In practice the current that flows depends not only on the number of electrons that are available, and their speed but also the ease with which they travel. If there are obstacles to their motion in the material, the electrons have to take a roundabout route and their mobility, and hence the conductivity decreases.

In every conductor and semiconductor, there is a basic speed at which electrons can travel. In silicon this is over two thousand miles per hour. We are used to using copper wire for conducting electricity in houses. Laboratory measurements tell us that each copper atom only provides approximately one electron for conduction. Other metals may provide more electrons, but have a lower conductivity because the electrons do not travel as quickly in the atom arrangement of that metal.

In addition to this basic speed, the mobility depends on the number of obstacles to the electron's motion. A pure metal is almost always crystalline (Page 65). In this ordered atomic arrangement there are nice clear paths between the atoms on which the electrons can move. Anything which disrupts this order will interrupt the electron flow and decrease its mobility, thus lowering the conductivity.

Conductivity in metals

There are several ways in which we can change the mobility of electrons in a metal, all of which involve slightly moving the atoms out of their normal ordered positions. The electrons then bump into these displaced atoms as they pass through the material and are scattered from their straight paths. The voltage is still pushing the electrons in the same direction, but they are forced to take a roundabout path through the material. Here are the most common ways we affect the electrical conduction of a metal.

1. **Heating** the material causes the atoms in the solid to vibrate (see diagram on Page 61) and this makes the electron's path through the crystal more difficult. The atoms move into the clear paths and deflect the electrons as they attempt to move through the crystal. For this reason, metals become worse conductors when they are heated and better conductors when cooled.

2. **Bending and deforming** a metal produces dislocations. We've seen (Page 68) that these dislocations introduce distortions in their neighborhood and these too disturb electron motion. The effect is not great, but the conductivity drops slightly when we work harden a metal.

3. **Impurity atoms** also produce distortions in their surroundings (Page 76). This is a very effective way of reducing electrical conductivity. This is why the copper used for the first transatlantic telegraph cable had only ten percent of the conductivity of pure copper.

4. **Smaller crystals** can be produced by different processing methods (see for example the HSLA steels - Chapter 13). This introduces many more crystal boundaries into the metal and these too disrupt the electron flow and thus reduce conductivity. The crystal on the other side of the boundary has a different orientation and the straight electron path in one crystal does not continue in the second (see figure on Page 119).

Of these four methods the greatest effect is produced by impurity atoms, and these are easily added to the metal when it is molten. We already mentioned some of these effects in talking about thermal conductivity (Page 162). Remember that in metals the electrons are responsible for carrying both heat and electricity, so we can expect a decrease in thermal conduction to be accompanied by a decrease in electrical conduction.

The concept is amazingly simple. Electricity is carried by electrons, and the fewer obstructions to their movement in the crystals the better the conductivity. One would therefore expect conductivity in amorphous metals to be very poor, and it is.

Another way of looking at this property of metals is the converse. If we want good conductivity we want a good pure material with large crystals. Some wires manufactured for connecting hi-fi components claim to have this feature, thus producing lower distortion to the sound. Some people claim to be able to hear the difference, although many people are skeptical. While the claim for better sound may or may not be true, the claims about conductivity should be valid. It is also worth noting that the connectors at the ends of these wires are often gold plated. This metal does not react with the oxygen in the air so there is no poorly conducting oxide layer on the surface.

Conductivity in semiconductors

Everything we have said above concerning electron mobility in metals is also true in semiconductors. However, in silicon and other semiconductors we have seen that we can change the number of charge carriers. Impurities may donate free electrons or provide electron holes which allow electron motion, and heating can also increase the number of electrons and electron holes able to carry the current by providing enough energy to release electrons from the bonds (or jump the energy gap). In most cases this increase in the number of available electrons to carry the electrical charge overwhelms the lower mobility which also occurs because of the impurity atom displacing surrounding atoms or of increased atom vibrations, just as in metals. Because of this, the conductivity of semiconductors usually increases when semiconductors are heated or have impurities added to them.

It should not be surprising that free electrons move faster through the material than do the electrons moving from bond to bond (hole motion). In semiconductors we therefore consider these as two different carriers, electrons and holes.

In computers and some other electronic devices the speed at which they can operate is limited by the speed at which electrons can move through the electronic components. Increased speed of operation therefore needs increased electron mobility. Although, as discussed above, there are some ways we can make sure the electron's mobility is a maximum, it is ultimately determined by the material itself. Electrons simply have different mobilities in different materials.

Modern research has discovered a material in which the electron mobility is increased. It is gallium arsenide (GaAs). If you look at the part of the periodic table shown earlier (Page 237), you will see that gallium and arsenic appear each side of germanium. Gallium has three outer electrons and arsenic has five. They form a compound which is identical in crystal structure to diamond and silicon except that the atoms are alternately arranged, one gallium, one arsenic, etc. They pool their electrons (five and three) to give the eight electrons typical of the four covalent bonds around a silicon atom. The result is a compound with the same properties as silicon except that the electrons travel faster. This new technology is already being seen in radar detectors (look out for GaAs in advertisements) and should eventually produce much faster computers. We mentioned gallium arsenide in the previous chapter as also having the potential for higher efficiency solar cells.

Faster computers may not be important for our everyday applications: they are already fast enough. The major driving force for their development has probably been military. If your enemy fires a missile at you, it is most important that you calculate its trajectory as fast as possible so that you can fire your missile to intercept it. This has been one of the driving forces for miniaturization in electronics. In any computer it is electrons shunting around the circuits which are responsible for its working. If you can't make them travel faster, you can at least make the distances they have to travel as short as possible. Here again we benefit from research which was not really aimed at our convenience. The fastest computers will use light beams rather than electrons, because nothing travels faster than light. Although there have been some exciting recent developments, the development of optical computers is still many years away.

Another limitation of semiconductors is temperature. At high temperatures the thermal energy quanta become large enough to free electrons from the covalent bonds in which they normally exist (Page 240). The material then becomes a conductor. For a high temperature semiconductor we need a material with a larger energy gap. Such a material is diamond (carbon). Notice that it is immediately above silicon in the periodic table and has the same crystal structure. In the last few years there has been much research on the production of diamond films for electronic components. The diamond is produced by causing a carbon-containing gas such as methane (CH_4 - a hydrocarbon) to decompose under special circumstances (CVD again!) so that it forms diamond rather than soot. Diamond films are probably one of tomorrow's new materials.

27. SUPERCONDUCTORS

You will certainly have seen mention of superconductors in the news in recent years, often accompanied by some very prophetic statements. To understand a little about these materials, we should first understand what is meant by the term **super-conductivity**. When metals are cooled the atoms vibrate less and less (see diagram on Page 61), the amount they scatter electrons decreases, and the electrons find their paths through the material much easier to negotiate. The electron mobility therefore increases and the electrical conduction increases. This continues as we continue to decrease the temperature, but in some metals we reach a temperature at which the resistance to electron motion suddenly drops to zero.

This means that if we apply a voltage to set an electron moving in a loop of wire, it will continue to circle the loop until we do something to make it stop. The temperature at which the electrical resistance of the metal suddenly drops to zero is called the **critical temperature**.

The reasons for superconductivity are complex and are not really understood; they need not concern us. The history of the phenomenon is, however, of some interest. The effect was first discovered in 1911 by a Swedish physicist, K. Onnes, who found that the electrical resistance of mercury suddenly dropped to zero at -269°C (very, very cold). In the following 75 years scientists sought for materials which would be superconductors at higher temperatures but improvements (increases in the critical temperature) were very slow. In 1986 the record critical temperature was still only -250°C for a niobium-germanium compound.

In 1986, came news of a major breakthrough. Scientists working at IBM laboratories in Zurich, Switzerland, discovered that superconductivity was shown by a special type of ceramic at temperatures higher than had previously been possible. Not that the temperatures were high relative to our everyday experience; they were still only -237°C. This relatively high critical temperature surprised most scientists because ceramics are usually thought of as insulators. The material was a copper oxide containing some lanthanum and strontium. Some later juggling with the **atomic structure** of the material by adding impurities of barium, yttrium, scandium, etc., produced further increases in the criticaltemperature to -183°C so that there are now materials for which it is above the temperature of boiling liquid nitrogen (-196°C). This is significant because it allows us to cool the conductor using a rather (comparatively) cheap liquid (liquid nitrogen costs approximately $1 per liter), but superconducting installations which would carry electricity over hundreds of miles using power lines cooled with liquid nitrogen would still be prohibitively expensive, and certainly not cost effective.

The search goes on for a material which will exhibit superconductivity at room temperature. Whether one will be found is not certain. The combination of elements used in the current highest temperature superconductors seems rather strange. Remember that there are about 80-90 elements to choose from and picking four or five to produce the compound, if it can be done, is like picking numbers for a winning state lottery ticket. In addition, with chemical compounds we not only need to pick the elements but also arrange them in the right proportions in the correct crystal structure. Physicists are nowadays exploring almost every combination of metal oxides in the hope of finding the sought-for breakthrough. One promising candidate uses thallium, barium, calcium, copper and oxygen, a rather nasty mixture because thallium is toxic. The research problem is obviously formidable.

The diagram on the following page illustrates the increases in the critical temperature over the last 80 years, and the compounds discovered at each major step. Future projections are purely speculative.

There are two major problems with these new ceramic superconductors which we should mention. First, we know that ceramics are usually brittle. Making wires that we can bend like metal wires is obviously a problem. We have already mentioned (Page 172) a way of possibly overcoming this problem by making the crystallites very small (the so-called nanophase materials). Another way of overcoming the problem is to make the superconductor in the form of a powder and then pack it into a silver tube. The silver is ductile so the whole may be drawn down into a fine wire. Many companies throughout the world are working on this powder-in-wire approach. Unfortunately these ceramic super-conductors are not isotropic in properties. They consist of alternating layers of copper oxide, which carry the current, and layers of the other elements. It is therefore important that the particles have these superconducting layers aligned along the wire. At present we do not know how to do this very efficiently.

The second problem is that, even below the critical temperature, these materials lose their superconducting ability if we pass too much current through them. There is a **critical current** above which they revert to their usual ceramic

Improvements in the critical temperature for superconductivity during the last century.
(K. Easterling, *Tomorrow's Materials*, The Institute of Metals, London, U.K., 1988. Fig. 48)

insulating property. Laboratory experiments have shown that some of these ceramic superconductors can carry currents of over 100,000 amps per square centimeter. The significance of this is best seen by stating that a copper wire can carry about 500 amps per square centimeter. In a house you have to use thicker wires if they are to carry higher currents; there is a much thicker wire to your range than to a light bulb for this reason.

Of course all superconductors also lose their peculiar property if we allow them to become too warm. The new superconductors can work at temperatures above the temperature of boiling liquid nitrogen, but there are obviously still many problems to be solved before they can be used for electric power distribution. The immediately important aspect of their discovery is that we have been given hope for superconducting materials at higher temperatures. What we now need to do is to understand what causes these ceramics to have this special property. Once we have done that, we may see the way to produce new materials with even larger critical temperatures and currents.

There are already some special uses being put into practice. One device which has already been announced is based on something called a squid (superconducting quantum interfering device). It is a medical instrument which can detect and measure the minute magnetic fields created by muscles as they move to make the heart beat. It has a great advantage of doing this without being wired to the patient, and could, for example, be used to simultaneously monitor the heartbeats of a mother and her unborn infant. The device is said to be able to detect magnetic fields close to one billionth of the earth's. Other possible uses are said to be detecting cracks in oil pipelines, and predicting earthquakes.

QUESTIONS: Chapters 24-27

1. If an electron needs 2 eV of energy to reach the next energy level it can be attained by giving it _____.
   (a) 2 quanta (packets) of 1 eV (b) one quantum of 2 eV (c) one quantum of 3 eV
   (d) both b and c (e) any of these

2. Which of the following would increase the conductivity of a semiconductor?
   (a) addition of impurities (b) removal of impurities (c) heating the material
   (d) both a and c (e) both b and c

3. All of the following are true of a rectifier except _____.
   (a) an n-type material borders a p-type material (b) conductivity can occur in both directions (c) donor electrons from the n-type material jump into electron holes in the p-type material (d) a rectifier has a net neutral charge (e) all of these are true

4. When we add donor dopant atoms to silicon we change the _____ structure.
   (a) atomic (b) electronic (c) crystal (d) both a and b (e) both a and c

5. Which of the following is true for both p-type and n-type pieces of silicon?
   (a) conduction occurs through electron hole motion (b) materials have a net neutral charge
   (c) nitrogen or phosphorous could be used as dopant impurities (d) both b and c
   (e) none of these is true

6. If we add a donor impurity to silicon at room temperature we will produce a(n) _____.
   (a) vacancy (b) free electron (c) electron hole (d) rectifier (e) both a and c

7. In order to have a metal with good electrical conduction we want the electrons to have as clear a path through the material as possible. Which of the following is (are) therefore undesirable in a good conductor?
   (a) dislocations (b) precipitates (c) impurities (d) both a and b (e) all of these

8. Which one of the following has a lower electron energy band which is not completely full of electrons?
   (a) silicon (b) germanium (c) gold (d) diamond (e) silicon carbide

9. Which one of the following has the largest gap in its energy diagram?
   (a) silicon (b) germanium (c) gallium arsenide (d) diamond (e) they are all nearly identical

10. In a piece of doped silicon, the donor impurity level is _____ the empty band while the acceptor level is _____ the full band.
    (a) close to, close to (b) close to, far from (c) far from, close to (d) far from, far from
    (e) none of these is correct

11. Gallium arsenide is a _____.
    (a) superconductor (b) metal (c) insulator (d) semiconductor (e) polymer

12-18.   __12__ conduct electricity better as they are cooled because the __13__ increases as the atoms vibrate less and cause less interference with the conduction. As it is being cooled, the __14__ of the metal drops to zero at a certain temperature. At this point, the metal has become a superconductor. Surprisingly, the best superconductors are __15__. If they are to be used as superconductors , __15__ must be made __16__ enough to be made into wires. The way this may be accomplished is by making __15__ with ultrafine grains. These materials are called __17__ materials. Unfortunately, no materials have been discovered which exhibit superconducting properties at __18__.

12. (a) polymers (b) semiconductors (c) glasses (d) metals (e) all materials
13. (a) impurity content (b) number of vacancies (c) electron mobility
    (d) phonon activity (e) electron speed
14. (a) conductivity (b) strength (c) thermal expansion (d) ductility (e) resistivity
15. (a) polymers (b) ceramics (c) metals (d) semiconductors (e) composites
16. (a) brittle (b) strong (c) ductile (d) stiff (e) pure
17. (a) composite (b) alloy (c) nanophase (d) oxide (e) intermetallic
18. (a) room temperature (b) low voltages (c) low light conditions (d) both a and b
    (e) all of these

19-28.   A rectifier uses two different types of _____19_____ in the form of a p-n junction. In the p-type material the electrons move _____20_____ while in the n-type material they move _____21_____. Motion is usually faster in the _____22_____ type material. Electrons can only move from the _____23_____ type to the _____24_____ type because if they try to move in the opposite direction they are stopped at the _____25_____ because _____26_____. One way of making faster computers is to make electrons move faster. This happens in a material called _____27_____. The fastest computers would use _____28_____ to carry the signals rather than electrons.

19. (a) plastic (b) gallium (c) alloy (d) activator (e) silicon
20. (a) from hole to hole (b) randomly (c) freely (d) at the speed of light
    (e) from nucleus to nucleus
21. (a) from hole to hole (b) randomly (c) freely (d) at the speed of light
    (e) from nucleus to nucleus
22. (a) n (b) p (c) normal (d) junction (e) none of these
23. (a) n (b) p (c) normal (d) junction (e) none of these
24. (a) n (b) p (c) normal (d) junction (e) none of these
25. (a) n-type end (b) p-type end (c) impurity atoms (d) anti-reflective coating
    (e) junction
26. (a) there are no electrons to join up with (b) there are precipitates in the way
    (c) they are scattered (d) there are no holes to drop into (e) they don't fit
27. (a) gallium (b) germanium (c) niobium carbide (d) gallium arsenide
    (e) none of these
28. (a) light (b) heat (c) neurons (d) protons (e) none of these

29- 43. Silicon is the most common element in the earth's crust. A silicon atom has _____29_____ valence electrons and forms four _____30_____ bonds to surrounding atoms which sit on the corners of a _____31_____. These units are joined together to form a(n) _____32_____ crystal. It takes about _____33_____ of energy to free an electron from a _____30_____ bond in silicon. This can be easily accomplished by a quantum from _____34_____, and when silicon is exposed to _____34_____ it is a(n) _____35_____, because the silicon now contains _____36_____. The atomic number of silicon is 14, which tells us that an atom of silicon contains 14 _____37_____s. When a phosphorus atom, which has an atomic number 15, is added to silicon it is a(n) _____38_____ impurity, and because it has an extra _____37_____ the silicon _____39_____. However, the extra electron provided by the phosphorus can be freed by an energy quantum of _____40_____ which can be provided by _____41_____. We call silicon which has been doped with phosphorus a(n) _____42_____ semiconductor. At really high temperatures silicon-based electronics fail to operate properly because _____43_____.

29. (a) 14 (b) 6 (c) 0 (d) 2 (e) 4
30. (a) ionic (b) covalent (c) weak (d) directed (e) both b and d
31. (a) cube (b) square (c) tetragon (d) tetrahedron (e) rectangle
32. (a) HCP (b) FCC (c) BCC (d) CCP (e) both b and d
33. (a) 0.03 eV (b) 5 eV (c) 10^{-23} eV (d) 1.1 eV (e) you cannot free an electron in Si
34. (a) thermal energy at room temperature (b) visible light (c) normal (120V) electrical voltages (d) microwaves (e) none of these
35. (a) superconductor (b) electrical insulator (c) electrical conductor (d) resistor (e) rectifier
36. (a) vacancies (b) free electrons (c) electron holes (d) both a and b (e) both b and c
37. (a) positron (b) neutron (c) electron (d) proton (e) both c and d
38. (a) existential (b) substitutional (c) interstitial (d) residential (e) combinational
39. (a) remains electrically neutral (b) becomes positively charged (c) becomes negatively charged (d) becomes very reactive (e) none of these
40. (a) 0.03 eV (b) 5 eV (c) 10^{-23} eV (d) 1.1 eV (e) you still cannot free an electron
41. (a) thermal energy at room temperature (b) visible light (c) microwaves (d) normal (120V) electrical voltages (e) none of these
42. (a) regular (b) irregular (c) p-type (d) n-type (e) there is no special name for it
43. (a) electrons find it more difficult to move (b) impurity atoms evaporate (c) electrons begin to be freed from Si-Si bonds (d) atoms vibrate too much (e) atoms form ionic bonds

44. All of the following are true concerning solar cells except _____.
    (a) high cost (b) low efficiency (c) large, single crystals of silicon are difficult to produce (d) solar cells only produce DC current (e) silicon is extremely rare

45-60. Solar cells convert light energy into _____45_____ energy. They basically consist of a thick p-type layer of _____46_____ with a thin n-type layer on the surface. In the n-type _____46_____ _____47_____ energy quanta give electrons on the _____48_____ level enough energy to jump up to the empty band. At the boundary between the n- and p-type layers some of the electrons from the n-type layer cross over and _____49_____. The result of this is that there is a thin volume at the boundary where there is/are _____50_____. This causes a(n) __51__ across the junction because there is a net _____52_____ charge in the n-type region near the boundary and a net _____53_____ charge in the p-type region near the boundary. Since _____46_____ has a band gap of approximately _____54_____ eV, _____55_____ light which penetrates the thin n-type layer will produce _____56_____. The electrons move under the influence of the _____51_____ thus producing an _____57_____. Unfortunately, solar cells produce very little power and are not very efficient. In night vision goggles we convert _____58_____ energy into_____59_____ energy and in a fluorescent tube we convert _____60_____ energy into _____59_____.

45. (a) thermal (b) electrical (c) radioactive (d) ultraviolet (e) free
46. (a) silicon (b) carbon (c) germanium (d) phosphorus (e) nitrogen
47. (a) electrical (b) free (c) radioactive (d) thermal (e) all of these
48. (a) interstitial (b) acceptor (c) donor (d) valence (e) full
49. (a) become free electrons (b) conduct electricity (c) fill vacancies
    (d) become substitutional impurities (e) fill electron holes
50. (a) no free electrons (b) no electron holes (c) free electrons (d) both a and b
    (e) both b & c
51. (a) voltage gradient (b) electrostatic field (c) magnetic field (d) electic current
    (e) heat sink
52. (a) positive (b) negative (c) neutral
53. (a) positive (b) negative (c) neutral
54. (a) 0.03 (b) 1.1 (c) 1.7 (d) 3.1 (e) 7.0
55. (a) red (b) yellow (c) green (d) blue (e) all of these
56. (a) donor electrons (b) vacancies (c) electron-hole pairs (d) both a and b
    (e) all of these
57. (a) voltage gradient (b) electrostatic field (c) magnetic field (d) electic current
    (e) heat sink
58. (a) thermal (b) electrical (c) ultraviolet light (d) mechanical (e) visible light
59. (a) thermal (b) electrical (c) ultraviolet light (d) mechanical (e) visible light
60. (a) thermal (b) electrical (c) ultraviolet light (d) mechanical (e) visible light

28. THE OPTICAL BEHAVIOR OF MATERIALS

Some thirty years ago, we hardly gave much thought to optical materials. Glass had been used for centuries to make vessels, ornaments and window panes, and more recently we had used them as lenses in cameras, eye glasses, microscopes and other optical instruments, but that was about all. Today we are well aware of the publicity there has been for optical fibers used for telephone communications. We may also be aware of optical fibers being used in medical instruments, automobiles, etc. The development of optical fibers used for these applications has required a much greater understanding of the properties of glass and the discovery of ways to produce special high purity glass materials. We shall therefore devote some time to exploring the science behind this material's development in today's world. We shall specifically consider the manufacture and working of an optical fiber for telephone transmission in the following case study. First we need to consider the basis of their operation.

Background

If you were asked what x-rays, gamma rays, light, microwaves, and radio and TV waves had in common you would probably say "nothing". You would be wrong because they are all basically the same thing. They are simply different parts of what we call the **electromagnetic spectrum**. Just as yellow is part of the spectrum of visible light, so is light part of an even larger spectrum. We have already seen (Page 214) that visible light stretches from the low energy red light (1.7 eV) to the high energy blue violet light (3.1 eV). What distinguishes this range of energies is simply that it is what our eyes are able to see. Below these energies are the infrared rays (down to 0.01 eV), microwaves (10^{-4} eV) and radio and TV waves (10^{-8} eV). Above are the ultraviolet rays (up to 100 eV), x-rays (10,000 eV) and gamma rays (10^6 eV). In other words our eyes are only able to see a very small part of this electromagnetic spectrum. (Note that we shouldn't say that they are not sensitive to other parts of the spectrum. Because of their high energies a direct beam of x-rays will destroy your eyes. We are sensitive to them but we just don't see them.) You may never have thought that the microwaves which cook your food and the x-rays which allow doctors to see inside your body are really the same thing as light, but they are. The only difference is the size of the energy quantum associated with them.

What is an electromagnetic wave?

What do we mean by an electromagnetic wave? The answer is very complex but for our purposes we can simply say that as the wave passes through materials it produces magnetic and electrical disturbances. When you drop a pebble in a still pond you can see the waves spread out as concentric circles from where the pebble hit the water. This is a mechanical disturbance. The pebble hitting the water caused the water molecules to move in this way. We have also talked about a phonon wave (Page 162) where atoms are caused to vibrate by heat. The electromagnetic wave produces small oscillating magnetic and electric forces in the material, and because electrons have a charge and are very lightweight, they are the particles in the material which are most influenced by this wave. You will of course remember that an electric field is what causes electrons to move.

When light enters a transparent material it loses some energy by moving the electrons, or rather the electric and magnetic fields cause them to oscillate. The light therefore slows down. You can imagine the electrons in the material as something the light wave has to push through. You can walk through air with little difficulty. If you try walking under water (with suitable equipment of course!) you find that you cannot go as quickly. Now if you did the same experiment with molasses your progress would be even slower. The same thing happens in materials. The more electrons the light has to push through, the slower it travels.

We often use the phrase "the speed of light"; indeed we may have heard that nothing moves faster than the speed of light. Most people are unaware that light changes its speed when it moves from one material to another. It is this change in its speed which causes light to bend when passing from one material to another. Its velocities in the two media are different.

When a beam of light hits a transparent material some of it is reflected from the surface. We mentioned earlier (Page 246) that we can put a coating on the surface to reduce this reflection, but in normal circumstances a significant amount is reflected. The remainder of the light enters the material and starts to make its way through, albeit at a slower speed and in a different direction. As it passes through the material it may lose some of its intensity by absorption, very often acquiring a color, because some colors (energies) are absorbed more than others (Pages 227-230). Eventually the light passes out of the material as what we call transmitted light. The following diagram illustrates these different phenomena.

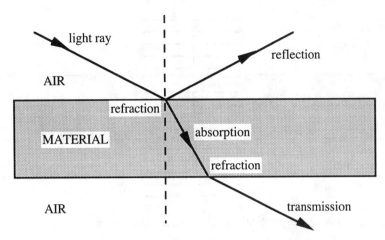

The various interactions of light with materials.

We have already talked about the way light interacts with some materials to produce color (Chapter 23). Some light can be absorbed by the electrons in the solid, lifting them to higher levels on the energy ladder. We have also seen that absorption is often due to impurities in the material. We usually think of window glass as clear, but if we try to look at it through an edge we find it impossible to see anything but a blue-green color. This color is caused by iron impurity in the sand from which the glass is made. It takes only a very small amount of impurity to produce this kind of absorption, in fact it is extremely difficult to eliminate.

As we said earlier, light is a wave and can be simply represented as shown below. The distance between identical points on the wave is the wavelength, λ. On the diagram we have drawn vertical lines through the crests of the wave and we shall now use these lines, which are perpendicular to the direction of the wave motion, to represent the wave rather than draw the waves. When such a wave enters a material along a path perpendicular to the surface, as shown in the diagram on the following page, the speed changes but not the angle. The slower wave is shown below by lines which are closer together.

Definition of wavelength (λ) of light.

Light entering a material perpendicular to the surface slows down but is not bent (refracted).

When the light wave is at an oblique angle to the surface, as shown in the following diagram, one end of the wave enters the material before the other so that one end slows down while the other end is still going fast. This is exactly what happens when a marching band turns a corner. One end of the line slows down and the whole line rotates. Note that the light wave bends so that it is closer to the perpendicular to the surface. When it emerges at the bottom face it is bent in the opposite direction so that it is now parallel to the original wave.

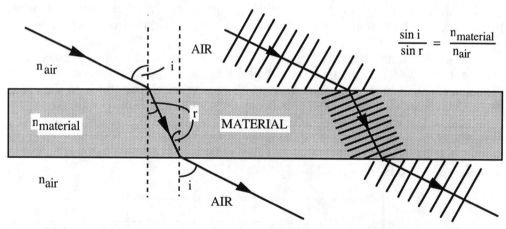

$$\frac{\sin i}{\sin r} = \frac{n_{material}}{n_{air}}$$

Light entering a material at an oblique angle is bent when it enters the material because it is slowed down by the higher electron density. See later text for definition of refractive index, n.

This bending of light is what we call **refraction**. Note that the light ray leaving the material is parallel to the original ray, but is displaced from it. This is what makes things appear to be where there really aren't. The amount by which the light is bent, or slowed down, is characterized by a property known as the refractive index (n) of the material which is given by:

$$\text{refractive index (n)} = \frac{\text{velocity of light in a vacuum}}{\text{velocity of light in the material}}$$

This quantity is always greater than one, because light always travels fastest in a vacuum, and its speed is related to the number of electrons in the material, or more exactly the number of electrons in a certain volume of material, something we call the **electron density**. In general, the larger the atoms in the material, the more electrons there are, and the larger the electron density and the refractive index. Some typical values of refractive index are:

air	1.0003
hot air	1.0001
ice	1.33
silica glass	1.45
lead glass	1.65
diamond	2.42

By definition the refractive index of a vacuum is one.

We can also assign a mathematical formula to the refractive index, as shown in the previous figure.

$$\frac{\sin i}{\sin r} = \frac{n_{material}}{n_{air}}$$

Because the refractive index of air is approximately one, we can write $\sin i / \sin r = n_{material}$, which can be rewritten as $\sin i = n_{material} \cdot \sin r$.

The maximum value of the sine of any angle is 1 (angle = 90°) so the maximum value of $\sin i$ is 1, when the angle i is equal to 90°, which we know is equal to $n_{material} \cdot \sin r$. When this happens, the emitted beam is traveling parallel to the boundary between the material and the air and

$$\sin r = \frac{1}{n_{material}}$$

This formula tells us the maximum value r can have for there to be a value of i, i.e. for the light to pass through the boundary. The angle r simply cannot be any greater than this value if the light is to escape from the material.

Some of you are not mathematical so don't worry if the previous two paragraphs are not readily understandable. We shall consider the result we are aiming at a little differently later.

What happens if the angle r is greater than this **critical angle**? The fact is that the beam is reflected back into the material by the boundary. We call this effect **total internal reflection**. All three words are important. It is reflection which happens inside the material as the light ray is trying to leave, and it is 100% (**total**). We earlier mentioned that some partial reflection occurs at the surface when light enters a material. However the reflection we are talking about here is 100% (**total**). It is this fact which becomes very important in designing optical fibers. We shall mention the partial reflection of the light at the top surface at the end of this section.

Let us look at this situation in another way. When the light goes into the less dense material (air) it is bent away from the perpendicular to the boundary as shown in the following diagram. As we increase the angle r, the angle i also increases. Three different situations (1,2,3) are shown. For ray 3 the emerging beam is just grazing the surface. Now if we increase the angle further (beam 4) the beam cannot emerge from the material and is totally reflected inside the material. The angle for beam 3 is the **critical angle**. Any light rays approaching the boundary with angles greater than this angle (measured from the perpendicular to the surface as shown) will be totally internally reflected. Notice that in this case the angles between the surface and both the reflected and incident rays are equal.

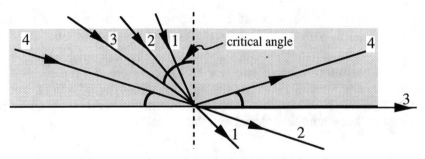

Illustration of what is meant by the critical angle.

For light going from silica glass (n = 1.45) into air (n = 1.0) this critical angle is just over 43°. When going from ice to air the critical angle is 48°. Notice that for total internal reflection to occur the light must be traveling in the material with the higher refractive index (slower speed) and be trying to enter a material with a lower refractive index (higher speed). In this general case the critical angle is given by

$$\sin r = \frac{n_{\text{material 1}}}{n_{\text{material 2}}}$$

The most common optical material is simple silica glass (SiO_2). By choosing impurities that only add extra levels to the band gap which do not allow the absorption of visible light, we can change the refractive index of the glass without affecting the color. These impurities will change the number of electrons in the material, i.e. they will change the electron density, and hence the refractive index. What we referred to in the table on page 269 as lead glass is what is often commonly known as lead crystal. It is not crystalline (it has no crystal structure) but is an amorphous glass whose refractive index has been increased by additions of lead. This increases the bending of the light and also increases the reflection of light from the surface of the glass. Its refractive index is nowhere near that of diamond but it is significantly larger than that of regular silica glass.

Improvements in camera lenses have resulted from the formulation of new glasses, but the major development in glass affecting us is that for optical fiber communication. Because of the phenomenon of total internal reflection, a light beam can be sent down an optical fiber with almost no absorption and will continue to pass down the fiber for large distances so long as it never meets the surface at an angle smaller than the critical angle. You must remember that we always measure the angle from the perpendicular to the surface. The material around the fiber must have a smaller refractive index than the fiber. It too can be glass.

In a typical fiber arrangement, shown in the following figure, the core is made of a glass with a high refractive index (say 1.6) and is surrounded by a glass with lower refractive index (say 1.55). This gives a critical angle of around 75° so that the light will stay in the fiber so long as it never hits the surface at an angle greater than 15°. We shall discuss how we ensure this condition is satisfied in the next chapter.

Illustration of total internal reflection in an optical fiber.

*Note carefully that the angle drawn on the figure is **not** the critical angle. You have to be careful whether you are measuring angles from the surface, or from the perpendicular to the surface. Remember that the critical angle is defined as the angle from the perpendicular.*

The development of suitable glasses with almost zero absorption for optical fibers was a major research problem. Some details of these materials and their advantages will be given in the case study in the following chapter.

Notice that the glass fiber is surrounded with another glass. Before leaving the subject we should mention why this cladding is necessary. We have said that the light never escapes from the fiber unless it hits the surface at an angle to the normal less than the critical angle. The core glass (fiber) is surrounded by a cladding glass to protect the fiber from scratching. A scratch would allow the light to escape as shown below. Indeed if you can see the light passing down the fiber it is because it is escaping through surface imperfections. It may be difficult to imagine that if a bare optical fiber cable carrying all sorts of light signals, even high power laser light, were suspended across a totally dark room, you could sit in that room and see nothing. To see the light, some has to escape and reach your eyes. The major point about optical fibers is that they are designed to not allow any light to escape, not even the slightest amount.

Scratch where ray hits nearly perpendicular to surface and escapes

A scratch on the surface of a fiber can allow the light to escape.

There is one illustration of this phenomenon of total internal reflection with which we are all familiar. When driving along a straight road in hot weather we often see what appears to be a pool of water in the distance, something we call a mirage. The black road becomes very hot from the sun's rays and the air layer immediately above the surface is heated by the road so that its refractive index is decreased. Sunlight coming onto the road therefore passes from a higher to a lower refractive index, and total internal reflection is possible. Using the values given in the table on page 269 we can calculate the critical angle to be around 89°. If we look down the road a long way this angle is exceeded. Near to us the reflection angle is much lower. If our eye is four feet above the road surface the mirage will be seen about 75 to 100 yards in the distance and of course it always stays that far away.

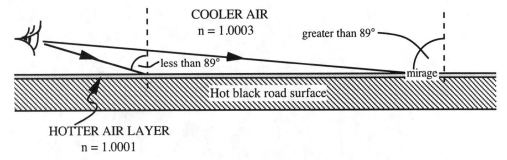

Production of a mirage in the distance on a hot road.

Reflection of light from the surface of a transparent material

While this subject is not really relevant to our discussion, we have mentioned it, and should perhaps explain it a little more. If a **transparent** material has a refractive index n, the amount of light (R) reflected from its surface as the light enters it is given by the following formula:

$$R = \frac{(n - 1)^2}{(n + 1)^2} \times 100\%.$$

Using this formula and the values for refractive index given on page 269 you can calculate the amounts of light reflected from the surfaces of these materials. You will find that only 2% is reflected from ice, while 6% is reflected from lead glass ('crystal') and over 17% from diamond. It is this high reflection combined with strong refraction which make diamond an attractive, and hence valuable gemstone.

29. CASE STUDY: OPTICAL FIBERS FOR TELECOMMUNICATIONS

Background

Advertising has done its best to convince us of the superiority of optical fibers for the transmission of telephone conversations. The first transatlantic fiber optic telephone cable began operation in late 1988 and with it has come increased clarity and the loss of other people's conversations audible in the background. Let's try to understand something of the way this new materials development uses some of the scientific principles we have already considered and puts them into practice.

First we should explain that any sound can be put into a digital code. The way this is done need not concern us here but it is a technique which is used in modern compact disc records (CD's). During recording, the sound is sampled many times in a second and at each time the signal picked up is translated into a number which is expressed in a binary form. This simply means that the number uses only the digits 0 and 1, rather than the ten digits we normally use for counting. This binary number can then be expressed as a series of pulses transmitted very rapidly at fixed intervals, maybe a ten thousandth of a second apart. If a pulse is transmitted we have the digit 1, and if no pulse is transmitted we have the digit 0. On a CD these digitally coded sounds are in the form of very small pits on the surface. In the player a very finely focused beam of light from a laser hits the surface and is reflected from these pits. The pattern of pits is thus translated into a pattern of reflected light pulses which are then somehow converted back to reproduce the original sound. The details of these translation mechanisms are not of importance here. We are here interested in how the sound of our voice can be transmitted thousands of miles through an optical fiber after it has been turned into a series of light pulses.

What is a typical optical fiber like?

We have already seen (Page 271) that our optical fiber must satisfy two important criteria. First is must contain the light, i.e. it must be designed to produce total internal reflection and have no defects at the surface to let the light out. Second it must allow the light to pass through large distances without significant loss of intensity, i.e. there must be almost no absorption of the light in the glass. Sometimes this light loss is called **attenuation**. We therefore say that the glass must have a low attenuation factor.

A typical optical fiber has three components as shown in the following diagram. First there is an inner core of glass with a relatively high refractive index. This is the fiber along which the light travels. This fiber is surrounded by a sheath of glass with a lower refractive index. This arrangement satisfies the criterion that light traveling in the core is in the higher refractive index material, while the outer glass layer ensures a smooth surface and serves to protect the surface of the core from scratches and other surface imperfections. An outer polymer coating adds strength and protects the whole fiber from damage. The entire three-layer unit has a diameter of about a quarter of a millimeter (250 microns).

Diagram illustrating the three layers in an optical fiber.

You will see from the next diagram that the light ray must enter the fiber within a certain acceptance angle. Light rays which enter the fiber at greater angles will strike the surface of the fiber at an angle that allows them to cross the boundary between the two glass layers and thus exit the fiber.

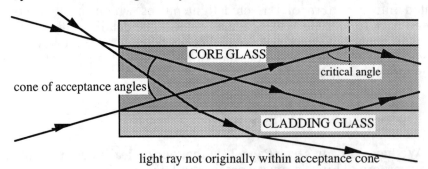

Illustration of how a light ray entering the fiber at an angle outside the acceptance cone leaves the core when it reaches the cladding glass.

How do we make a fiber?

Our earlier discussions of the interactions of light with materials have shown that impurities can produce light absorption (Page 228). A pane of window glass appears very clear when in the window, but try looking through it from the edge! You will be lucky to see anything even through a piece an inch thick. The reason for this is the impurities in the glass. The silica sand from which glass is made contains some iron, not much, but enough to cause considerable light adsorption and give the glass a blue-green color. The secret to producing an optical fiber which will allow light to be sent over long distances with very little absorption is therefore to get the impurities out. However this is easier said than done.

Solids are notoriously difficult to purify (Page 78) and getting the iron and other metallic impurities out of silica sand is no exception. To get what we need we take a rather roundabout way. Compounds of metals and the halides (chlorine, bromine and iodine) often have very low melting and boiling points (we mentioned this on pages 79 and 214) and these temperatures differ according to the compound. Thus, if we react our impure sand with chlorine to produce iron chloride and silicon chloride we have two different compounds which have different boiling points. If we now heat this mixture, the iron chloride will boil at a different temperature than the silicon chloride and we can collect and condense the vapors separately. This process is the same we mentioned in the production of pure chromium (Page 79) except that here we are using chlorine rather than iodine, and is essentially the same as used in the distillation of whiskey and other alcoholic spirits. In the same way, in any cooking with wine or spirits there is almost no alcohol in the finished sauce, etc., because the alcohol evaporates at a lower temperature than the water.

To make the super-pure glass required for optical fibers we therefore first change the silicon oxide into silicon chloride, purify it as a gas and then change it back into the oxide by reacting it with oxygen. With this background we can understand one of the common manufacturing methods for optical fibers. Note that the cladding glass is not responsible for the light transmission so its purity is not critical. It simply serves to provide a smooth defect-free surface for the fiber which is carrying the light.

The manufacturing technique involves a process known as chemical vapor deposition (CVD). A mixture of the ultrapure silicon chloride ($SiCl_4$) vapor and oxygen (O_2) is heated to a temperature where they react to form chlorine and silicon oxide (SiO_2), the basic component of glass. Of course this chlorine can be collected and used to form more $SiCl_4$ by reaction with more of the impure sand, so it is recycled and not released into the atmosphere.

A tube of regular silica glass is held in a piece of equipment similar to a lathe so that it can be rotated. Around the tube there is an furnace, or oxygen-hydrogen torch, which encircles the tube and slowly moves back and forth along its length. The pure $SiCl_4$ and O_2 flow into the tube and react to form SiO_2 where the tube is being heated by the flame, and the particles of silica glass which are formed are deposited on the tube walls. The rotating tube and the moving furnace all help to give a coating of uniform thickness in the tube.

At this stage you may be asking how the deposited glass has a higher refractive index than the silica tube in which it is formed. The answer is quite simple. Remember that the refractive index is a measure of the slowing of the light's speed in the material. The higher the refractive index of a material the more it slows the motion of the light as it passes through. This slowing is caused by the electrons in the material. The more electrons it has to pass through, the slower the light travels.

We can make the light move more slowly, i.e. increase the refractive index, by replacing some of the silicon atoms with atoms having more electrons, i.e. with a higher atomic number. However we must ensure that these impurity atoms do not cause any absorption of the light we wish to transmit. A suitable impurity atom is germanium, which you may remember has the same number of *outer* electrons as does silicon, but has a *total* of eighteen more electrons (32 versus 14). Remember that it is also a semiconductor and has the same crystal structure as silicon. This large increase in the number of electrons produces a significant increase in the refractive index when only a small amount of this germanium impurity is added.

Now the question is how we can add small amounts of ultra pure germanium to our glass. The answer is again quite simple. We produce pure germanium chloride ($GeCl_4$) in the same way that we produce the pure silicon chloride and mix a small amount into the gas stream of $SiCl_4$ and O_2. This is sometimes called the **dopant** for the glass, just as we refer to impurities in semiconductors as dopants. Notice that in both cases the word refers to impurities we have *intentionally* added to change the atomic structure of the material and hence its properties.

As the furnace moves up and down the tube it not only causes more glass droplets to be deposited on the tube walls, but the heat also sinters, or fuses, the deposited particles of glass together so that they form a solid mass.

The next stage of the process is to increase the temperature so that the glass softens, and the tube collapses to form a solid rod consisting of a core of higher refractive index glass and a surrounding sheath (the original silica glass tube) of lower refractive index glass. The rod is then placed in a high temperature furnace where it is softened and drawn out into a thin fiber in much the same way as one pulls taffy. A thin protective plastic layer is then placed on the surface to complete the manufacturing process.

Deposition of the germanium-doped silica glass.

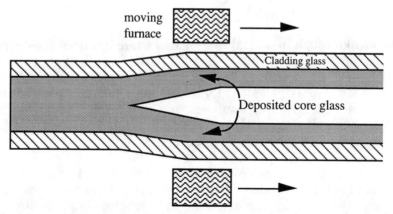

Furnace made hotter to soften the glass so that the original tube and the deposited glass collapse to form a solid body which can be drawn into a fiber.

Glass being pulled to produce fiber.

The breakthrough in optical fiber manufacture has been the development of methods for producing pure glass. In 1970 only 1% of the light entering a one kilometer length of the best available optical fiber was transmitted to the other end. Today that figure is better than 95%. Quite a difference! The following diagram illustrates the dramatic improvements in transmission in optical fibers from 1968 to 1980. The tremendous increase in the early 1970's was due to the manufacturing techniques we have outlined above.

Of course even these improvements do not allow light in an optical fiber to cross the Atlantic Ocean unaided. This means that the transatlantic cable has to have light amplifiers built in at intervals along its length. There are also problems with splicing, or joining, such fine glass fibers. However these subjects are beyond this discussion.

Improvement of transmission through optical fibers since 1968.

You may be thinking that this method of producing the core glass for a fiber goes to unnecessary extremes to get rid of impurities. It is most important to realize that even very small amounts of impurity produce significant absorption. Using the criterion which we mentioned in the previous paragraph, the following concentrations of impurity atoms (given as the numbers of atoms per *billion*) would only allow 1% of the light to reach the end of a one kilometer length of fiber: cobalt, 2; iron, 20; copper, 50.

Just think how much purer than this we need the glass to be in order to be able to get 95% of the light through this 1km length!

Fibers used for telephonic transmission have a core diameter of only about 10 microns, a thousandth of a centimeter. Why do we make the fibers so thin? There are two important answers. The first is that when we bend a fiber, the outside stretches and therefore sees a tensile stress. The thicker the fiber the greater the stress and the greater the chance of fracture. Thin fibers are therefore more flexible. The second is that, if the fiber is thin, there is less chance of the light hitting the fiber wall at an angle less than the critical angle, and therefore escaping. The following diagram show a light ray entering three fibers of different thicknesses at the same angle, and the paths that these rays take through the fibers. In the thick fiber the light ray makes only one reflection in the fiber and hits the fiber wall at a smaller angle (measured from the perpendicular to the surface) than any angle of incidence in the medium thickness fiber. In the thinnest fiber the angles of incidence are the largest. As a result of these two factors really thin fibers can be bent more and have less change of losing the light than do thicker fibers.

Three parallel light rays entering different thickness optical fibers. In the thinnest fiber there is less change of the angle of incidence being smaller than the critical angle.

The advantages of optical fibers

What are some of the advantages of optical fibers over copper wires for telephone transmission? The two major ones are clarity of signal and the ability to carry many conversations in one fiber at the same time. In addition there are factors of weight and volume. Optical fibers are obviously much thinner than a copper wire and they have a much lower density. This means that the Atlantic ocean could be crossed with two shiploads of optical fiber as opposed to five of copper wire, which would not be able to carry as many conversations.

When an electrical current travels along a wire it produces a magnetic field outside and around the wire. This magnetic field in turn causes a small current to flow in an adjacent wire which is in the influence of this magnetic field. A signal is **induced** into the second wire which duplicates the signal in the first wire although at a much lower intensity. This is why one often heard a second conversation on the same line when making a telephone call. For obvious reasons the phenomenon is known as **crosstalk**. One conversation has crossed over to an adjacent line. With light waves in an optical fiber there is no such phenomenon. The light does not in any way cross over to an adjacent fiber, with the consequence of a better and clearer signal.

Another benefit related to the absence of crosstalk is the security of conversations carried on optical fibers. Telephone lines are tapped using the same phenomenon which causes crosstalk. A small coil of wire placed around the wire carrying the conversation will pick up the conversation because an identical signal is induced in the coil. With an optical fiber the only way to tap the light is to break into the fiber and allow some light to escape, a fact which would immediately be noticed. We should, however, note that the optical fibers only connect the main transmitting and receiving stations, and that connections between them and our houses is still by copper wires. It will only be when the total connection is by fiber optics that we can be certain that nobody is listening.

To understand the second major advantage of being able to carry many more conversations, one has to remember that the audio signal is transmitted along the optical fiber by a series of pulses (light flashes). These pulses need only be around a ten thousandth of a second (10^{-4} sec) apart. You may think that this means the pulses are very close together. True, but when you think that each pulse need only be around 10^{-8} seconds in duration (a ten thousandth of the time between pulses) it means that a thousand other pulses could easily be placed between two adjacent pulses from one conversation, and these thousand other pulses could each come from a different conversation. This slotting together of pulses from many different conversations can easily be accomplished nowadays with the electronics at our disposal. Such techniques allow over 10,000 simultaneous voice conversations to be carried over a single optical fiber. This technique of passing many signals down one fiber is known as **multiplexing**. An illustration of how this is done (not to scale) is given in the next diagram.

Illustration of how two different conversations (1 & 2) can be transmitted at the same time. Note that the time T is really over ten thousand times greater than the time t.

The first transatlantic fiber optic cable (many fibers), which is about the diameter of a garden hose, was capable of handling 40,000 simultaneous conversations, more than twice the combined number possible using the three previously existing copper cables. At that time each fiber could carry around 600 simultaneous conversations. Today's more advanced technology allows one fiber to carry 30,000 simultaneous conversations. There are now several transatlantic fiber optic links and more than one third of the capacity is unused! It is perhaps even more remarkable to note that the first transatlantic cable was completed in 1956 and could handle only 52 simultaneous calls! The last 40 years have brought tremendous changes. This latest quantum leap is due to the new materials technology of optical fibers.

Some other advantages of sound transmission by optical fibers are the lack of electrical interference and the absence of corrosion effects. Recent data also show that the maintenance costs of a fiber optic network are about a fifth of those using conventional wires.

Other uses

The use of optical fibers to carry light from one place to another with very little loss in intensity is finding so many applications in our daily lives that it is impossible to catalog all of them.

The illumination of the switches and dials in an automobile may nowadays come from one bulb in an 'easy-to-reach' location rather than from many small bulbs in awkward locations behind the dashboard. The light is carried to the instruments by optical fibers.

Many medical instruments for seeing inside the body use a bundle of optical fibers to carry the light to the area/organ to be examined, while another bundle of fibers fitted with a lens is used to see what is happening. There have also been experiments using fiber optics to carry fine laser light beams to burn out the fat in clogged blood vessels.

Research at Penn State University has examined the possibility of carrying sunlight into windowless rooms using fiber optics. Fluorescent light has an inherent flicker, which you may not notice, but it does affect some people. The flicker-free light brought into the room by the fiber optics seems to have significant advantages over fluorescent lighting, and of course consumes no electricity.

Examples could be multiplied but those given are sufficient to illustrate the importance of this new materials technology. Remember that the major developments have taken place in the last twenty years. Optical fibers are truly an example of the importance of new materials in today's world.

In future we shall almost certainly see optical fibers being brought into our homes. When that happens, they will not only carry our telephone conversations, but will bring us more radio and TV signals than we currently obtain via cable, and also give us computer connections to the bank, the supermarket, etc. One US company talks of providing 700 channels once their customers have the necessary optical linkages and decoding boxes! We can only begin to imagine the possibilities. Here is perhaps a materials development which we shall produce changes in the way we live comparable to the changes brought about in the last forty years by solid state electronics. In the last few years telecommunications companies have announced plans to 'wire' the USA with optical fibers at costs (under)estimated in the billions of dollars! It is anybody's guess how long it will be before such plans reach fruition.

QUESTIONS: Chapters 28-29

1. Which of the following electromagnetic waves has an energy of approximately 10 eV?
   (a) blue light (b) gamma rays (c) infrared rays (d) ultraviolet rays (e) microwaves

2. Light will travel the <u>slowest</u> in _____.
   (a) air (b) ice (c) glass (d) diamond (e) a vacuum

3. The core glass in an optical fiber is formed by _____ .
   (a) melting (b) zone refining (c) annealing (d) sintering (e) chemical vapor deposition

4. Which of the following is not true of the core glass of an optical fiber?
   (a) no cracks (b) higher electron density than the cladding glass (c) must be thin
   (d) no unwanted impurities (e) all of these are true

5. The distance between two identical points on a wave is called the _____.
   (a) wavelength (b) frequency (c) energy (d) speed of light (e) none of these

6. Light loss that occurs through absorption is sometimes called _____.
   a) refraction b) attenuation c) multiplexing d) crosstalk e) total internal reflection

7. When we make optical fibers we must make sure that the fiber is free of unwanted impurities and microscopic surface scratches. These correspond to processing the fiber to control the _____ structure (impurities) and the _____ structure (scratches).
   (a) crystal, micro (b) atomic, micro (c) crystal, macro (d) electron, crystal
   (e) atomic, crystal

8. Which of the following is not true of light ?
   (a) it is an electromagnetic wave (b) the wavelength of light is different in different media
   (c) the velocity of light is the same in different media (d) light incident on a material may
   be reflected and refracted (e) nothing can travel faster than light

9-11.   The bending of light when it enters a material is called ___9___. It is dependent on the
   ___10___ in the material. The ratio of the speed of light in a vacuum to the speed of light
   in a material is called the ___11___.

   9. (a) reflection (b) attenuation (c) refraction (d) reverberation (e) the critical angle
   10. (a) electron density (b) electron mobility (c) number of electrons (d) electron hole
   density (e) type of electrons
   11. (a) transmission coefficient (b) velocity gradient (c) reflective index (d) attenuation
   constant (e) refractive index

12-26. In the manufacture of pure optical fibers, impure sand (silicon oxide) is reacted with ____12i____ and the resulting mixture of ____12ii____ s is separated by a process of ____13____. The required glass is then made by a process called ____14____. In this process, a mixture of ____15____ vapor and ____16____ gas is heated to form ____17____ and ____12i____. In order to increase the refractive index of this glass, we add some ____18____ ____12ii____ vapor to the gas stream. The refractive index of the glass produced with this dopant is higher because ____18____ has ____19____ electrons than silicon. We use ____18____ as the dopant because it is a ____20____ impurity in glass and has ____21____ valence electrons. It is therefore neither an acceptor nor a donor. As a result we can increase the refractive index of the glass but it will still not ____22____ any light. An optical fiber carries signals by means of ____23____ and as many as a few hundred telephone conversations can be carried by one fiber at the same time using a technique called ____24____. A kilometer length of the best optical fiber loses about ____25____% of the light when it passes from one end to the other, but very little light would be ____26____ over distances of hundreds of kilometers.

12. (a) nitrogen, nitride (b) iodine, iodide (c) chlorine, chloride (d) fluorine, fluoride (e) oxygen, oxide
13. (a) distillation (b) zone refining (c) decimation (d) doping (e) annealing
14. (a) internal reflection (b) zone refining (c) chemical vapor deposition (d) melting (e) vitrification
15. (a) $NbCl_4$ (b) SiO_2 (c) $SiCl_4$ (d) TiO_2 (e) NaCl
16. (a) nitrogen (b) chlorine (c) hydrogen (d) oxygen (e) carbon dioxide
17. (a) TiO_2 (b) GeO_2 (c) SiO_2 (d) NbO_2 (e) none of these
18. (a) niobium (b) titanium (c) silicon (d) lithium (e) germanium
19. (a) a larger number of (b) a smaller number of (c) twice the number of (d) larger (e) slower
20. (a) refractive (b) interstitial (c) precipitate (d) large (e) substitutional
21. (a) 8 (b) 4 (c) 10 (d) 18 (e) 0
22. (a) transmit (b) absorb (c) diffract (d) reflect (e) refract
23. (a) electrons (b) phonons (c) neurons (d) light pulses (e) protons
24. (a) crosstalking (b) multiplexing (c) concentrating (d) superpositioning (e) complexing
25. (a) 10 (b) 0.2 (c) 20 (d) 4 (e) 0.01
26. (a) transmitted (b) reflected (c) absorbed (d) refracted (e) emitted

27-29. A mirage is an illustration of the phenomenon of the ____27____ of light. For this to occur, light must be traveling in the material with the ____28____ refractive index and the angle of refraction must be ____29____ the critical angle.

27. (a) refraction (b) total internal reflection (c) total internal absorption (d) total transmission (e) attenuation
28. (a) higher (b) lower (c) much greater (d) weaker (e) much smaller
29. (a) equal to (b) smaller than (c) half as much as (d) greater than

30. MAGNETIC MATERIALS

There is no doubt that magnetic materials play a vital role in our everyday activities in today's world, even though we may be unaware of their presence. At some time we have probably all played with magnets, or toys containing them, but if we were asked today to name a place where we could find them we would probably mention the little magnets we use to hold notes to the refrigerator door. If we take a simple magnet and walk around trying to pick things up with it, we are unsuccessful most of the time. We recognize very few materials as magnetic and the vast majority of those are based on iron. What makes iron or any other material a magnet? Or more generally, why are most materials not magnets? The answer to these questions can get very complex; indeed the magnetic behavior of materials is perhaps the most difficult to understand. We shall find a simple answer provided we are willing to accept two simple statements on faith. But, to be honest, we have to do that all the time.

Background

If we wish to magnetize a bar of iron we do so by placing it in a strong magnetic field. Usually we do this in the following way. We make a coil of wire and pass a direct current through it. The result of this is that the coil behaves like a magnet. If we slowly push our iron bar into the coil and take it out, as illustrated below, we find that it has been magnetized. The magnetic field of the coil has somehow magnetized the iron. Why is this?

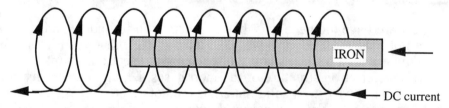

IRON

DC current

A piece of iron may be made magnetic (magnetized) by slowly pushing it into a coil through which a direct electric current is flowing, and then withdrawing it.

The first thing that we have to accept is that *electrons going round in circles produce a magnetic field*. This is certainly true of the coil of wire shown in the diagram, where the radius of the circles is the radius of the coil. It may seem quite a large change in scale, but electrons go round in circles when they orbit the nucleus of an atom and when they do this they also produce a small magnetic field. This is our first clue. We should therefore expect each individual atom to act like a little magnet. Physics tells us that in such a case the strength of the magnetic field is proportional to the area of the circle. Obviously this is very small for electrons orbiting an atomic nucleus.

Because magnets can attract and repel each other we might expect atoms to show some reaction to a magnetic field. In fact, if we take individual atoms and place them in a magnetic field we can easily show that they are moved by that field just as small weak magnets would be. The only exceptions are the inert gases. Apart from the inert gases every individual atom acts like a little magnet. Notice carefully that we are here talking about individual atoms, and for this the atoms must be separated as in a vapor, but this is often not difficult to accomplish. We are not really interested in the magnetic behavior of atomic gases, but they do give us the next clue that we need.

What is it that makes the inert gases different in their magnetic behavior, i.e. why, of all the atoms, do they not behave like little magnets? We have already seen that they are characterized by having eight electrons in their outer shell. These eight electrons have orbits around the nucleus such that for every electron going one way there is another going the opposite way , and the opposite directions produce magnets which are opposed to each other and therefore cancel each other out. This canceling of magnets is basically what leads to most materials being non-magnetic and it occurs at so many different structural levels. Here it occurs at the level of the electron structure. This leads us to the second fact we have to accept: *there are some atoms, including those with the electron structure of the inert gases, which do not behave as if they are little magnets.* In fact any atom with only full sub-shells of electrons behave the same way.

Now we have the necessary basic information to understand why most solids are not magnetic, because we have already seen that when atoms bond together they usually do so by sharing or exchanging electrons so that they both end up with the electron structure of the inert gases, i.e. eight electrons in their outer shell. This is why most solid materials are not magnetic. For example we saw that common salt (NaCl) consists of sodium and chlorine ions which each have an inert gas electron structure.

Now that we have seen why most solids are not magnets , we need to ask why it is that some materials manage to have atoms which do produce a magnetic field? For this we shall consider metal magnets and ceramic magnets separately.

Metal magnets

At this point, we need to look once more at the periodic table provided at the beginning of the book (Page 7). Across the middle of this table you will see the following elements:

Scandium Titanium Vanadium Chromium Manganese Iron Cobalt Nickel Copper Zinc
Sc   Ti   V   Cr   Mn   Fe   Co   Ni   Cu   Zn

These elements are called the **transition metals** and their major feature is that they contain electrons in their 4s level while the 3d level is only partly full. This is because the fourth electron shell begins to fill before the third shell has its full complement of 18 electrons ($2n^2$). In other words the energy ladder we drew earlier (Page 210) is a little more complex than we imagined. The 4s level shown in the diagram should be slightly below the 3d level, i.e. between the 3p and 3d levels. Don't let these details overwhelm you, just grasp the important fact that many of these transition metals have a 3d level which is only partly full while having electrons on the 4s level. When these atoms form bonds with themselves, or with other atoms, they usually use the electrons in the fourth shell for the bonding and leave the third shell unfilled. This is enough to make the atom a small magnet, because it is left with an unfilled electron shell.

This raises yet another question. If this is true for these transition metals, why are they not all magnetic? It **is** true that the atoms in these circumstances each act like a small magnet but, just as we have seen that the electrons in an atom can produce magnetic fields which cancel each other, so the individual atom magnets can be arranged to cancel each other. In some elements (e.g. titanium) each atom points its magnet in a random direction. As a consequence there is no resultant, or net, magnetic field. We call such materials **paramagnets**. In other elements (e.g. chromium) the individual atom magnets arrange themselves so that they alternate in pointing in opposite directions. Again there is no resultant magnetic field. Such materials are called **antiferromagnets**. The following illustrations may help you to visualize this. The arrows on the atoms are pointing in the directions of their atomic magnetic fields. In both these cases the magnetic cancellation occurs on the atomic level.

Within this group of transition metals there are only three which, in the solid form, arrange their individual atom magnets to all point in the same direction. These are iron, cobalt and nickel. We call these three elements **ferromagnets** (ferro = iron) and they are the only common metals which we consider to be magnetic. In some magnets we use combinations (alloys) of these elements to obtain a desired property.

On the left the atom magnets are systematically arranged to oppose each other, something called antiferromagnetism (e.g. chromium). On the right the atom magnets are randomly oriented to produce an effect called paramagnetism (e.g. titanium).

It is not possible for us to explain why the atoms arrange their individual atom magnets in the way that they do. We must simply note that the alignments are spontaneous and we cannot manufacture the materials so that they arrange their atom magnets in any other way. For example, we know that the chromium atom produces a stronger magnet than the iron atom, but we can't use chromium as a magnet because the atoms insist in pointing their individual atom magnets in alternating opposite directions so that they cancel each other. The material is antiferromagnetic.

There is one final point to consider. If the iron atoms in a crystal spontaneously arrange their atom magnets to point in the same direction, why are not all pieces of iron magnetic? Here again we have a situation where the magnets arrange to cancel each other. It is true that in a piece of iron the atom magnets align in the same direction, but even in one single crystal there are different regions called **domains**. In each domain the atoms point their magnets in the same direction but atoms in adjacent domains point their magnets in opposite or different directions so that they cancel each other. A typical illustration is given on the next page, where the arrows again show the directions in which the individual atoms point their magnets in each of the four domains.

In an iron single crystal there are regions called domains in which the atoms point their magnets in the same direction, but different domains point in different directions so that the magnets cancel.

Note that this diagram shows a single crystal, and a single crystal can contain many different domains. The atoms are arranged in a continuous ordered array throughout this piece of material, and there are no grain boundaries. The only difference between the domains is that the atoms point their magnets in different directions in different domains. This is simply the natural state of the material. Here we have cancellation on a microstructural level. Domains are a new feature of microstructure which we have previously not encountered. They only occur in magnet materials.

Note that we have now seen three ways in which magnets cancel each other. In single atoms the fields of the individual electrons may cancel. In titanium and chromium, for example, the individual atom magnets cancel, either by pointing in random or opposite directions, a situation that we cannot change. In the ferromagnets we can have whole regions of atoms (domains) which point their magnets in opposite directions, a situation that we shall now see can be changed.

When we place a piece of iron in a coil of wire, the magnetic field in the coil forces the individual atom magnets to turn to point in the same direction as the applied magnetic field of the coil. The way they do this is rather interesting because it tells us much about the way we can influence the magnetic behavior of materials.

In the above diagram we have shown four domains (not grains or crystallites), and just as grains are separated by grain boundaries, so are domains separated by domain boundaries or walls. However the domain boundary is a thin *volume* of material in which the individual atom magnets gradually change direction. The following diagrams illustrate what we are talking about, where the arrows represent the magnets of the individual atoms.

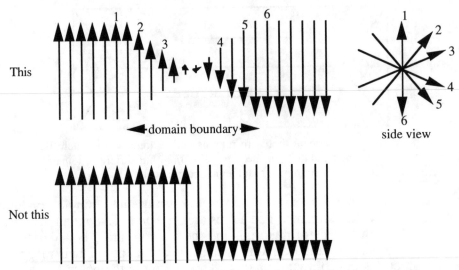

This

Not this

Atom magnets near a domain boundaries are changing direction gradually as shown in the upper diagram rather than suddenly as shown in the lower diagram.

When we place a piece of iron in our coil in order to magnetize it, the domain walls in the material move and this movement is accomplished by rotating the atom magnets in the wall a small amount. In some respects it's just like turning a screw; the wall moves forward as the magnets rotate.

Now think what this does. It allows us to change the direction of an atom magnet a little at a time rather than completely reverse it in one go. There is some similarity here with the dislocation which we discussed earlier (Page 68). The dislocation makes it easier for planes of atoms to slide over each other by moving a row at a time, while domain boundaries allow atom magnets to rotate more easily by doing this a little at a time. As the domain boundary moves we end up with more atoms pointing their magnets in the direction of the magnetic field acting on them. After the material has been magnetized, any supply of energy, such as heat or a sudden jolt, e.g. dropping the bar on a concrete floor, may cause the domain boundaries to return to their original positions and the net magnetism of the material to be lost. The following diagrams illustrate what happens when a domain boundary moves in a crystal. We must note that the domain boundary, which in the previous diagram is shown as only 10 atoms wide, is in fact about 300 atoms across. This means that the boundary has a width of close to 1000Å.

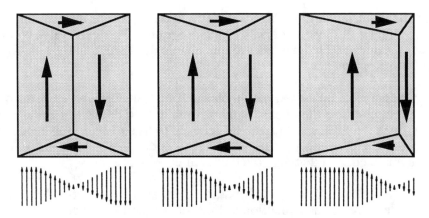

Material being magnetized in a vertical-up direction.

Using domain boundaries

Now we come to the interesting way in which the materials scientist can influence the properties of magnetic materials by way of these domain boundaries. There are some instances when we want to be able to quickly change the direction of magnetization of a material. For example in an electrical transformer the alternating current changes direction 60 times per second, which means that the magnetic field produced in the coils of the transformer also changes direction this frequently. We also need the magnets in the transformer to be able to change their direction in pace with this current change, which means that we want the domain walls to move very easily, because, as we have seen, they are what allow the atom magnets to change direction. On the other hand there are instances when we want our material to stay magnetized in a given direction and not be easily changed. An important example of this is on magnetic recording tape or a magnetic computer storage device. When we record information in the form of a magnetic signal on the tape or disc we don't want this signal to disappear just because we drop it, or the temperature gets too high.

It turns out that we can stop, or hinder, the motion of domain boundaries by putting small precipitates in the metal. If we do this, it becomes more difficult to move the domain boundaries when we magnetize the material, so we need much stronger magnets to do this, but conversely it is more difficult to move the boundaries back to their original positions, i.e. to demagnetize the material. Putting precipitates in the material helps produce a **permanent magnet**, one which does not readily revert to the unmagnetized state. Now you also know what other effect precipitates have on a metal: they stop dislocations moving, making the material harder (Page 99). The two effects are inseparable, and we therefore often call these materials **hard magnets**. This can really be taken to have two meanings. The materials are mechanically hard, and they are also hard (difficult) to demagnetize.

Of course, if we now want a material for a transformer we need a material without precipitates so that there are no obstructions to domain boundary motion. This is why you may see such material referred to as **soft iron**; it is mechanically soft because there are no precipitates to pin dislocations. Materials which are easily magnetized, and demagnetized are called **soft magnets**.

There is one other way of making permanent magnets which we must discuss. We have already mentioned that the domain boundary has a width of around 1000Å. If we now make our magnet using smaller and smaller crystals, we reach a point where the boundary occupies almost the whole crystal. Each crystal wants to divide itself into domains as already illustrated but the walls are now beginning to take up too much room. Just think how wasteful it would be to build a house using building blocks ten feet thick! We would end up with rooms that were so small as to be practically useless. We therefore use thinner walls. In a magnetic material the domain boundaries, or walls, are quite thick on an atomic scale (over 300 atoms across) and there is no way of reducing this thickness. As soon as the crystal becomes so small that a domain boundary would occupy a large fraction of its volume, the crystal gives up the notion of dividing into several domains and assumes the form of just one domain per crystal. In each small crystal all the atom magnets now point in the same direction. This means that there is now no easy way for the atom magnets to change their direction and they become small permanent magnets. We call these materials **single domain magnets**.

This is the technique we use on our magnetic recording tape and computer discs. The following photograph, taken using a scanning electron microscope, shows the particles on a disc. They are small, with a width of about two tenths of a micron (2000Å), so that each particle is only large enough to contain one domain. In some other magnets we manage to process them so that we have a microstructure something like the aluminum-lithium alloys we discussed earlier (Chapter 11). In this case there are very fine precipitates of magnetic metal surrounded by non-magnetic metal. The magnetic particles are so small that they are single domains. In order to get a really strong magnet, and to make sure that these domains don't all point their magnets in different directions, we solidify the material inside a strong magnetic field. This forces the atom magnets in all single

Photograph of small magnetic particles on a computer
disc. Each particle is a single magnetic domain.

domain particles to line up in the same direction when they crystallize, so we
obtain a material which is both a strong and a permanent magnet.

It is interesting to note that when we make metal particles as small as this
they are also too small to contain dislocations. If we make thin metal **whiskers**
(Page 97) and measure their strength, we find that they are about a thousand
times stronger than normal metals. This confirms our earlier statements that it is
the dislocations which weaken the metal. Unfortunately metal whiskers are too
small to be of much use to us.

Amorphous metal magnets

Here is a separate and very new type of metal magnet which has the
potential of being very important. We have already seen that amorphous metals
are very difficult to make (Page 64) but that they are of great importance for
magnetic materials. Of course the atoms have to be magnetic to start with, which
limits us to iron, nickel and a few others. To simplify matters we shall only
consider a piece of amorphous iron. Under normal circumstances the metal is
crystalline. At room temperature the iron crystals are body centered cubic, and
for a reason very difficult to understand, the atom magnets insist on pointing in
directions parallel to the crystal cube edges. They just don't like pointing in other
directions, a phenomenon we call **magnetic anisotropy**. However if we want
to reverse the magnetization direction, which is done via domain boundary
motion, we have to turn the atom magnets so that at some time they point in
directions where they don't want to be.

Atom magnet lies parallel to cube edge (1), but in order to reverse direction
(5) must pass through directions 2 and 4 which it does not like to do.

In the above diagram we show an atom magnet pointing parallel to an
edge of a cubic crystal (1). As the domain boundary comes up to this atom it tries
to turn the direction of the magnet to point in the opposite direction (5). Notice
that the atom is not moving, only the direction of its little magnet. In order to
reverse direction the atom magnet has to be made to point in directions (2 and 4)
which it doesn't like. It takes energy to move the magnet through these
directions. Turning the atom magnet is like moving a ball over a wavy surface, as
shown in the accompanying diagram. Energy is required to push the ball over the
humps just as it is required to move the atoms magnets around. It is this magnet
anisotropy which makes it difficult to move the domain boundary and hence
magnetize the material in a different direction.

We mentioned earlier that a transformer contains a magnet in which the
atom magnets reverse direction every time the current direction changes (60 times
per second). Each time this happens energy is used, and this energy comes from
the power we are transmitting, i.e. we have an energy loss. Now think what
happens if we replace this magnet with an amorphous magnetic metal. In this
material the atoms are randomly arranged. There are no cubic crystals and no
cube edges to align the atom magnets, so the atom magnets don't mind which
direction they point in. They can point equally easily in any direction and very
little energy is required to change this direction, i.e. they are truly soft magnets.
As a consequence there is not the energy loss that is found with crystalline metal
magnets.

It is estimated that by using amorphous metals in the transformers used in
power transmission in the U.S.A. we would save energy to the value of well over
$1 billion a year! These amorphous metal magnets are now being produced
commercially and are being used in new installations. It is of course not
economical to replace all existing installations with the new material, but it is
gradually making an impact in today's world.

Remember what we said about amorphous metals earlier (Page 65). They can only be produced in very thin sheets, so we have to make our magnets by laminating these sheets in the same way we build up a thick piece of plywood. Also, because they have no atomic order there are no straight paths for electron motion and electron mobility is low, making for a high electrical resistance. It turns out that this is an added advantage, because not only does the alternating current in the transformer produce a rapidly changing magnetic field, it also shunts the electrons back and forth in the metal magnet, producing heat. The random atom arrangement in an amorphous metal inhibits this electron motion and therefore reduces this effect.

There is one final curiosity about these new amorphous magnets. Because the atoms are randomly arranged there are no planes of atoms to slip over each other, and of course there are no dislocations, so the materials are quite hard and brittle. However, they are soft magnets. This combination of mechanical hardness and magnetic softness is quite unique because in crystalline materials anything we do to stop domain boundaries moving also stops dislocations moving. We therefore usually produce mechanical hardness and magnetic hardness at the same time. This is not the case here.

Ceramic magnets

Not only can the transition metals themselves be magnetic but so can some of their compounds. They also have the domain structure we have just discussed and exhibit many of the properties of metal magnets. However there are some really important differences.

Perhaps the earliest known, naturally occurring, magnetic material is known as lodestone which is an iron oxide (Fe_3O_4). The iron atoms give up electrons so that the four oxygens each have the extra two which they need to have their outer shells of eight. These eight electrons are obtained by two of the three iron atoms each losing three electrons and the third losing two electrons. In both cases, the iron atom (ion) is left with an unfilled outer electron shell which does not contain eight electrons and is therefore a magnet. In the crystalline solid the three iron atoms arrange their magnets in the following manner.

$$\uparrow \qquad\qquad \downarrow \qquad\qquad \uparrow$$
$$Fe^{3+} \qquad\quad Fe^{3+} \qquad\quad Fe^{2+}$$

Two of the three atom magnets cancel each other and the third iron ion (Fe^{2+}) produces a net magnetic field. Notice that the oxygen ions are not magnetic - they have an full outer shell of eight electrons. Therefore in each molecule (Fe_3O_4) there is no magnetic field from the oxygens, two of the irons are little magnets which cancel each other, leaving only one iron ion to produce the magnetic field. In a piece of magnetized iron, **all** the atoms contribute so the metal magnet is much stronger than the ceramic magnet.

What then is the importance of these ceramic oxide magnets if they are not as strong as metallic magnets? One answer to this question lies in the fact that ceramics are electrical insulators.

When we were talking about the advantages of using amorphous metals in transformers we mentioned that we lose energy for two reasons; as the individual atom magnets rotate, and as the free electrons are shunted back and forth in the material. Ceramics have no free electrons so there is therefore no energy loss produced by the second of these two effects. In circumstances where the magnetic field is changing direction extremely rapidly we therefore use ceramic magnets.

Perhaps the situation closest to you where this occurs is in the tube of your television set. A magnet at the back of the tube causes an electron beam to scan across the screen which is dotted with different phosphors. This electron beam is scanned very rapidly, 525 lines every sixtieth of a second. Using a ceramic magnet in this situation causes a much lower energy loss than would be the case for metal magnets. It also makes the TV set considerably lighter in weight.

Another advantage of ceramic magnets is that they are not as soft as metals. You may not realize that inside your portable tape recorder/player there is a magnetic recording head over which a rather abrasive magnetic tape passes. The chances are that this tape also uses ceramic magnet particles (iron oxide or chromium oxide). This recording head has to stand up to considerable abuse, and a metal magnet would soon wear away. You may have seen words such as ferrite used in describing the materials used for this purpose. Ferrites are simply a group of materials based on iron oxide magnets.

Ceramic magnets also have the advantage of being brittle and can be ground to very fine powders without loss of their magnetic properties. They are also corrosion resistant. They do not rust! Iron metal powder rusts very quickly, especially on hot, humid summer days. Because of these properties, ceramic magnet powders can be easily mixed into plastics to produce the material used for the door seal on your refrigerator and for some advertisements attached to car doors, etc. You will also find particles of ceramic magnet in the little decorative magnets you use to attach notes or bottle openers to the refrigerator door. This resistance to corrosion is why most recording tapes are made using ceramic magnets. We can easily grind them to single domain size and there is no need to protect them from the atmosphere.

The early recording tapes used iron oxide for this same reason, then came chromium oxide (CrO_2) tapes. Remember that we earlier said that a chromium atom is a stronger magnet than an iron atom, but that chromium was, unfortunately, antiferromagnetic. In the oxide we can take advantage of this stronger magnet. Metal recording tapes were a much later development because the problems of corrosion and making very small, single domain, particles had to be overcome. That's one reason why they are more expensive. Their advantage lies in the fact that metals are stronger magnets because, as we mentioned earlier, all their atoms can contribute to the magnetic field rather than some of them, as in the case of oxide magnets.

Conclusion

We encounter magnetic materials in many places during our everyday lives and they have grown very much in importance during the last 20-30 years. Unfortunately, there are not many materials in which this occurs.

Magnetic materials are an excellent example of the way structure affects properties. Remember that all magnets depend on the electrons orbiting the atomic nucleus. A magnet must contain atoms which have less than eight electrons in their outer electron shell (**electron structure**), and these little atom magnets must be arranged in the solid so that they do not cancel each other. We have also seen that the atoms in crystalline metals point their atom magnets along certain directions in the **crystal structure**, and that if we make the crystals very small (**microstructure**), we produce permanent single domain magnets. And of course, we are probably aware that if we want to produce a really strong magnetic field we place the two ends (north and south poles) of the metal magnet close together by bending the rod into a horseshoe shape (**macrostructure**).

We can also change the properties of magnets by replacing some atoms with others (**atomic structure**). This is especially true of ceramic magnets, but a discussion of these effects is outside the scope of this text.

QUESTIONS: Chapter 30

1-10   Magnets are important components of all electric motors, automobiles, tape recorders and computer memory storage devices. We can classify magnets as metallic or ceramic, although there are two different types of metallic magnets: crystalline and amorphous. Amorphous iron has the advantages that it can be magnetized easily in any direction and _____1_____ because _____2_____, but it has the disadvantage(s) that _____3_____. Ceramic oxide magnets have the advantage(s) of _____4_____ but compared to metal magnets have the disadvantages of _____5_____. A metal magnet contains crystals which are subdivided into _____6_____s and can be considered as either hard or soft, depending on how easily it gains and loses its magnetization. For an audio tape and magnetic storage devices we need _____7_____ magnets because _____8_____. This is accomplished by using single _____6_____ magnets. The early magnetic tapes were made using ceramic oxide particles because the inherent _____9_____ of ceramics made it easy to obtain single _____6_____ magnets. This is an example of the _____10_____ structure of the material.

1. (a) is stiff (b) is more shiny (c) has a high electrical resistance (d) both a and c
   (e) both b and c
2. (a) the atoms don't have 8 electrons in the outer shall (b) there is no crystal structure
   (c) it is always thin (d) its crystals point in all directions
   (e) it has more free electrons because the electrons are not used in bonding
3. (a) it is always in thin sheets (b) it is brittle (c) it rusts (d) both b and c
   (e) all of these
4. (a) good abrasion resistance (b) not corroding (c) a high electrical resistance
   (d) both b and c (e) all of these
5. (a) rigidity (b) lower magnetic strength (c) brittleness (d) low luster
   (e) both b and c
6. (a) precipitate (b) domain (c) grain (d) microcrystal (e) crystallite
7. (a) soft (b) amorphous (c) hard (d) either b or c (e) any of the these
8. (a) they do not rust (b) they are easy to magnetize (c) they hold sound easier
   (d) they are cheaper (e) they are difficult to magnetize and demagnetize
9. (a) rigidity (b) lower magnetic strength (c) brittleness (d) low luster (e) strength
10. (a) electron (b) atomic (c) micro (d) macro (e) crystal

11-20. Magnetism is produced by electrons moving in circular orbits. This can be demonstrated by passing an electrical current through a ___11___. In a magnetic material it is the motion of the electrons ___12___ which produces the magnetism. Metal magnets are usually ___13___ than ceramic magnets but have the disadvantage(s) that they ___14___. Recording tape uses very small magnetic particles because ___15___. Ceramic magnets are used in ___16___. Amorphous iron is a very important magnetic material which can be used to advantage in ___17___. It is produced by cooling molten iron at a rate of a ___18___. Unfortunately, it is only available in the form of ___19___ pieces and it is quite ___20___.

11. (a) rectifier (b) light bulb (c) coil of wire (d) ceramic (e) battery
12. (a) freely between the atoms (b) around the atom nuclei (c) from bond to bond
    (d) from one energy level to another (e) none of these
13. (a) magnetically weaker (b) magnetically stronger (c) more amorphous (d) larger
    (e) lighter
14. (a) oxidize (rust) (b) cannot easily be ground to a fine powder
    (c) do not transmit light (d) both a and b (e) they have no disadvantages.
15. (a) they do not rust as easily (b) they allow the tape to be flexible
    (c) they are cheaper (d) it is difficult to change the magnetization of such very small
    particles (e) both b and d
16. (a) refrigerator door seals (b) magnetic note holders (c) VCR recording heads
    (d) TV sets (e) all of these
17. (a) rectifiers (b) activators (c) transistors (d) transformers (e) both c and d
18. (a) million degrees per minute (b) thousand degrees per second (c) million degrees
    per second (d) billion degrees per second (e) these cooling rates are all too slow
19. (a) small (b) thin (c) large (d) thick (e) powdered
20. (a) expensive (b) brittle (c) ductile (d) both a and b (e) both a and c

21-24. There are some ceramic magnets and they are very important in today's world. One/some of their advantages is/are that they ___21___. As a result they can withstand the repeated passage of a recording tape in a VCR for years, and can also be mixed with a plastic for use as ___22___. Ceramic magnets do not rust because they ___23___. The big advantage of metal magnets is that they are ___24___.

21. (a) resist abrasion (b) can be ground to a fine powder because of their brittleness
    (c) are lightweight (d) both a and b (e) all of these
22. (a) magnets holding notes to refrigerator doors (b) recording heads for cassette players
    and VCR's (c) refrigerator door seals (d) both a and b (e) both a and c
23. (a) have ionic bonds (b) are very strong (c) are oxidized (d) are based on metals
    (e) both b and c
24. (a) less likely to oxidize (b) stronger magnets (more attraction)
    (c) free of dislocations (d) both a and b (e) both b and c

31. MATERIALS IN TOMORROW'S WORLD

What new materials are there left for us to discover? The materials scientist approaches his work with the attitude that there must be materials with the properties we want if only we can find the right elements and put them together in the correct proportions (atomic structure) in the correct crystal structures. The scientist never takes 'no' for an answer. We may not be able to speculate wisely about the unknown, but there are many materials we already know about: our current problem is getting them to work.

Five years have elapsed since the first edition of this book and, while researchers have been very active. there have been no new major materials developments which have shown up in our everyday lives such as was the case in the previous fifty years. The following brief discussion points out some of the exciting materials developments we are still expecting. It is anybody's guess how long we shall have to wait.

Ceramics

We have already mentioned some of the anticipated developments in ceramics. Superconducting ceramics, nanophase materials which are not brittle, and strong, tough fiber reinforced materials are but a few of the possibilities. We expect to see tremendous advances in all these areas in the coming years. For the general consumer perhaps the greatest advance would be a ceramic automobile engine.

Japanese researchers have already found it possible to manufacture such an engine by using ultrafine, ultrapure ceramic powders. It exists in an automobile which has already been track tested for a few thousand miles. It is a basic fact of physics that engines are more efficient the higher the temperature at which they operate. A ceramic engine could operate at temperatures around 1400°C (2500°F) and would not require a radiator. Imagine being able to get rid of a heavy cooling system, replace the heavy steel engine with a smaller, lighter one made of ceramic, and increase efficiency at the same time! Surely an automobile manufacturer's dream, and experts predict it will come true before the end of the century.

Already some cars are using silicon nitride rotors for turbochargers. Here it is the lighter weight which is an advantage. The rotor reaches its required velocity earlier because it needs less energy to turn it, and as a consequence, turbo lag is reduced, and the turbocharging effect is more immediate.

The catalytic converter in today's automobiles is also a recent ceramic material called cordierite. It is made with a very fine honeycomb structure which is coated with a very thin layer of the catalyst. The exhaust gases pass through this honeycomb which must not present much of an obstacle to the gases otherwise a significant back pressure would build up. Ceramics are also used as spark plug insulators, oxygen sensors, sensors that turn on the windshield wipers when rain falls, sensors that turn on the lights when it gets dark, etc. More and more ceramics are being used in today's cars, and the trend will certainly continue in the years ahead.

There is no doubt that as ceramics are made to be less brittle and stronger there will be many areas of our everyday lives where they will be used, especially where resistance to heat is required.

Metals

The demise of the vast North American steel empires has caused some people to speculate about metals being supplanted by polymers or ceramics in almost all applications. However, we have discussed two metallurgical developments of recent years (HSLA steels and aluminum-lithium alloys), both of which give considerable weight savings on automobiles and aircraft, respectively.

You may remember that in aluminum-lithium (Chapter 11) we produced a fine precipitate of something we called delta prime which had the chemical formula Al_3Li. Compounds of two or more metals with exact chemical formulae like this are called intermetallic compounds, i.e. compounds produced between two or more metals. Combining nickel with aluminum produces a new, strong, heat-resistant metal called nickel aluminide (Ni_3Al). Yes, it has the same atomic arrangement as our delta prime (Page 108); just replace the Al with Ni, and the Li with Al. This is just one of a number of new metallurgical developments to compete with the heat resisting properties of ceramics. There is also much current interest in titanium aluminide intermetallics. Unfortunately, these new metallic materials are very brittle (you should readily appreciate that atom planes composed of two different atoms cannot possibly be as smooth as those containing only one type of atom) and their properties resemble those of many ceramics. Here again, we need to learn how to harness these materials and tailor their properties to our needs.

Recent years have seen many advances in the fabrication of metal parts from powders. Making metal powders is sometimes quite difficult, but when it can be done, the required part can be made by making a mold, filling it with the powder and then sintering in the same way we produce ceramic parts. The result is a part which is very close to the final size and shape so that little, if any, machining is required, and there is no metal waste. Savings in the cost of the amount of metal used and in the machining labor costs more than compensate for the cost of producing the powder. You would be surprised how many metallic automobile components are made using this technology nowadays.

We also mentioned when talking about Al-Li that there was usually a solubility limit of one metal in another. This limits the compositions of the alloys we can make. By using the powder metallurgy approach we can blend powders of different metals and then sinter them. This gets round the solubility limit which exists when metals are melted together. In this way we can produce new, interesting materials. The process, known as mechanical alloying, is already being used to produce some parts for jet engines.

There is little doubt that there will be even more use of powder metallurgy techniques in the future.

Another way round the solubility limit for some metals is to cool them very quickly from the melt, a process known as **rapid solidification**. While not fast enough to produce amorphous metals, the cooling process is fast enough to stop the different atoms from separating, and the larger solubility which exists at higher temperatures is frozen in.

New, so-called "superalloys" using nickel with quite large amounts of chromium, cobalt and tungsten as alloying elements, are also likely to see increasing use at high temperatures in the years ahead. But here again, the immediate need is in jet engines, especially in military applications, and it is unlikely that we shall encounter them in our everyday lives.

Finally, one must mention the continuing quest for metal matrix composites. At present there appear to be exciting possibilities for reinforcing aluminum with polymer fibers known as PBT. Who would of thought of reinforcing metals with plastics twenty years ago?

Polymers

Here is a group of materials which have become the bane and blessing of today's society. Cheap, easy to handle, very serviceable, non-toxic, etc., are but some of their advantages. It is remarkable that such a thin plastic bag can be strong enough to hold the garbage and be so cheap.

Polymer chemists can arrange the chains at their disposal into configurations not thought of only a few years ago. We can have chains radiating from a central nucleus in star (several chains radiating from a center like spokes in a wheel) and starburst patterns (the same but with the chains continually branching as they go further from this center), make long chains composed of a variety of shorter different chains, etc. No wonder six or so new plastics are sent to Underwriters Laboratories for testing every week.

Every year over 30 million tons of polymers are made in the U.S.A. Much is used in products which have a long life, but a large amount is used for hardly more than a minute, especially in containers for fast food and supermarket prepacked-meat trays. It may be used for only a minute or two but it will survive for a couple of centuries. If it were not so cheap we would perhaps say it was over engineered. A recent study suggests that over 18% of the landfill volume today is occupied by plastics.

Degradable plastics are the focus of much attention nowadays and, at the time of writing, have shown up in bags for packing one's goods at the supermarket. There are several forms of degradability: by biological activity (biodegradable), by light (photo-), usually ultraviolet, and water (hydro-). The new biodegradable plastic bags contain a little less than 10% starch, which is consumed by microorganisms in the water or soil. The plastic then falls apart. In the future we shall certainly see the starch content increased to over 50% and the introduction of polymers degraded by one or a combination of the above degradation mechanisms. At present there are some claims which seem to be suspect. A bag clearly labeled "photodegradable" has been sitting in the author's window for five years now with no signs of decay. Of course, even if such a bag were photodegradable, it would not help to have it placed in a landfill.

There are however other polymer developments in the offering which will probably have a greater impact on our lives.

We have used plastics for electrical insulation for years but there are now polymers which conduct electricity. The discovery of conducting polyacetylene

(Page 141) was another scientific accident which occurred in the early 1970's. The reason for its conduction has something to do with the fact that the molecular chain has alternating double and single bonds along its length, as illustrated below, but an explanation is beyond the scope of this discussion. The prospect of conduction along a single polymer chain introduces the concept of molecular wires about one atom in diameter. Just think of what this can do for electronic miniaturization!

$$=C-C=C-C=C-C=C-C=C-C=$$

A chain of polyacetylene.

New polymers also show some strange reactions to light. The fastest computer would use light rather than electrons to transfer information; nothing travels faster than light! Polymers may provide the switches for the light. There are also new polymers which transmit normal intensity light, but become opaque when exposed to high intensity laser beams. This material could be used to protect a person's eyes from damage by laser light beams.

Finally, as already mentioned in this chapter there are new lightweight, high strength, high modulus polymer fibers which are stable at temperatures above the melting point of aluminum. Just pour molten aluminum around the fibers and you have a valuable composite.

Semiconductors

Very early in this book (Page 8) we mentioned the importance of the production of high purity silicon. It is this which has made all of our modern electronics possible, ranging from the radio built into a small headphone to complex computers and medical instruments, etc. We have seen how impurities can affect the properties of semiconductors, and it is this which we control in their applications. The purest silicon available to us has about ten trillion impurity atoms in one ounce (Page 80) and apparently this is something we can live with. After all, the devices we make from this material do work! We have also mentioned the potential use of gallium arsenide in computers and solar cells (Pages 250 & 256). Its advantage is that its 'chips' would run five to eight times faster than silicon ones and consume one tenth the power. This is a very attractive possibility, especially for supercomputer manufacturers such as Cray and IBM.

For over ten years there have been attempts to use GaAs chips for computers, but without success. This is apparently because GaAs does not tolerate impurities as does silicon. Its electrical performance is greatly reduced by impurity atoms, and the best vacuum we can create on earth is still too dirty to produce material of sufficient purity. This is one example of where the processing of materials in space may have some real advantages. Space-based manufacturing has always been one of NASA's goals, but it is just too expensive at present - a shuttle flight costs close to a billion dollars. Perhaps space factories for materials processing will become a reality in the next century?

Conclusion

Our ability to fulfill our dreams and visions is often limited by the materials at our disposal. We live in exciting times, when new materials which expand our vision are always becoming available. New materials have changed our lives in the last few decades, especially semiconductors and polymers. The immediate future is difficult to predict. In this author's opinion the only development which is likely to have such a tremendous effect on us as have these two materials in the optical fiber. If indeed every house is wired with this technology there will be radical changes in the way we need to do many of our everyday chores. Whether these will really be beneficial is a matter for debate, and is perhaps a subject for the sociologist rather than the scientist.

SUMMARY QUESTIONS

1-3.   The processing of a material can involve ____1____. By changing these manufacturing stages one can significantly change the ____2____ which in turn changes the ____3____.

    1. (a) annealing (b) heating (c) quenching (d) rolling (e) all of these
    2. (a) structure (b) size (c) density (d) properties (e) both b and c
    3. (a) structure (b) properties (c) shape (d) melting point (e) color

4-7.   Throughout the book we have encountered some elements which are probably new to us. What applications (materials) did we mention which used the following elements?

    4. cobalt   5. gallium   6. europium   7. niobium

    (a) HSLA steels (b) magnets (c) TV screen phosphors (d) optical fibers
    (e) high efficiency solar cells

8. Select the true statement from the following:
    (a) all polymers are ductile at room temperature
    (b) the core glass of an optical fiber is pure SiO_2
    (c) tempered glass contains very small crystals
    (d) impurities are important in determining the color of a phosphor dot on a TV tube
    (e) a broken fiber cannot be tolerated in a composite

9. Select the incorrect statement from the following:
    (a) some metals are non-magnetic
    (b) most metals are ductile
    (c) no metals are liquid at room temperature
    (d) metals contain ions but do not have ionic bonds
    (e) metals are lustrous because they contain free electrons

10. Which of the following is not one of the ways to strengthen polymers or ceramics?
    (a) flame polishing (b) precipitation hardening (c) compressive loading
    (d) vulcanization (e) crystallization

11-14.   What applications do you identify with the following materials?
    11. cordierite   12. gallium arsenide   13. polyacetylene   14. chromium oxide

    (a) magnetic recording tape
    (b) a catalytic converter
    (c) a conducting polymer
    (d) optical fibers
    (e) high speed electronics

15-24. Getting impurities out of a material is a challenge for the materials scientist. We discussed how chromium could be purified by first reacting the chromium (and all its impurities) with _____15i_____ to produce _____15ii_____ s. The resulting mixture of _____15ii_____ s is then purified using a process called _____16_____. Purified chromium _____15ii_____ is then decomposed by passing it through a very hot furnace where pure chromium is produced by a process called _____17_____. We also saw how the _____18_____ of carbon-carbon composites can be formed from the _____17_____ of carbon from _____19_____. In optical fibers the core glass is also produced using _____17_____. A gas mixture of purified _____20_____ and _____21_____ passes through a hot tube and glass is formed. To increase the _____22_____ we add a small amount of purified _____23_____ to the gas mixture. This adds an impurity to the glass which increases the _____22_____ but produces no light _____24_____.

15. (a) chlorine, chloride (b) iodine, iodide (c) sulfur, sulfide (d) bromine, bromide
    (e) oxygen, oxide
16. (a) distillation (b) vitrification (c) annealing (d) chemical vapor deposition
    (e) sintering
17. (a) zone refining (b) chemical vapor deposition (c) polycondensation (d) doping
18. (a) matrix (b) surface (c) precipitates (d) filler (e) both a and d
19. (a) carbon dioxide (b) chlorine (c) acetylene (d) methane (e) diamond
20. (a) titanium oxide (b) geranium chloride (c) silicon chloride (d) silicon oxide
21. (a) nitrogen (b) oxygen (c) helium (d) both a and b
22. (a) density (b) reflectivity (c) electron density (d) strength (e) crack resistance
23. (a) chromium iodide (b) gallium arsenide (c) geranium iodide (d) iron
    (e) germanium chloride
24. (a) reflection (b) absorption (c) transmission (d) emission (e) refraction

25-26. The electrons in a certain material have a full band of possible energies separated from a completely empty energy band by an energy gap of 7 eV.

25. This material is a(n) _____.
    (a) semiconductor (b) insulator (c) electrical conductor (d) none of these
26. What color is a single crystal of the material?
    (a) red (b) violet (c) yellow (d) colorless (e) none of these

27-29. An impurity atom is added to the material of questions 25-26 and introduces an energy level 2.1 eV below the empty band. _____27_____ kick(s) an electron from the full band to the empty band, and when the electron returns to the full band via this impurity level _____28_____ light is _____29_____.

27. (a) microwaves (b) infrared light (c) blue light (d) ultraviolet light (e) radio waves
28. (a) red (b) yellow (c) violet (d) orange (e) green
29. (a) transmitted (b) reflected (c) emitted (d) adsorbed (e) absorbed

30-46. Impurities in materials are very important. As single atoms they can be _____30_____ and sometimes they occur in large groups called _____31_____. Regular window glass is opaque and a blue-green color if you try to look through a few inches thickness. This is because of the presence of _____32_____ impurity which produces some _____33_____ of light. Glass for optical fibers is pure _____34_____ which has been doped with _____35_____. This impurity is chosen because it produces no _____33_____, and because it is a _____36_____ impurity with more _____37_____ it increases the _____38_____ of the glass. In making Corning Ware we add _____39_____ impurity to act as nuclei for the formation of _____40_____. This process of forming _____40_____ from glass is called _____41_____. Corning Ware is very strong because of the presence of very small _____40_____, and does not break when taken straight from the freezer and placed on a hot burner. We call this property _____42_____. We add the impurity _____43_____ to rubber to produce _____44_____. The important impurity in HSLA steels is _____45_____; the impurity making silicon a p-type semiconductor is _____46_____.

30. (a) substitutional (b) interstitial (c) intrinsic (d) both a and c (e) both a and b
31. (a) dislocations (b) point defects (c) interstices (d) precipitates (e) chains
32. (a) silicon (b) germanium (c) iron (d) carbon (e) oxygen
33. (a) refraction (b) transmission (c) aberration (d) emission (e) absorption
34. (a) silicone (b) silicon oxide (c) geranium (d) lead silicate (e) silicon carbide
35. (a) silicon (b) germanium (c) iron (d) carbon (e) oxygen
36. (a) substitutional (b) interstitial (c) intrinsic (d) both a and c (e) both a and b
37. (a) photons (b) phonons (c) bonds (d) neutrons (e) electrons
38. (a) hardness (b) refractive index (c) absorption (d) internal reflection
    (e) conductivity
39. (a) titanium oxide (b) aluminum oxide (c) lead oxide (d) niobium carbide
    (e) gallium arsenide
40. (a) voids (b) crystals (c) precipitates (d) both a and c (e) both a and b
41. (a) solidification (b) hardening (c) devitrification (d) deregulation (e) sintering
42. (a) thermal shock resistance (b) impact resistance (c) shear strength
    (d) chemical inertness
43. (a) boron (b) carbon (c) sulfur (d) nitrogen (e) oxygen
44. (a) chain stiffening (b) crystallization (c) amorphization (d) crosslinking
    (e) relaxation
45. (a) germanium (b) aluminum (c) niobium (d) iron (e) nitrogen
46. (a) germanium (b) aluminum (c) niobium (d) iron (e) nitrogen

47-56. Metals consist of atoms held together by metallic bonds, whereas ceramics can contain _____47_____ bonds. Polymers have chains of carbon atoms with _____48_____ bonds along a chain but _____49_____ bonds between adjacent chains. In polymers it is the _____49_____ bonds which are usually thought of as the weakness in the material. Metals can often be strained several percent in tension because of _____50_____, whereas polymers often can be strained much more than metals because of _____51_____. Ceramics cannot be strained very much because the _____50_____ cannot move easily. One reason for this is the _____52_____ bonds which are _____53_____. Usually ceramics break catastrophically because of _____54_____. Polymers break in a similar manner when they _____55_____. It is important to remember that in all materials, fracture involves the breaking of _____56_____.

47. (a) covalent (b) hydrogen (c) ionic (d) metallic (e) both a and c
48. (a) covalent (b) van der Waals (c) hydrogen (d) ionic (e) metallic
49. (a) covalent (b) secondary (c) ionic (d) metallic (e) directional
50. (a) grain boundaries (b) dislocations (c) precipitates (d) impurities (e) weak bonds
51. (a) chain sliding (b) chain straightening (c) steric hindrance (d) both a and b
    (e) both a and c
52. (a) covalent (b) van der Waals (c) hydrogen (d) ionic (e) metallic
53. (a) strong (b) directional (c) non-directional (d) rotating (e) both a and b
54. (a) surface flaws (b) weak bonds (c) vacancies (d) impurities (e) dislocations
55. (a) contain fluorine (b) are compressed (c) are above the glass transition temperature
    (d) are copolymers (e) none of these
56. (a) grain boundaries (b) crystals (c) atoms (d) bonds (e) any of these

57-65. Metals are _____57_____ because they have rather fluid metallic bonds and _____58_____ motion occurs when metals are stressed, causing deformation. Ceramics deform very little under stress because they either have _____59_____ bonds or ions which repel each other if moved. Both of these interfere with _____58_____ motion and as a result, ceramics _____60_____ under stress. Ceramics can be strengthened by eliminating surface cracks and scratches or keeping them from propagating. One approach used to strengthen glasses is _____61_____ where the surface is remelted to get rid of small surface cracks. Another method is to cool the surfaces of the hot glass quickly, setting up _____62_____ stresses at the surface. _____63_____ ceramics may be strengthened by _____64_____. The _____65_____ in ceramics blunt cracks in the same way that the _____65_____ in metals stop _____58_____ motion.

57. (a) brittle (b) soft (c) weak (d) strong (e) ductile
58. (a) grain boundary (b) impurity (c) dislocation (d) precipitate (e) bond
59. (a) strong (b) weak (c) directional (d) both a and c (e) both b and c
60. (a) bend (b) fail catastrophically (c) stretch (d) blunt (e) slip
61. (a) ion implantation (b) hot rolling (c) flame polishing (d) tempering (e) layering
62. (a) tensile (b) shear (c) compressive (d) yield (e) no
63. (a) amorphous (b) dense (c) light weight (d) crystalline (e) layered
64. (a) making the grains larger (b) stopping dislocation motion (c) making the grains
    smaller (d) scratching the surface (e) adding pores
65. (a) grain boundaries (b) pores (c) bonds (d) tensile stresses (e) both a and c

GLOSSARY

Acceptor impurity: An substitutional impurity in an insulator or a semiconductor which has (usually) one less electron than the atom it replaces. Because of this there are insufficient electrons to form the covalent bonds and an electron hole is produced.

Alloy: A mixture of two or more metals. Mixing usually occurs in the molten state. The solid may contain more than one phase, as in aluminum-lithium alloys, and each phase often contains some of each metal. There is no need for the two atoms each to be arranged in a repeat pattern (see 'Intermetallic compound').

Alloying element: An element added to another to produce an alloy. It is usually the element which is present in the smaller proportion. Example, niobium in HSLA steels.

Amorphous: Refers to a material in which the atoms are arranged almost randomly. There may be some short range order, such as the silicon/oxygen tetrahedra in glass, but the order does not extend further than a few atoms. Often considered the opposite of crystalline. In polymers it means that the carbon chains are not arranged in an ordered manner.

Angstrom unit (Å): Small distance measurement, being 10^{-8} cm. An atom is around 2Å across. This unit is gradually being replaced by the nanometer (10^{-9} meters). One nanometer is equal to ten angstrom units.

Anion: An atom which has acquired one or more electrons so that it has a negative charge.

Anisotropy: A characteristic of a material showing quite different properties in different directions. Example, graphite is strong parallel to the planes of carbon atoms but weak in the perpendicular direction. Caused by the crystal structure of the material.

Annealing: Process of heating a material to a high enough temperature for the atoms to move around and thus eliminate defects. Used to soften materials after work hardening or precipitation hardening.

Anode: The positive electrode or terminal of a battery. It attracts anions: negative ions.

Antiferromagnets: Materials such as chromium in which the atoms are magnetic but arrange their individual magnets so that they are aligned in opposite directions and therefore cancel each other.

Atomic number: The number of electrons and the number of protons in an atom. Equal numbers make the atom electrically neutral. Each element has a unique atomic number.

Atomic structure: Refers to features of the material which are of the size of atoms, e.g. impurity atoms, vacancies, interstitials. When we substitute one atom in the material with another we are also changing the atomic structure, i.e. the atoms which compose the material.

Atomic weight: The weight in grams of 6.02×10^{23} atoms of an element.

Austenite: The face centered cubic (FCC) form of iron which exists at temperatures above approximately 912° C. It is the form of iron which can dissolve the most carbon. When iron is heated to form austenite it becomes softer because the carbon dissolves . When cooled, the carbon forms precipitates with the alloying elements causing the metal to become harder.

Band energy diagram: Diagram showing the energy steps in a solid which are so close together that they seem to form continuous bands of possible energies.

Benzene ring: A hexagon of six carbon atoms. When it exists as benzene, each carbon atom is covalently bonded to a hydrogen atom. In polystyrene there are only hydrogen atoms on the five carbon atoms which are not directly attached to the polymer chain.

Block copolymer: A material in which the polymer chain consists of two or more mers which occur in blocks along the chain.

Body centered cubic: Arrangement of atoms, all of the same type, which has them sitting on the corners and at the geometric center of the cube.

Calorie: Unit of energy being the amount of energy required to raise the temperature of one gram of water by 1° C.

Carbonization: Process of heating a material, often a polymer, to decompose it and drive off the elements other than carbon, and therefore leave a carbon residue. The heating must be done in the absence of oxygen so that the carbon does not burn.

Cathode: The negative electrode or terminal of a battery. It attracts cations: positive ions.

Cation: An atom which has lost one or more electrons so that it has a net positive charge.

Charge carrier: An entity which carries the electrical current in a material. The two major types are electrons and electron holes. In some ionically bonded materials the ions may themselves move and thus transfer charge.

Chemical vapor deposition: Process for producing a solid material from vapors. Sometimes it involves only one compound which decomposes when heated (methane to produce carbon or soot) whereas in other cases it involves the reaction of two or more gases to produce a solid and another gas (silicon chloride and oxygen react to produce solid silicon dioxide and chlorine gas).

Close packing: Arrangement of atoms in which they are packed like balls racked up for a pool game. Usually only used for metals, and solid inert gases, where all the atoms are the same size. Two types exist, cubic close packed (CCP) and hexagonal close packed (HCP).

Composites: Materials made by intentionally mixing two different materials to produce one which is superior to both. Nowadays this term is usually taken to refer to materials made with fibers of one component embedded in a matrix of another.

Critical angle: Angle measured from the perpendicular to the surface at which a light ray in a material can just escape parallel to the outside surface of the material.

Light rays at angles greater than the critical angle suffer total internal reflection.

Critical current: Maximum amount of current which can be passed through a superconductor with it retaining its superconducting property.

Critical temperature: Maximum temperature at which a superconductor is superconducting.

Crystals: Volumes of material in which the atoms are arranged in a discernible repeat pattern in three dimensions. The repeat unit is known as the unit cell.

Crystal structure: The arrangement pattern of atoms within a unit cell, e.g. the BCC and FCC crystal structures. Materials can have the same atomic structure but different crystal structures (glass and quartz, diamond and graphite).

Devitrification: Process of heating a glassy material to a temperature where the atoms begin to move around and arrange themselves to form crystals.

Dimensionless quantity: A number obtained by dividing two quantities with the same units, e.g. strain is length divided by length.

Dislocation: A linear defect in a material often described as the termination of a partial plane of atoms in the material. It is the defect which allows planes of atoms in metal crystals to slide over each other a thousand times easier than they otherwise would.

Domain boundary: Volume between two magnet domains in which the individual atom magnets gradually change orientation from that of one domain to that of the other.

Donor impurity: A substitutional impurity in an insulator or a semiconductor which has (usually) one more electron that the atom it replaces. Because of this it has enough electrons to form the bonds and then has one left over. It donates this electron to the structure.

Doping: Process of intentionally adding impurities to a semiconductor.

Elastic strain: A change in shape or dimensions of a material which disappears as soon as the force producing it is removed.

Elastomer: A polymer which has elastic properties like rubber.

Electromagnetic wave: A wave such as light or x-rays, which has associated magnetic and electric fields. Because of this it causes electrons and other charged particles to move.

Electron density: Parameter which indicates the relative number of electrons in a certain volume of a solid. A higher electron density produces a larger refractive index.

Electron hole: A missing electron in a bond which allows electrons to move by hopping from bond to bond. The hole appears to move in the opposite direction to the electron.

Electron-hole pair: Defect produced when an electron is pulled out of its bond to produce a free electron and an electron hole.

Electron structure: The smallest structure level in a material referring to the arrangement and density of electrons, number of free electrons and electron holes, etc.

Electrostatic attraction: Attraction between opposite electrical charges, e.g. an anion and a cation, and an electron and a cation.

Electrostatic field: An influence which exists between negatively and positively charged entities so that charged particles are accelerated from one to the other.

Entropy: A physical parameter of a material which describes its disorder. The tendency to increase entropy is responsible for the spring of a polymer rubber chain.

Equiaxed microstructure: Microstructure of a material in which the crystals have approximately the same size in whichever direction you measure.

Extrinsic defects: Defects which come from outside the material, usually in the form of impurities (interstitial or substitutional).

Face centered cubic: Arrangement of atoms, all of the same type, which has them sitting on the corners of a cube with one in the center of each cube face.

Ferrite: **1.** The low temperature (BCC) form of iron.
   2. Name given to ceramic magnets in which some of the ions produce a net magnetic field.

Ferromagnets: Materials in which the individual atoms are magnetic and spontaneously align their magnets in the same direction to produce a magnetic field. Iron (ferro) is the most common example. Nickel and cobalt are others.

Flame polishing: Process of passing a flame over the surface of glass to melt a thin layer of the surface. This gets rid of surface cracks, which do not form again on cooling because of the thinness of the melted layer.

Fluorescence: Property of a material in which it absorbs high energy ultraviolet light and emits visible light. The emission stops as soon as the ultraviolet light is turned off.

Glass ceramics: Materials which started as a glass but which have been devitrified so that they now contain very fine crystals cemented together with a little remaining glass.

Glass transition temperature: Temperature above which many polymers are quite plastic or rubbery, but below which they are brittle and will break like glass.

Graft copolymers: Polymers which have a main chain of one mer and side branches of a different mer.

Grains: A term used interchangeably with 'crystals' for the individual crystals in a polycrystalline material. Adjacent grains have different orientations and are separated by **grain boundaries**.

Grain refining: Process of treating a metal (hot rolling in HSLA steels) to produce a very small (fine) microstructure.

Heat treatment: Term used in metallurgy to describe the various heating and cooling processes the material may be subjected to during its manufacture.

Intermetallic compound: A compound of (usually) two metals in which the two atoms are each arranged in a regular repeat manner, see e.g. Al_3Li in aluminum-lithium alloys. (Different from an alloy where one atom may be randomly substituted for another in the crystal.)

Interstice: A small hole which exists between atoms in a crystal. Sometimes it is large enough to accommodate a small impurity atom (usually a non-metal such as carbon or nitrogen).

Interstitial: An impurity atom in an interstice (extrinsic) or sometimes an atom from the material itself which has been displaced into an interstice (intrinsic).

Intrinsic defects: Defects arising within the pure material itself, such as a vacancy (common) or an intrinsic interstitial (rare).

Ion implantation: Process by which ions (charged particles) are accelerated from a source by an electrostatic field and fired into the surface of a material. Large ions cause distortions which can close surface cracks and thus strengthen glass and ceramic materials.

Luminescence: Collective term for the emission of light by fluorescence and phosphorescence.

Macrostructure: The largest structure level of a material, referring to its overall shape and engineering design.

Magnetic domains: Small volumes of a material in which all the individual atom magnets point in the same direction. A single crystal can be divided into many different domains.

Materials science: Scientific discipline which seeks to understand the relationships between the properties of a material and its different structure levels, and then to change properties by modifying the structure through different processing techniques.

Matrix: In a two phase material the matrix is the continuous part of the structure which contains the precipitates (as in Al - Li alloys) or the fibers (composites).

Mer: The unit which repeats to make up the polymer chain.

Metal whiskers: Very thin (1000Å) crystals of metal which are not wide enough to allow dislocations to form. They are not more than a few microns long.

Micron: Abbreviated form of the length measurement known as a micrometer (10^{-6} meters). One micron is equal to ten thousand (10^4) angstrom units or one thousand (10^3) nanometers.

Microstructure: Structure level in a material which relates to the size, shape, and orientation of the crystals (grains).

Molecular weight: Value obtained by adding the atomic weights of all the atoms in a molecule. For example, a water molecule (H_2O) has a molecular weight of (2 x 1.008 + 15.999). Polymer chains are considered long molecules and can have molecular weights of tens of thousands up to a million.

n-type semiconductor: A semiconductor which has been doped with donor impurity atoms.

Nanophase materials: Solid materials which have an exceptionally fine grain structure.

p-type semiconductor: A semiconductor which has been doped with acceptor impurity atoms.

Paramagnets: Materials such as titanium in which the atoms are magnetic but arrange their individual magnets so that they are aligned in random directions and therefore produce no net magnetic field.

Permanent magnets: Magnets which are not easily returned to the unmagnetized state, either because their domain boundaries are locked in position or because they are composed of single domain magnets.

Phase: A distinguishable portion of matter. The distinction may be because of atomic structure (e.g. aluminum-lithium solid solution and delta prime, Al_3Li) or crystal structure (e.g. FCC and BCC iron) differences. A material may consist of two or more phases.

Phonon: A cooperative motion of atoms in the form of a wave which moves through a material carrying energy from one place to another. Phonons transport heat in materials which are held together by covalent and/or ionic bonds.

Phosphorescence: Property of a material in which it absorbs high energy ultraviolet light and emits visible light. The emission can be seen to continue for some time after the ultraviolet light has been turned off.

Photon: Term used for an energy quantum of light. Light comes in discrete energy packets (photons) with each a different energy for each color.

Pile-up: Name given to the crowding of dislocation on a slip plane where they are stopped by a grain boundary.

Plastic strain: A change in the shape or dimensions of a material which remains after the force which produced it has been removed. It is the result of the movement of a large number of dislocations.

Point defects: Defects in a material which are concerned with the atomic structure, i.e. they are approximately the size of atoms. Vacancies and interstitial atoms are examples.

Polar molecules: Molecules in which there is a non-uniform distribution of electrons, causing one end of the molecule to have a positive charge and the other a negative charge.

Polycrystalline: Term used to describe a crystalline material which is made up of many small grains.

Powder metallurgy: Process of producing metal parts by compressing a powder into a mold of the desired part and then sintering.

Precipitate: Small particle of a different phase which is often produced in a material by the motion of atoms during heat treatment.

Precipitation hardening: Process of hardening a material by heat treating it so that a large number of small precipitates are formed, which impede dislocation motion during plastic deformation.

Primary bonds: The three strong bonds: covalent, ionic and metallic.

Quenching: Process of cooling a material very quickly with the aim of freezing the movement of atoms so that they stay in the positions they were in before quenching.

Rapid solidification: Term used for the rapid cooling of a metal from the liquid (molten) to the solid state. Cooling is not quick enough to produce an amorphous metal, but can produce solid solutions with compositions which cannot be achieved with slow cooling methods.

Recrystallization: Process which often occurs inside a metal during annealing, when atoms move around enough to produce new and more perfect crystals than the previous ones which were dislocated and defective.

Refractive index: Parameter of a material which is the ratio of the velocity of light in a vacuum to its velocity in the material. It determines the amount of bending (refraction) of a light ray when it enters a material.

Secondary bonds: The two weaker bonds: van der Waals and hydrogen.

Single domain magnets: Magnets whose grain size is so small that each grain can only exist as a single domain because there is not enough room for domain boundaries.

Sintering: The fusion of ceramic or metal powders into a solid when heated to high temperatures. Occurs because of vacancy motion allowing atoms to move around. Sometimes a high pressure is also applied to push the particles together.

Slip planes: The planes in a crystal which slip over each other by dislocation movement during plastic deformation. They are usually the planes containing the highest atom density, i.e. the planes with the closest atom packing. (Sometimes called 'close-packed planes' even though they may not be close-packed in the strict sense of the word.)

Solid solution: An intimate mixture of two or more types of atom in the solid state with no special spatial arrangement between them. Analogous to a liquid solution but in a frozen form.

Steric hindrance: Term used for the situation where a polymer chain cannot move or twist because there are large groups of atoms on it which get in each other's way.

Strain: The fractional change in a dimension of a material. Usually expressed as a percentage of the original length.

Stress: The force or load per unit area on a material.

Substitutional: Refers to an impurity atom taking the place of an atom of the pure material in its crystal structure, i.e. the impurity substitutes for the original atom.

Superalloy: A metal alloy, usually made using nickel or cobalt, which is resistant to high temperatures.

Superconductor: A material showing no electrical resistance.

Thermal shock resistance: Property of a material which indicates its resistance to cracking and fracture when subjected to large, sudden temperature changes.

Thermoplastic: A polymer which becomes soft at high temperatures so that it can be plastically deformed.

Total internal reflection: Phenomenon used in optical fibers in which a light ray is 100% reflected at a boundary between the material it is in and a material with a lower refractive index.

Ultimate tensile strength: The stress at which a material fails or breaks.

Vacancy motion: Important method for atom motion in a material in which the atom moves into an adjacent vacancy. Material is transported by the cooperative motion of a large number of atoms.

Whiskers: Small metal crystal which are about 1000Å in diameter and no more than a few millimeters long. Their small size does not allow dislocations to form in them, hence they are very strong.

Yield strength: The stress at which a material begins to deform permanently, i.e. show plastic deformation.

Young's modulus: Physical parameter of a material which is a measure of its stiffness. Calculated by dividing stress by strain.

SOLUTIONS TO QUESTIONS

Chapters 1 - 5

1.d	2.c	3.d	4.a	5.e	6.c	7.d	8.d	9.b	10.b
11.d	12.a	13.b	14.e	15.d	16.d	17.a	18.b	19.d	20.d
21.b	22.b	23.a	24.d	25.c	26.a	27.a	28.a	29.a	30.c
31.c	32.e	33.d	34.e	35.c					

Chapters 6 - 8

1.e	2.d	3.a	4.a	5.b	6.c	7.c	8.c	9.d	10.d
11.a	12.a	13.a	14.e	15.b	16.d	17.d	18.e	19.a	20.a
21.c	22.b	23.c	24.a	25.c	26.b				

Chapter 9

1.b	2.d	3.c	4.d	5.d	6.b	7.e	8.c	9.c	10.c

11. (a) 100 p.s.i. (b) 0.1% (c) 100,000 p.s.i. (d) 300 p.s.i. (e) yes

Chapters 10 - 13

1.d	2.e	3.b	4.d	5.e	6.b	7.d	8.b	9.d	10.c
11.a	12.a	13.d	14.b	15.e	16.c	17.b	18.d	19.e	20.b
21.c	22.d	23.b	24.c	25.e	26.c	27.a	28.d	29.b	30.c
31.a	32.c	33.e	34.c	35.d	36.a	37.a	38.d		

Chapters 14 - 16

1.e	2.e	3.d	4.d	5.b	6.e	7.c	8.b	9.c	10.a
11.e	12.a	13.c	14.d	15.c	16.e	17.c	18.a	19.e	20.d
21.a	22.c	23.b	24.d	25.b	26.c	27.e	28.a	29.b	30.b
31.b	32.b	33.d	34.d	35.a	36.b	37.d	38.a	39.c	40.b
41.a	42.c	43.a	44.b						

Chapters 17 - 19

1.e	2.d	3.d	4.b	5.a	6.a	7.c	8.e	9.b	10.e
11.e	12.e	13.c	14.d	15.d	16.e	17.b	18.c	19.c	20.a
21.d	22.c	23.b	24.b	25.b	26.e	27.e	28.e	29.a	30.b
31.a	32.a	33.b	34.c	35.b	36.c	37.a	38.d	39.b	40.b
41.c	42.a	43.c	44.e						

Chapters 20 - 21

1.c	2.b	3.c	4.d	5.c	6.d	7.d	8.d	9.c	10.b
11.d	12.c	13.a	14.e	15.b	16.d	17.d	18.b	19.b	20.d
21.d	22.b								

Chapters 22 - 23

1.e	2.d	3.a	4.a	5.e	6.e	7.d	8.a	9.e	10.d
11.e	12.e	13.b	14.c	15.b	16.d	17.b	18.b	19.d	20.a
21.d	22.d	23.a	24.a	25.e	26.a	27.e	28.b	29.a	30.b
31.c	32.b								

Chapters 24 - 27

1.d	2.d	3.b	4.d	5.b	6.b	7.e	8.c	9.d	10.a
11.d	12.d	13.c	14.e	15.b	16.c	17.c	18.a	19.e	20.a
21.c	22.a	23.a	24.b	25.e	26.d	27.d	28.a	29.e	30.b
31.d	32.b	33.d	34.b	35.c	36.e	37.e	38.b	39.a	40.a
41.a	42.d	43.c	44.e	45.b	46.a	47.d	48.c	49.e	50.d
51.b	52.a	53.b	54.b	55.e	56.c	57.d	58.b	59.e	60.c

Chapters 28 - 29

1.d	2.e	3.e	4.e	5.a	6.b	7.b	8.c	9.c	10.a
11.e	12.c	13.a	14.c	15.c	16.d	17.c	18.e	19.a	20.e
21.b	22.b	23.d	24.b	25.d	26.a	27.b	28.a	29.d	

Chapter 30

1.c	2.b	3.e	4.e	5.e	6.b	7.c	8.e	9.c	10.c
11.c	12.b	13.b	14.d	15.e	16.e	17.d	18.c	19.b	20.d
21.e	22.c	23.c	24.b						

Summary

1.e	2.a	3.b	4.b	5.e	6.c	7.a	8.d	9.c	10.c
11.b	12.e	13.c	14.a	15.b	16.a	17.b	18.a	19.d	20.c
21.b	22.c	23.e	24.b	25.b	26.d	27.d	28.b	29.c	30.e
31.d	32.c	33.e	34.b	35.b	36.a	37.e	38.b	39.a	40.b
41.c	42.a	43.c	44.d	45.c	46.b	47.e	48.a	49.b	50.b
51.d	52.a	53.e	54.a	55.e	56.d	57.e	58.c	59.d	60.b
61.c	62.c	63.d	64.c	65.a					

INDEX

(numbers in italics refer to glossary entries)